D0098991

Magnolia Library

Tango Lessons

TANGO
LESSONS

A Memoir

MEGHAN FLAHERTY

Houghton Mifflin Harcourt

BOSTON   NEW YORK

2018

Copyright © 2018 by Meghan Flaherty

All rights reserved

For information about permission to reproduce selections
from this book, write to trade.permissions@hmhco.com or to
Permissions, Houghton Mifflin Harcourt Publishing Company,
3 Park Avenue, 19th Floor, New York, New York 10016.

hmhco.com

Library of Congress Cataloging-in-Publication Data is available.
ISBN 978-0-544-98070-9

Book design by Kelly Dubeau Smydra

Printed in the United States of America
DOC 10 9 8 7 6 5 4 3 2 1

Lines from "the mockingbird" are from *Mockingbird Wish Me Luck* by
Charles Bukowski. Copyright © 1972 by Charles Bukowski. Reprinted
by permission of HarperCollins Publishers.

Excerpt from "I have not lain with beauty all my life . . ." (no. 10) by
Lawrence Ferlinghetti, from *A Coney Island of the Mind,* copyright
© 1958 by Lawrence Ferlinghetti. Reprinted by permission of New
Directions Publishing Corp.

For my dad,
my first and dearest friend

Prologue

YOU'VE SEEN IT DANCED, ONSTAGE OR IN THE MOVIES. A blind man leads the scent of a young woman around the bar in march tempo, to music saccharine with strings. A lady in a backless dress, her silky hair bunned low, cleaves to a suited man. You hear the *da Dum dum Dum*: the orchestra soars, the *Dum* thumps out the rhythm of four patent leather shoes across a marble floor. You see the glissandos and the ritardandos — with each silk-stockinged knee slid up a pinstriped thigh. Maybe a dozen half-naked courtesans in corsets take the stage for the finale. Spins and dips and final tableaus. Thunderous applause. Tango, the dance of passion, dance of love!

But this is showman's tango, staged fedora tango for the tourists. This is ballroom competition tango, the stuff of sequins, rigid choreography — the music secondary to the flashy moves. This is tango as the mating dance of prostitutes and pimps. It is pure seduction: a dramatic tussling across an empty stage, a bodice-ripping stare.

Forget your fishnet fantasies and take the rose out of your teeth.

Real tango is plainer, and more punishing, with a deep and tidal pull. It isn't glamorous. It isn't posed or planned. It happens when two people meet on one small patch of hardwood floor and take their place in a line of other dancers moving counterclockwise. It's a quiet thing. The gentleman opens up his arms and takes the lady's right hand in his left. They step toward each other, torso to torso, heart to heart, and they listen — they stand still — until the music tells them where to go.

You might miss it if you aren't looking close enough. There are no prescribed steps. Through subtle tensions, evanescent shifts of weight, two dancers converse. The music tells them how, and it will never be the same dance twice. Tango is the only partner dance in history to be wholly improvised. There is a leader and a follower and, between them, an intricate and wordless conversation. The best parts of the dance remain invisible, like the inner growth of trees.

It is, above all, bittersweet. Enrique Santos Discépolo, beloved tango poet and composer, said it best: *"El tango es un pensamiento triste que se baila."* Tango is a sad thought danced. But it is also pure and buoyant pleasure. A man and woman moving, half-possessed, to music. In their fusion, the sad thought is relieved.

Chapter One

THE STUDIO WAS IN AN ORDINARY OFFICE BUILDING, ON the second floor. I had only just enrolled myself, by index card and golf pencil, and now I stood in one of several rooms walled off by dark pink curtains, strapping on a pair of grandmotherly pumps. The maestro entered, heels slapping as he thrust himself across the floor. He wore a suit over a black T-shirt, like an eighties stand-up comic, and a ridge of curls hugged his slightly horsey neck. Immediately, he started giving orders in a clipped and thinly eastern European accent. *The dance yes is to walk. Okay, begin.*

We didn't walk. We practiced standing—with all our weight on one foot then the other, watching our ankles wobble in the mirror. My classmates were a pair of forty-something Asian women and some shrinking, balding men in stripes. We didn't speak. The ladies were asked to stretch up on the forefoot—balanced on the ball, heels elevated—a task that only made us wobble more. Then the maestro demonstrated foot trills, little flicks, one foot around the other. *Your feet caress the floor,* he said. *You hear the difference.* A dozen ears tuned to the tidy sweeping sound of leather sole against hardwood. *Now the other. You try.* And we stood there, one foot wobbling, the other undertaking little decorative missions. We tipped and steadied ourselves, like toddlers playing teapots, until we could approximate the maestro's tight ellipses. *Lápices.* Spanish for "pencils" — the step named after circles drawn on the sketching paper of the floor.

We lined up at the curtain blocking one class from the next. To walk. This meant transferring weight from foot to foot as we had practiced, and then slinking forward, hauling ourselves across the floor as if on ski machines, lugging one leg forth to meet the other. *I will hear your feet,* the maestro said, cupping a hand over one ear and listening for the swish of our soles across the boards. *Always, the ball of the foot must caress the floor.* The way he kept saying "caress" struck me as slightly lewd, but I ignored this. The practice of our toe-first trudge across the room required perfect concentration. We each grunted quietly as we tried to heave our weight around on tiptoe. I imagined my classmates as ailing jungle animals trying to relearn how to stalk their prey.

One slow and somber instrumental played on endless loop, its beats as clear and heavy as the tides, its melody a wisp of seaweed between waves. "Bahía Blanca," it was called. The white bay. I did not know that then. I only knew the awkwardness and effort of this tango class: the buckling of my ankles, the threat of sliding into accidental splits. The song plinked to a close and then repeated. I pursed my lips and shut my eyes to everything but the ocean rhythm of the strings, trying to will my body into grace, into the tango walk — and thinking, even as I stumbled, *this is why I'm here.*

I had taken tango classes once before, when I was sixteen, on a term abroad in Argentina. I was a lonely, oddball kid, and thus spent half my time there by myself, on park benches, furiously scribbling impressions into a composition book: the taste of diesel fumes and city grit baked into empanadas, the feeling of having fallen to the bottom of the world map in the picture frame, of being under glass and in plain sight. The other half I'll call my teenage education: hitchhiking, staying out past seven in the morning dancing *cumbia,* and drinking daintily from liter bottles of *cerveza* on unlit dirt roads.

South of the equator, vast and varied, Argentina was unseasonable and unreasonable. I loved every thorny inch of her. The weather and the months ran backwards. The provinces — sandy, grassy, frozen under feet of salt or ice — were systematically ignored, and poor. They stretched a geographic patchwork quilt across the lap and shoes and shoulders of the country, while Buenos Aires, squatting on the Rio de la Plata delta, got all of the attention. I'd been devastated to leave the foothills of the Andes for the capital, but she was the *distrito federal,* the port, the Paris of South America, and, by happy accident, she created tango, with which I fell in love.

On Tuesday afternoons, I took the *subte* from my homestay in the Buenos Aires outskirts to meet my tenth-grade Honors Spanish II teacher in the basement café of a discount bookstore on la Avenida Corrientes. He called himself José Barretto, his alter ego, the mask behind which Joe Barrett buried every trace of his midwestern self. He'd spent ten years in the Dominican Republic and been reborn as an adopted member of his host family. Señor Barretto was robust where Joe was ordinary, open where Joe was closed, and an unmitigated dork. He devoured Argentina every bit as hungrily as I did. In Buenos Aires, at least, that required an appetite for tango. He'd found the class by chance, during his afternoon perambulations. There was no sign, no neon stiletto blinking outside on the sidewalk. Just a handful of businessmen and blue-collar workers spending their lunch break clumped around a boom box, learning how to dance.

Our instructor was a gentleman named Alfredo, with a bristly mustache and a salt-and-pepper pompadour. José took notes on scraps of paper stuffed into his breast pocket and, every few minutes, fished out a handkerchief to mop his brow. José didn't quite have what it took for tango; there was something missing that I noticed even then — some heat, perhaps, or some dark depth of pessimism. He held me gingerly, with all the anodyne sterility that his position as my septuagenarian chaperone required. He smiled every so often, as if embarrassed by his forehead sweat. Or as if waiting for tango to become more jubilant, waiting for the sound of upbeat drums.

I, however, was enchanted by the mournful music — as by any other antique treasure, intricate, threadbare. It sounded like old lace draped across the table of a century. Beautiful, but thinned from age. You had to turn the volume up to hear the old songs underneath the static and the dust. But there the tango surged — keening and crooning, darkly beckoning, and sad.

The class moved by mathematic increments, painfully precise. *One*, the first step, backwards for the leader, forward for the follower. *Two*, a side step, opening out together. *Three, Four*, the couple walking — him in forward, her reverse. *Five*, he leads a cross, left over right. *Six*, the exit. *Seven*, another side step to resolve, then back to one, the feet together, *Eight*. *Lo básico*, Alfredo called it. The basic eight. All steps were accessed from this grid, wrought from the cross and meant to lead back into it. Forward to a side step, or *salida;* backwards to the cross; then resolution.

After four weeks of lunchtime lessons, Alfredo took my hand to test my comprehension. *"Entonces,"* he said, and asked in Spanish, "So, you have the basic?" He steered me from the fray. His knees were almost as sharply pointed as his sleek black polished shoes. He was all angles, but moved supplely, as if by master puppeteer. "Show me," he said.

He led me through eight steps, the box. Years later, I would learn this pattern was an arbitrary one. *There are no steps in tango.* But back then, as long as there were things to master, I would master them. He led. I followed.

"Good," he said. "Now close your eyes."

The old *tangueros* often spoke of leading this way, a transitive verb. *"La bailo,"* they would say. "I dance her." Swallowing my nascent feminist dismay, I disregarded that paternalism and embraced, instead, the thrill of dancing without steering. The blind leap. Alfredo moved through me like a prow parting water, and the lead made sense. The follower was supposed to cultivate something called *la ignorancia sagrada,* her sacred ignorance, which felt a bit like flying in the dark. A leader, he told me, should give her room only to do the thing he wants. There could be no second-guessing if the lead was clear; his chest, his arms, the shapes he made would show a lady where to step, by magic alchemy. A follower must close her eyes and trust. And that's what I was doing then — sixteen and newly in the honking, vivid world: learning to trust.

This lesson, a decade later, was not at all like that, and I was not that dewy-hearted girl. This lesson and I both were disappointing. For a few futile moments, I pretended I was not in SoHo, New York City, but in Palermo Soho, Buenos Aires, lost inside that old framed photo of the world. But I was not. I was twenty-five years old and flailing. A failed actress and the daughter of a doubly broken home. By day, I languished in a cubicle; by night, beside a man who didn't want me. I knew I needed to do something, however bold or blind. This class, Basic Argentine Tango, Section A, was it.

I'd built it up. Stockpiled my nerve. Checked the website every day for months, vowing to sign up for the next cycle and then the next, until here I finally was: in ugly shoes on an ordinary Tuesday, teetering around an unassuming studio not six blocks from my office with a bunch of strangers. And all because I wanted to be different than I was. I wanted to be the kind of woman who took tango lessons.

I stood in line behind the maestro, trying to do what he did with my feet. Trying to feel something, anything, that wasn't lost. But then the hour struck. The maestro killed the music. Class was over. There had been no chivalry, no sacred ignorance. We hadn't so much as partnered up.

I left the studio that first Tuesday evening and met a man for dinner. My boyfriend. The third in a line of men who wouldn't touch me. The first I'd called the Hobbit, a baker and fellow Chili's server in our former Massachusetts college town who had refused to kiss me out of sheer politeness. He was five foot six to my five foot seven, pathologically respectful, and emotionally stalled. I was attracted to his gentle kindness, though I misread each of his signs. The second was a theatre designer with a Homer Simpson alarm clock — a consummate lost cause. I called him Non-Date. We'd spend hours bantering over rounds and rounds of hoppy beers at baseball bars, and wandering laps around Manhattan. I was sure that it was destiny. The merest idea of him made my insides spin. I walked beside him with my hand loose, dangling at my side. It took him three years to reach for it, and once he did, he spooked and changed his mind.

Number three was accidental. My best friend. Our lack of chemistry was not his fault. But once we'd tried to call ourselves a couple, we couldn't untry; we were stuck. He loved me like a sister, and his folks were family to me when I really needed one, after mine had come apart. He was a failed actor too; we understood each other's unfulfilled ambition. We both wanted to be better than we were. He came from money; I did not. I worked meaningless jobs that left me drained while he stayed home and filled his days with weightlifting and errands.

There was a deep and inborn sadness in him that I cradled, a chaos in me he steadied. There wasn't passion. We took care of each other. He paid for groceries, I found his socks. We were fiercely codependent, two lost kids skipping through the adult woods. He called me Biscuit. I called him Peter Pan. We cared for each other very deeply, but we were not in love.

We should have pushed each other off the nursery sill, but we were both too frightened of the world, and I was desperate not to be alone. My life was better with him in it. Perhaps the solace we took together made up for the sacrifice. Perhaps, I thought, the sloppy lusts of teenage lip-lock were meant to be outgrown. I knew just enough about desire to understand I wasn't very good at giving rise to it. By the time I came to tango, I had forgotten what it felt like to be touched.

The pivot back was partly Peter's fault. He'd sent me on a second trip to Buenos Aires some months earlier, to accompany and translate for his mother on a one-week tour. Her treat. The fool idea had come to me while she and I sat sipping Malbec somewhere in San Telmo, watching two *porteños* twirl and kick their legs around each other in a tango show. I watched the way the dancers moved together — making geometry or making love, and dragging silent steps across the floor like cat burglars. Tango had never looked like sex to me, more like an elaborate stage battle between exhausted nemeses. Their smiles bent in anguish, their wan cheeks aflame.

"You and Peter ought to do this," she whispered.

I watched his long and rippling dress pants, her midriff flexing into every turn. My arches ached from effort, watching theirs. Fond memories of modest tango steps evaporated in the heat of their sweating and spinning. Their strong legs anchored, loose legs letting go. The whole effect was breathlessly and wordlessly alive. Peter would never want to do this

— with me or without. I found myself wishing he might want to, and wanting to myself. My toes tensed under the table. I felt my ribcage swell.

In the taxi back to our hotel, night wind thrashed my hair through open windows. The driver swerved along the pothole gauntlet up 9 de Julio, the widest street on earth, zooming from lane to lane toward the Obelisco. The city had fallen apart a bit since last I'd seen her, but the radio still blasted tango, and the night still sparkled with the chill of reverse spring.

That was the April a smoke cloud invaded Buenos Aires from brush-burn fires set by ranchers forty miles upwind, and my lungs were full with it. Talking, even breathing, stung. That night, lying on my twin guesthouse bunk beneath the open window, I drank it in — more than a little tipsy from the Malbec, more than a little melancholy, charmed.

I lay there remembering the night when, ten years earlier, I'd snuck into a tango club deep in the bowels of the city. From a folding chair on the outer edge, I watched the dancers, like a flock of aging birds, as they swirled together in one stately counterclockwise loop. There were centuries contained in all their steps, lifetimes of agony and joy traced in their shared path around the floor. I stayed for one drink only, one glass of inky wine — but that had been enough.

I remembered, too, the nunnish handmade tango shoes that I'd procured in haste at the Flabella factory on Suipacha in the city center the next day, desperate to take home an artifact of tango. Black leather, with a closed toe box coming to a military point, they were the only pair available in size 43. I thought that when I looked at them, I'd conjure back that old wood-paneled room made beautiful by live musicians and by all those men and women gelled and coifed and dressed in black. I thought the shoes might make me elegant like them, their eyes closed and contemplating, with some unnamed pleasure, something very sad.

Then again, I was sixteen. What something very sad was there for me to contemplate with so much untrammeled life ahead? I stuffed the shoes into my suitcase, said goodbye to Buenos Aires and to Argentina, and flew the fourteen hours back to ordinary adolescence. Tango was soon abandoned with the box of souvenirs beneath my bed: ticket stubs and candy wrappers, the unassembled scrapbook of my months abroad. A time capsule of myself at age sixteen. Now here I was again in Argentina, with a suitcase full of woodsmoke, aching for the wonder I had lost.

Back in New York, the idea haunted me. I still had the dusty dance shoes — unworn and wrapped in tissue paper. What better way to cure my spinning wheels, I thought, than to dig them out and learn the dance of endless loops? I wanted what I'd seen onstage — a woman and a man who wore each other out like nemeses — and the dance I'd seen old couples do in basement clubs, with wrinkled foreheads pressed together, their eyelids lowering to sad, sad strains of *bandoneón*. I wanted to close my eyes and trust.

Tango was to be my trapdoor into transformation. Instead, I found my first class awkward and unbeautiful, the way I'd always seen myself. Instead of mettle, it required only minor calisthenics. And while it held enormous promise, I had not envisioned spending the entire fifty minutes standing like a lame flamingo in a pond.

My doubts reverberated. This tango was stern and cold. Anticlimactic. Nothing about that harshly lit lesson felt like flying in the dark — more like a rehabilitative gym class. I wasn't standing around in fishnet stockings hoping to be ravaged, but I was waiting for some kind of benediction.

By the time I stepped into that January night and met Peter for dinner, I had resolved to swallow my deflated feelings and concentrate instead on acing Basic Section A in hopes of one day making it to Basic Section B. My schoolgirl egotism demanded I not fail, again, at this. I would not put the shoes back in their box. There was something necessary buried in that tangled footwork — swirling in that dark — and it was buried still. Terrible and beautiful as a brushfire burning miles upwind. I couldn't see it yet, but it was there. Where had she gone, that girl who braved two city buses and a train to take a tango lesson in another tongue halfway around the world? I wanted to be her again.

I wanted other things I didn't know enough to name.

I played up the glamour of my first grown-up tango class to Peter, my first grown-up boyfriend, though I knew the truth of both was more banal. I wanted him to see me differently. I wanted him to be a little jealous, a little threatened by my newfound poise. I sipped wine with affected mystery. I thought tango had the power to make him fall in love with me in earnest, so I babbled away about the music and the melancholy and the foot muscles required. Though every detail seemed to bore him, I pontificated on. I wanted to see me differently as well.

When you say "thank you" to an Argentine, he sometimes says "please" back. *Gracias. Por favor.* Partings are marked with *suerte,* luck. And when you aren't sure of something, he will say *por las dudas,* for the doubts. Here's another dish of butter for your bread. One last splash of wine. You know, *por las dudas* — just in case. I started dancing tango for the doubts.

Chapter Two

THEN AGAIN, THE TRUTH IS MUCH MORE COMPLICATED THAN a boom box and a box of shoes. The folded memory of Argentina in a winter coat ten years forgotten is a pretty thought, perhaps the best one. But tango was more to me, even then, than artifact or curio. And I knew more of sadness than I knew how to admit.

I sometimes say I started dancing tango because I had forgotten what it felt like to be touched. That's true, except, if I am honest, I had never really let myself be touched, not in that unguarded, pleasure-seeking way. I also say I started taking tango class in spite of all the overt sensuality, and consciously, that's also true. But somewhere in me, even then, some small voice must have fought through all the cotton wool and known enough to ask for what it whispered in the dark.

There is another story, one I almost never tell. A story I carried with me into tango, and carry with me still. It is the story of a very little girl, hiding from her male relations in a life already half-forgotten. That little girl was me and, for the longest time, a ghost I spoke of only in third person. I'd wait, sometimes for years, until I was sure enough of someone, then I'd share the scant details: how I lived mostly with my birth mother until I was six years old. How she wasn't stable, wasn't well. How she'd forget to pick me up from school. How she would leave me in her dark apartment, vanishing for hours or days; and when she was there, she was never present—just a lolling silent thing in rumpled sheets, with naked breasts and legs under a nightshirt, barely moving from her bed.

I never felt it was her fault. She herself had been abused —by threat of vengeful God, by cruel mother, forceful father, and by her brothers' grown-up lusts. I would explain about their sad eyes and leather belts, about their calloused fingers and their nails black with grime. How they would stare at her, at us. I would explain about the cocaine and her deep disso-ciation. Half the time, you see, she could not know that I was there to be forgotten.

I tell myself she hid beneath the decades, under mounds of substances and men and money. She chose oblivion. I pic-ture whole pieces of her going blank and disappearing, until there was not much woman left, certainly not enough to call a mother. Just a collage of empty, censored places held by skin, amnesia, cigarettes.

This woman, tied to me by accident of birth—she did the best she could. She was smart and worked in sales, for a while at least, and must have managed to pay bills. She sent me early to a private kindergarten. The same school where, in my red tartan pinafore that reeked of menthol lites, I was sometimes abandoned overnight, left to the kindness of the staff. She made enough to pay for cocaine, smokes, and diesel for her rust-col-ored sedan. She made enough to buy me Barbie dolls, then left me playing with them in her empty shag apartment while she went on a two-day bender. There was usually a small amount of food among the bottles of champagne in the fridge; I learned to work the electric range before I was tall enough to see the top of it. I learned to curl up in my closet with a Teddy Ruxpin and a book whenever she brought people home and end tables were littered with white talc and butts. I learned to hold my tongue while driving through the wide flat frozen nothing of Nevada to her parents' trailer, for the holidays, avoiding the chicken coop one bearded uncle had made his home. Most weekends and for two weeks every summer, she did the humane thing and passed me to my dad, who wanted custody but wanted confrontation less. He drove three hours each way up the California coast, and carried me with him through his world of contractors and daiquiris and backyard barbecues and paperbacks. To him, my weekdays were a bad dream he did not wish to see, but soothed.

His best efforts could not protect me from the edges of the darkness she had weathered. That darkness had disgusted him during the two years they were married: the old man's meanness, his perverted rage, his great displays of piety — as his children, brother and sister, disappeared together behind locked bedroom doors. Dad caught them at it, maybe more than once. That's when he finally left. Too noble-hearted to imagine such things would affect a little girl.

Her darkness became my darkness, shading over innocence by innocence. Her cruel mother was my cruel grandmother, and her father's hand, on occasion, forced its gnarled way upon me too. Her brothers looked at me with that same stare, and I felt enough of their sour breath to fear them more than any other thing. I remember grizzled hair and greasy cuffs and, over all their clothes, the grit of ash. I hid behind the cityscapes of green glass bottles cluttering the coffee table, but was never small enough to disappear.

I was six years old, nearly seven, when my dad remarried. A recent heart attack had scared him sober. No more daiquiris. No more pretending I was safe. His new wife could not bear children, but she could help him save and raise the daughter he already had. They fought for custody and won. I never saw my birth mother again. Months later, when summoned for questioning, she didn't show. We left the state. At seven, I went into therapy two afternoons a week until I turned thirteen and shut the door on my past.

It could have been much worse. I was rescued young and plastic; and of all the horrors perpetrated upon children, I was spared the most severe. A state exam confirmed this. They'd been careful; there was no lasting harm. The telling was almost worse than what had happened. Telling brought with it too much fuss, too many concerned adult faces and unfastened secrets. All that shame loosed in the air and caught and kept in documents and folders. I was certain they would come for me because I'd told — the birth mother, the prurient old man, the uncles; they'd told me that they would. They'd told me they would know. Therapy helped, but it was years before I sat in public places without fear.

When it came time for the official case against my birth mother, part of me wanted to lie. To say to the policemen that my therapist, or I, had made the whole thing up. Then I would never have to say out loud what Dad and I could not discuss: That she had let them hurt me. That I had been tampered with. That he had left me there each week. To this day, as if in mutual embarrassment, we rarely speak of it.

His new wife was the one to soothe my horror dreams and tell me I had courage. To steer me through a youth spent mostly in the backseat of a minivan as the three of us boomeranged from state to state, chasing my father's job. She taught me valor, honesty, and how to pack a suitcase. Soon she was my mother, in both act and name. I called her what she called her mother: Mum. The word felt awkward in my mouth at first, then absolutely true. I was hers. We were a family. In exchange, I was as crowd-pleasing a kid as I could muster: good grades, good behavior, handiness in the kitchen. I had their love but I wanted their pride.

Children are resilient. Still, the darkness left a stain, a shame I have no memory of not feeling. I was afraid of men. At first it was their pleated pant legs, heavy tread, their voices thick with threat. Then their attention. I was afraid of kindness, which I knew could curdle overnight.

The only man I did not fear was my father. I remember doubting only once or twice, and feeling all the more ashamed for it. But he was mine to trust, my dad. I hugged him, face against his cotton pullover, swooning in his scent of shaving gel. He'd hoist me up onto his shoulders, hold my ankles to his chest. We kissed goodbye as innocently as other parents and their children kiss: a quick peck on the lips. We had this unspoken pact: *You never blame me for getting you into this, and I'll be an honorable dad.*

Sometimes, when I was very young, I cringed to hear him out of bed at night. The sheet rustling, the toilet flush. A floorboard shifting underfoot. I had no need to fear. His steps were heavy, but they never found their way into my room with any bad intentions. He wasn't like those other men, the grandfather and uncles. He would not do those things. He didn't drink beer out of cans, and leave his cigarette stubs floating in the lukewarm dregs. He didn't hit or yell. He read to me. When I called his desk phone in his temporary cubicle, he answered, almost every time. He loved me almost as much as I loved him, which was worshipful, immense. I loved him perfectly.

Soon the contrast between my new life and the old was so intense, the old one started to feel false. We moved from coast to coast, and up and down the Eastern Seaboard. I felt safer in each new place, within the sanctuary of the three of us. My family. It didn't matter where we were. With each routine supper served on plastic mats, with each day running errands, reading, swimming alongside them; with every good report card, every fistful of tinsel on a Christmas pine, and every passing uneventful year, the darkness was diluted. Books were my refuge. I read story after story, willing myself into the lives of others. I learned what words could do—obscuring some truths, laying others bare. I read widely, darkly—perhaps beyond my age. I peered into the worst recesses of the world and came out wheezing with relief. I had parents, and both assured me I was special, bright, and safe. I'd been given all of the advantages, and every gift. I had all the luck and love I needed to overcome, to render those early years insignificant. They didn't have to be my story anymore. Outgrowing them, I thought, as one did school clothes, was the only way to show my gratitude.

By the time I started high school, I was ready. We'd moved fourteen hundred miles away from where I'd started, and not one soul knew me there. I no longer needed to explain why I did therapy instead of sports. I lost my baby fat and built a better version of myself—a girl who studied hard and sang in chamber choirs with her eyes shut because the music was too beautiful, who tried to talk and flirt like people did in the old black-and-whites. A girl who could win mid-sized roles in school plays, and try on other dresses, other aspirations, and come to love the stage paint and the lights. My past no longer felt like mine. I was just another teenage girl; I didn't need a handicap for what I had survived. I'd done the work and wanted to be judged on different metrics than that tired story of a wounded child. When I did let on, and tell a trusted friend or two about my past, I reveled in their shock. *But you're so well adjusted!* they would say, and I would smile. I was.

But shame, the residue of what came before, is what persists. Mum saw this coming. When I placed out of mandatory therapy, and moved to reinvent myself, she tugged me by the ponytail to hold me back. No matter how well I deflected, or how hot my face would flush, she kept me tethered to those roots. She knew better than to allow me to forget, no matter how seductive the forgetting. She'd seen the statistics, and was worried I might fall victim to the adult traps of early tampering: promiscuity, low self-esteem, seeking an abusive partner, or — worse — becoming one. She wanted to be sure the cycle, from adult to child, ended with me.

There were a lot of ways in which I hid: isolation, burrowing into family, eating myself to chubby sexlessness, a bowl cut and a beefy-T. Mum took one look at me and knew that it was up to her to teach me sex was not something to fear. She made an early choice, to overshare. To show little-girl me a frank and healthy view of human sexuality. To teach me about pleasure. She knew that I did not like looking backwards, so she kept the focus on herself: she kept it effervescent. She started small — as I was small — describing my parts and womb as a kind of pink, inviting beau parlour, and spiraled through the years into treatises on penis sizes relative to nationality (French: passable; Middle Eastern: grand; and German: might as well not bother). She made jokes of all the things I found most terrifying, until those things were harmless, comical appendages, subject to gleeful ridicule.

She made it sound so wondrous: two people who loved and found each other so delicious that they simply had to shuck their clothes spontaneously and groan. I had been so full of hope that, at first blush, I'd join her priestess temple, that it would make me feel honored, make my body feel good. That didn't happen. First blush was brief and painful, with an undeserving boy who vanished afterward and broke my adolescent heart. I didn't feel that he had robbed me, but I felt then, more than ever, that I must have been repulsive to him somehow, because I wasn't pure.

My next attempt was with a nice boy I deflowered, clumsily. He didn't vanish; he stared straight into my eyes and tried to love me, but the smell of us together like that made me ill. I never told a soul about my nausea. I left him for college, embarrassed and ashamed. And after four years sequestered in the bosom of a same-sex education, where I fell so hard and fast in love with a woman that I thought the male subject moot, the project fell apart.

Meanwhile, I lost myself onstage. After one college production, I declared my very unwise major. I could have aimed at anything I wanted — scholar, lawyer, engineer — but I picked theatre. Like an addict, a maenad tripping after Dionysos, I found myself insatiable, subsumed. Mum wasn't thrilled. *I think,* she said on more than one occasion, *that you are hiding.* She was right. She thought I should own my fractured life, and "share my story," not keep on pretending that it wasn't mine. I was never certain why. She also thought that I should study something practical. I much preferred to hide. I slunk into the brick, windowless theatre, where, term after term, role after role, I could be anyone. I wore prostheses, swimsuits, hoopskirts, a papier-mâché wig. I was a psychiatrist, a drunk, a mother, a nurse, a Scottish schoolgirl, Susan B. Anthony's muse. When I wasn't asleep or studying, I was there in the dark, watching beaches, stables, platforms built around me. I stepped into other memories. I spoke other people's words. Performing was a strange and self-obliterative rush. I hid in full view, beneath the blinding lights that I'd helped hang. Invisible while everybody watched. Dizzyingly present, somewhere else. And burning purely at the center of me, which was no one. There was a roar of sound, a heavy curtain, silhouettes of friends and strangers filling empty seats. Then it was over. I smeared another face from mine and left the ghost light burning on another empty stage.

. . .

Just before my senior year, my father left my mother. In the aftermath of my redemption, their greatest shared wish come mostly true, they'd fallen out of love. As though they'd sucked the ugly out of all my wounds and it had poisoned them. Each of us — our little unit — came apart. There was a blast of acrimony, a short and vicious war. Dad shoved the contents of his closet into a plastic garbage bag, clicked closed the sliding-glass back door, and walked away. Mum crumpled in a heap of swallowed sobs, with blood rage in her eyeballs. The dog whined at the door. All three of them were lost to me that day, and I to them. I spent the last weeks of my summer watching Mum implode, pleading with her to believe he would come back, standing helpless in their bedroom doorframe as she keened, replenishing the water glass beside her bed. And when September came, I turned my back and drove to school. I took on another role, and dug down into it, until I couldn't hear her pain.

A few months later, our dog died of sudden cancer in her arms, on the lawn. We were each of us, again, alone. She sold the house and moved to Florida. He went back out on the road. I finished school and moved to New York City, where people go when they can't think of somewhere else, and did what people do there when they want to make it in the theatre: I wasted half a decade waiting tables.

I pretended to be sexually well adjusted, sexually adept — even, and especially, to Mum. I'd been trying to impress her since the day the ink dried on the adoption papers, and felt that I, that we — our family — had failed her. Now she'd hauled herself to Florida and started over, found a two-bedroom rental condo and a job. She was a one-woman revival, suntanned to leather, with a closet full of rhinestone sandals and a dance card full of beaus. And she spoke fluent sex — never cringing at the clinical, always celebrating appetite. She'd model, say, her haul of clearance pink-feather-and-leopard underpants for me on Skype. I rolled my eyes, but deep down I was awe-struck. Sex came so easily to her — and she was good at it, virtuosic. I know because we were that close, perhaps too close; part of our mother-daughter bargain had always been to share the truth and bear it jointly. But despite my trying, and despite her expert ease, I remained a disappointment, a knot that no one could untie.

By the time I came to tango, I'd turned all of my romantic failures into punch lines — three men in a row who wouldn't touch me! The Hobbit, Non-Date Guy, now Peter Pan — the joke that I was somehow cursed. They each had their own excuses. What remained constant was me: wanting so much to be desired, and to desire in return, but feeling impotent, off-putting and offput. Despite my mother's best attempts to make the act of human coupling seem beautiful, it never felt that way to me. The mechanical effort of it pumped me dry of tears. I was too embarrassed, too daunted by the flesh, the sweat, the squeaking springs, and all that dreadful vocal indecorum. Being cursed, I thought, was better than being undesirable. Not loving anybody fully was preferable to being left — and not being touched much easier than weathering the aftershocks of shame. I was disappointed when I failed to live up to my mother's hopes for me, but more than that, I was relieved.

When I say Peter wouldn't touch me, I mean that literally. His feelings for me weren't physical. I don't just mean that we did not have sex. I mean that he would bristle when I tried to take his arm. If he took my hand to hold it walking down the street, he would extricate himself in seconds. He would hug me sometimes, earnestly, but back away abruptly — so abruptly that I'd fall forward into vacant space and have to catch myself from falling farther. He meant no malice with his lack of physical affection. I assumed the fault was mine.

There were some men who wanted me, but turned my stomach. There were others whom I wanted, but they turned their backs. I chose the ones who didn't want me — at least not in that way. For someone who had never fathomed how it ought to feel, giving up was no great sacrifice. My relationship with Peter gave me all the comfort of companionship without the challenge of unknotting my most twisted parts. Deep down, I wasn't sure I wanted to be touched at all.

Still, I chose tango. You might ask why, given the state of me — and I have no cogent answer. So I tell that story about Argentina, about being sixteen and in a foreign place. About bravery, or about trust. But it's more about the fact that sixteen-year-old me, the girl who fell in love with this staid dance half a world away, was an accomplished little obfuscator, and I wanted her to win. That pretty story could have been her story, were it not for what had come before. Maybe, somehow, now it is. Or maybe it's as simple as: I steered into the wind.

Chapter Three

I BLINKED AND THREE YEARS HAD UNRAVELED. I WASN'T ACT-
ing much, and when I was, I somehow always ended up in leak-
ing church basements on Ninth Avenue, performing poorly
written one-acts in my underwear. Real roles were ever out of
reach. Casting bulletins called for crones or cartoon women,
manic pixies or "model types" in sexpot catsuits. Still, I tried. I
spent all the money I'd accumulated serving steaks and vodka
tonics to the business class on headshots, self-promotion seminars, and postcards advertising shows no one would see. My
odds of "making it" had long expired, but I held on to the memory of dropping into character, scratching art out of a dark and
empty theatre. Standing center stage in front of strangers, disappearing in plain sight.

I worked double shifts and spent late evenings in an Irish
pub across the street, drowning in pop music and beer. Peter sat at my bar some nights; I served him scallops, twenty-
dollar drinks, and sped through sidework to accept his cab
ride home. Frustrated fellow servers came and went, book-
ing shows only to come back three months later, mortified and
broke. An alarming number turned to teaching yoga. Eventually, for health insurance, I took an entry-level desk job in non-
profit marketing, doing work that made me miserable (asking
rich people for money), but was better perhaps than failing to

land auditions and smelling perpetually of restaurant, which is to say, of steak and bleach and raw onions. Helping recovering homeless men and women transition from sobriety to employment was work, at least, that mattered. I lived paycheck to paycheck in a studio apartment in Astoria, still shelling out for acting classes, just in case. I put on pumps and tried to feign being a grown-up, which was sometimes acting job enough.

While I furrowed my brow and wondered where my life had stalled, Dad took up with his high school sweetheart, and Mum was in the throes of midlife renaissance. It was, ostensibly, the happiest either one of them had been in years. I seemed to be the rotten egg. I'd done this gutsy, foolish thing, and moved to the big city by myself to try and earn a living doing art. But I was still the same scared, melancholy girl, always a little quiet, even when performing, always a little ill at ease. I wore grey and read books and tried to fade into the background, best I could.

My life was functional, but ordinary. I got promoted beyond the pool of cold callers, but my boss was borderline psychotic and the office left me feeling empty. Part of me missed the hustle and the flexibility of slinging oyster platters and martinis, the constant crises, the sore-footed dance of customer appeasement. Now I sat all day in a six-by-six-foot office cubby, unjamming staplers and redrafting press releases, listening to tango records in hopes that they might bring me closer to the hologram of me, a younger, better self. I counted down the minutes spent arranging donor databases until lunch bought me an hour of freedom to eat my salad on the greasy metal stairs of SoHo loading docks. Nights and weekends Peter and I went out to dinners I could afford only because he always paid. I learned the luxury of well-made food consumed at normal mealtimes, which felt good after years of trough-style afternoon employee meals. Every evening felt elaborate, like an unearned treat, a holiday from lives we were not living. We went to shows and films, and tried to will ourselves onscreen. We watched pickup softball matches in the park. We enjoyed the consolation of each other's company — the joking ease, the tacit understanding — but we were filling time.

Peter was also in a rut. Too often, I forgot about his quiet desperation in attending to my own. He wasn't performing either; he too had a pile of expensive card-stock headshots. He too cringed each time he kicked them farther underneath his bed. He drank too much, to drown the harpies of his own self-loathing. And, maybe to avoid the ambush of his own depression, he was at the gym six days a week, alternating between training others, which made him miserable, and slogging from weight machine to weight machine, torturing himself. As if his fitness level marked his barest minimum of pride. He and I were both big-hearted, wide open to the world like wounds, and unremittingly frustrated with ourselves. We lived in privilege and plenty — mine borrowed, his bequeathed — yet we were merely plodding through. Not ungrateful, but rather contrite. And conscious always of our opiate inattention to our dreams.

Tango felt like insurrection. As if those fifty minutes once a week, however tedious, could burn the whole thing down. The following Tuesday, a week after that first class, I went back to the studio and stood again behind the maestro in my unfortunate Flabellas. The same song looped. The same group stared down at their feet. The same winter seeped in through the windowpanes. We stood and shifted, and continued our martial stalking, back and forth across the room. Any delusions I had harbored of being good at this were duly quashed, but I surrendered. My mother, after all, had raised me to be braver than I felt. She'd always warned me against the fear of looking stupid. *How else do you learn,* she'd say, and throw me out into the deep ends of new languages and schools and singing solo.

She was not afraid of looking foolish, nor of starting over. In her world, there were always second chances: for motherhood, for daughterhood, for post-marital romance, and — I hoped — for being twenty-five. All I had to do was let myself look just a little stupid.

In tango class, for a beginner, this was easily achieved. Beginners learn with other beginners, in a quarantine of skill. For the first few classes, you dance by yourself, changing your weight in place from foot to foot, plodding back and forth between two mirrored walls, and — on special occasions — doing shadow exercises with a stranger standing several feet away, matching his footing and the way he moves his legs, and staring at him so hard he becomes your own reflection and you forget who's imitating whom.

Eventually, you're deemed ready for the practice hold. A leader holds his arms out and you, the follower, place your hands onto his elbow crooks. You attempt to walk together, toe-first, dragging your legs across the floor pedantically on every downbeat *whump*. For followers, this is almost always backwards. And both of you are almost always looking down.

After the technique of toe-first walking and the practice hold, you learn the cross, or *la cruzada*, where one foot hooks across the other. I'd learned this move as "position five," but it is infinitely versatile. The leader uses it to change direction, or to steer the follower to change which foot walks first. You shift your weight onto the crossed foot, slightly lift your heel, then scoot your back foot free. The cross moves the couple from two shared ski tracks to three, from parallel legs to opposite, where the dance is like a graceful version of a three-legged race. It is the punctuation of the tango sentence. The pause in the momentum of the walk. For a few weeks at least, we practiced pausing. Walking. Pausing.

Pause. Walk. Pause.

Thinking back, retracing steps and milestones, I've tried to put my finger on precisely when addiction claimed me, precisely when pursuit became preoccupation. Because, despite the Sisyphean labor, I became obsessed. Walking, breathing, thinking, sleeping tango. I became tedious to anyone willing to listen. I practiced with the pillar in the break room at the office, while the coffee brewed. I drilled footwork at the copy machine, to the rhythm of the stapling and collating, startling to a halt whenever I saw someone pass the printing room. I bought a pair of red suede T-straps from a dance outlet in Chelsea, and stuffed them into my purse to carry with me everywhere. *Por las dudas.*

I called my mother with momentous news of my new hobby. At first she was relieved. "Oh, good," she said, no doubt remembering me, at sixteen, trying to demonstrate what José and I had learned when we returned from Argentina. Dance itself meant little to her; her most advanced move was the disco bump. But she was on a whole renascent tear. She'd changed all of her passwords to "freedom," shed thirty pounds, and had recently spent a Saturday afternoon tailgating at a country concert with champagne in plastic flutes. "You need to live more, Meg," she said.

She was thrilled about the shoes. The rest of it confused her. "No one speaks?" she asked, when I explained that I knew nothing about the classmates whose elbows I clasped every Tuesday night. As a talker, she was immediately wary of a social scene where people touched, but no one spoke. "I thought you said it was a social dance."

"It is, Mum. It's just a quiet one."

"Jesus, Meghan." If she'd been fretting about my lack of purpose, she hadn't really said. Not beyond a comment here and there about dreams and distraction. But tango was just too dreary, and impossible for her to comprehend. Sometimes, I think, so was I.

Mum was certain tango men were closet perverts. To her, the class was really just a covert sex club, and I was too naïve or too polite to notice. She also assumed that any able-bodied of-age man must want to sleep with me; that I had managed to unearth three consecutive specimens who didn't only made her worry more. *Men just don't seem to want me that way, Mum,* I'd say. But she was sure that I was not, in fact, defective as an object of desire. Just, perhaps, defective in my taste. And understandably confused. I wanted to be wanted. I was afraid of what that meant. *There's nothing wrong with you,* she'd say; though there was surely something wrong with them. Her best guess was that they preyed upon some deep ambivalence in me.

My father, however, was tickled by tango. *Well, good for you,* he said. He thought it was a healthy outlet, something constructive I could do, all by myself, to get my city legs back underneath me. Whether or not he found the thing salacious, he withheld. But tango wasn't like that — at least not until Pre-Intermediate. And that was months away.

Tango came of age in tenement or *conventillo* courtyards and in dance halls called *academias*. Its unsavory reputation probably stemmed from the array of tough guys — *malevos, malandrinos, compadritos* — and loose women who frequented those halls. But sex was not the game. Among the louts were good, God-fearing patrons wanting nothing more than to move to music. *Porteños, criollos.* Immigrants — three million men in twenty years — who'd left everything behind and garrisoned themselves upon the citizens of Buenos Aires and Montevideo.

Argentina, ever bigoted and vain, built herself in Europe's image. Her seventh president, Domingo Faustino Sarmiento, and his aspiring statesman friends penned xenophobic rants against his country's people — those of mixed, indigenous, and Afro-Argentine descent. This distinctively "American race," as he considered it, was idle, muddy, and unfit to constitute a country. And so began the great whitewashing of Argentina, the state-sponsored culling of black populations. Sarmiento and his cohort, the Generación del '37, championed the salvation of Argentina through the aggressive solicitation of "more civilized" European labor. These workers came in droves — Italian, Spanish, Polish, Russian, French, German, Austrian — descending on the booming city, which was then more margins than metropolis. By the 1914 census, the capital was well over 40 percent foreign-born. Outer barrios and slums spilled into countryside to accommodate the newcomers. In a crush of castes, the poorest were pushed into the *arrabales,* poor quarters on the edge of town.

Joining them on the periphery were gauchos: nomad hunters, cattle herders among the rural populations; also a mingling of Spanish, Amerindian, and African descent. You might call them "cowboys" or *vaqueros,* these horse-master dwellers of the pampas, the vast, impossible green plains of the interior. As commercial cattle ranching interests drove the gauchos closer to the city borders, the upper classes pushed the ever-growing wave of immigrants against them. The *arrabales* overflowed to form a labile band around the bustling city. Tango's breeding ground.

In Spanish, there is a neat word for this, *choque* — crash, or clash, or shock. Crash, for the collision of cultures thrashing their great plates together underground. Clash, for conflict: discrimination, poverty, and the vanishing Old World. And shock, for the tectonic blast of it. The dance that shook the globe.

Tango, at least at first, was the dance of the unwanted classes. Pastime of dreamers — foreign, forgotten, poor, and unattached — herded to the edges of a city run by oligarchs. A home in music for the home-deprived. As a member of New York City's artist caste — the servers, clerks, and child minders who couldn't quite afford the life there, but who shuttled daily to and from the city proper to their homes in outer boroughs, at all hours, with folk from everyplace around the world — I found the richness of this history compelling. Here I was, the daughter of divorce, in my own port city made by immigrants — in my own country built by slaves. Adrift, and seeking thrills. Traveling from squat, three-story Astoria into a midtown labyrinth of shining glass. Feeling ever in awe of all the industry around me, ever a little dingy, ever on the edge. It wasn't Buenos Aires on the eve of a new century, but there were certain legacies these cities shared, for good or ill. A history of corruption, longing, striving, cruelty. Present excess, endless want. The abiding quiet of street corners late at night.

Still, I was no *porteño;* I was a college-educated white girl, poor perhaps largely by choice, deluded when it came to my ability to make a living doing art. And there were no *academias* here. No neighborhood centers teeming with tango life. Only the studio with its fluorescent light strips and its soporific atmosphere.

As if either to nullify or reinforce my mum's sex club cliché, my classmates were mostly single, taciturn, and middle-aged. After nearly a dozen classes, we still hadn't learned one another's names. Most of the men had concave chests and sweaty palms, and either grabbed too hard, held on too tight, or barely touched my arms. Some had breath that reeked of pungent meals; this I forgave. Neither looks nor halitosis made much difference under those fluorescent lights. We were generous with one another. We rotated partners, touched forearms, and agreed to bob together, back and forth across the floor.

The maestro ended every class with foot drills. After an hour of infernal walking practice, we would all line up behind him. He did not call out his movements; he simply stabbed one foot this way or that, and drew his *lápices,* then switched and stepped and frilled. Our ragtag group stumbled behind him, struggling to keep up. We lost our footing, teetered, bit our lips in concentration. Then, with even less warning, he'd stop and cut the music. Class dismissed.

The weeks advanced. The maestro changed the music. We were no longer subject to "Bahía Blanca" droning on repeat, as beautiful as it was. We had graduated to the great parade: Di Sarli, Fresedo, D'Arienzo, Pugliese, Biagi, Canaro, and Caló. Tango today is danced almost exclusively to staticky recordings from its golden age, roughly 1935–1952. There is other, newer music, but nothing since has ever equaled those great orchestras. The sound quality is often poor, but if you squint your eyes and try to shut out every other noise, you can hear the moment, decades in the past, when the magic synthesis occurred.

Tango was always all about the music. The advent of the 2/4 *milonga* beat, which prefigured tango, was wrought from the bass line of the Afro-Cuban *habanera,* the speed of polka, and the poetry of the gaucho *payador* — a sung improvisation accompanied by guitar. *Milonga* steps spun from the Afro-Argentine *candombe,* a group dance to drum music (from the Ki-Kongo *ka,* "pertaining to," and *ndombe,* "the blacks"). Lower-class *porteños* of every race toyed with these rhythms on whatever instruments they had. The first orchestras were portable: guitar and flute and violin, sometimes a clarinet or *candombe* drums. Occasionally, tunes were played on solo piano, for entertainment in the clubs and cabarets. The lyrics were still largely improvised, and the dance a mix of Afro-Cuban *cortes* and *quebradas* — moves that froze or "broke" the dance — and *gauchesco* embellishments: heel-stomping *taconeos* (of North African and Andalusian influence) and *arrastres* — percussive slurs and drags.

The more newcomers surged into the capital, the more the music changed. Italian immigrants brought compositional and lyric prowess on the violin. And Germans brought the *ban-*

doneón, a polygonal bellows instrument, like a concertina, which is perversely difficult to play but gave the tango its distinctive, plaintive, almost human voice. Picture an accordion with seventy-one invisible buttons, played like musical Braille, and spanning 142 tones across five octaves. Then take away the keys.

Tango music developed over decades, from bawdy romps and martial instrumental ditties to sweeping, lovesick orchestrations, driving labyrinths of beat. The result is visceral and sad and yet somehow relieves you of the very sorrow it inspires. Sebastián Arce, contemporary tango superstar, calls it a demonic mixture, says it feels "as if the violin and bandoneón met by chance and had this diabolical marriage." The sound is unmistakable. "Tango starts rhythmically," he says, "ends crying, and in the middle stabs you twice in the heart."

That's how it felt to me. Even standing five feet from another human being, in a strange bright studio in SoHo, pacing the room and trying not to trip. The music pierced through the mundanity of our exertions, striking somewhere sharp and deep. We were each slumped in our private reverie, entranced. As our progress built, so did the aural education. We danced to music I had heard before, old songs I'd brought home from Buenos Aires, but which seemed to come unlocked when paired with movement. We kept walking. We learned the all-important ocho, a cross-system figure eight done mostly by the ladies, the trademark of the tango. It felt at first like figure skating on a very tiny rink, propped up by a leader's elbows, gliding in a loop, forward or back. The leaders delighted themselves when they got us going on our little circuit, tracing infinity before their feet. To guide us out required the careful insertion of a foot to break our ocho flow—one careful step with all the timing and precision of a double-Dutcher. The leader halts the follower's step, takes her through the cross and back to walking. This took another week or two to learn.

Tango as a whole is made of loops. Two dancers turning, separately, together. A swirl of couples dancing in that counterclockwise circle we call, of course, the "line" of dance — in yet another echo of Ki-Kongo dance traditions and the sun's path across the surface of the earth, *nzila ya ntangu*. Each couple shares the floor with dozens, often hundreds, following that path.

This was the last piece of Basic Tango — how to dance among the other dancers. How to rock in place to turn and navigate the corners. We began to practice all these building blocks in sequences — the walk, the cross, the *ochos,* and the turn — in rhythm. Until we could list convincingly around the room for the duration of a song.

Our boom box fought another boom box, just behind the curtain separating our class from the other classes in the studio. Thumps of syncopation, wafts of melodies and strings from different songs competed for our ears. The maestro gently nudged the volume for us so that we could hear. *Listen,* he urged, *with your feet.* The music, when brought above the swallowed warble of the stereo, had weight and a delicious pull. I filled my lungs with it.

Deep in the strangled wails of the *bandoneón* were fated loves and sainted mothers, satire and subversion, continents forgotten. Music full of yearning, boasting, and berating. Preening, promising, and despair. It was both alien and familiar. We walked through the fog of it. My legs felt heavy, trudging, reaching each beat as if through floodwater. Listening, I moved, and began to understand the architecture of the instruments: the basement of the thwapping beat, the main floors of the melody. There are no percussion instruments, as such, in tango. The piano, the bass, the *bandoneón,* even the strings all share the rhythm and the tune. It is music made of ocean currents churning, building to a crest only to slink away, defeated. The dancers are the shore.

Only then, submerging myself in the music, did I begin to disappear. I flickered, felt my edges blur, however briefly. I left class each Tuesday night a little changed. It didn't matter whether I was going back to Peter, takeout, television, or the tedium of fund-raising at work. I had this private thing. I could listen to the music on the subway, at my desk. I had dead men crooning in my ears, a constant serenade. Osvaldo Pugliese, secular saint and king among composers, hero to the working class. Osvaldo Fresedo, author of elegance, as full of joie de vivre as a Parisian stroll. Juan d'Arienzo, *"El Rey del Compás,"* king of the beat, who saved tango's staccato foot-pulse for the people. And Carlos di Sarli, tango's Cyrano, whom they called *"El Señor."*

Di Sarli, the gentleman writer of besotted melodies, was the last piece of the tango puzzle, uniting warring trends within the music by composing tangos worthy of both listening and dancing. There is a rich refinement to his orchestrations, almost cinematic, but his *compases* are clean, dependable — ideal for novice dancers.

"Bahía Blanca," with its surf-like sway, was one of his — a love song to the city of his birth. I understood now why our maestro chose it for those first few Basic classes: to teach our ears to walk against the swimming syncopation in the instruments, to find the gentle plodding meter underneath. To walk, simply, charting our course across the downbeats.

This was the soundtrack of our tedious beginning, this homesick melody with its defiant beat. Often, in those first few weeks, we had to strain our ears against the wide sweep of the song in order to internalize the structure underneath. This taught us patience, which is tantamount to talent in beginning tango class. No matter how we yearned to charge full tilt into the fray, we had to walk straight lines where our hearts were turning circles, ebbing and flowing with the strings. I understood: We had to keep our hopes in check. We had to learn to walk before we danced.

Chapter Four

BUT THIS WAS SOLITARY WORK, AND LONELY-MAKING. NO matter how I begged Peter to join me, he refused. Friends who were more dance-inclined also refused; tango, for all the sex that shrouds it, is an acquired taste. Like power walking, it does not appeal to everyone — and to some it looks more than a little strange. Not everyone can be prevailed upon to spend their evenings speechless, sipping water out of paper cones and occasionally touching elbows with a middle-aged divorcee.

"It's like you're living out my fifties for me," my mother joked, "and I'm living your twenties!" She went for dock-side happy hours. I sat on grimy city benches as the evening drained, my purse loaded with books, a toothbrush, shoes, waiting for class to start. I throbbed with solitude — my body shrunken, senses dulled, my fingers curled in.

I looked forward to class, but every week I found it was a struggle not to skip. Every week, Peter would forget, and ask when I'd be home for dinner and our routine television. "I have tango," I would say. "Oh, right," he'd pout. "So you're still doing that?" At first he'd meet me afterward, for dinner; then he lost interest. I told myself tango was worth the time that I spent sitting, waiting, second-guessing. And worth the money — funds I could not have hoped to muster had Peter not handled most of our expenses, everything beyond my rent and bills and clothes. Still, I didn't have much extra, and what I had I spent in part on monthly dues. Every week, I pushed through the door into the crush of dancers coming, going. I signed my name at registration, walked through a blast of sweat and hustle tunes, and hid out in the changing closet, where I buckled on my dancing shoes.

Not speaking was a mercy. Not being spoken to. Communicating in a series of shy smiles. Occasionally we mumbled "thank you" to each other as we changed partners and the followers rotated one leader to the right along the room. Otherwise, I learned the tango fundamentals mute, obedient, self-punishing. I soldered the soles of my feet to the floor and skied and skated, turned, skated and skied. And when class was over, rode the empty subway back to Peter's place. The irony of this — learning the world's most intimate partner dance in almost perfect isolation — was not lost on me.

I wasn't lonely just on Tuesdays. I was lonely all the time. Peter and I had reached a sibling-level shorthand with each other; we hardly spoke. There was no need. To stand beside each other was enough. We didn't really want to be together, but we didn't want to be apart. I remembered our first week as a couple, when we'd been so exhilarated by our ingenuity — by the idea of becoming "us" — that we stood beaming at each other in the subway car, and kissed because we couldn't think of what to say. He was so handsome that I sometimes stared at the biceps underneath his shirt, and blushed. We looked right together, like adults — and our fondness, our intensity of friendship, read like romantic love. We played pretend.

We didn't hold each other, but my sororal presence next to him in bed was vital to him — even when he fell asleep facedown and clothed after several martinis. I crawled into his queen-sized bed and lay there, schoolmarm-still, reading my book. And as my mother boffed her way through southern Florida in an effort to regain lost time, I clicked off my bedside lamp and went to sleep. Comforted by his breathing, there beside me in the dark.

We were hardly ever intimate. When we did have sex, our lack of chemistry made both of us a little sad. We tried, that whole first week, and found the motions almost comical. We gave up trying; I felt immense relief. It was an ideal situation for a girl afraid of men — to go everywhere with this picture of a man, this Ken doll in the flesh, and call him mine, knowing that he would not touch me. That I didn't need to guard my body anymore.

But after months of this, and years of flinching, keeping myself to myself, I'd gone a little cold inside. I was no longer physical; I'd lost my animal response. When touched, however casually, I recoiled.

Group instruction, once we graduated from practice hold to close embrace, was therefore quite discomfiting. Elbows were one thing. Now I had to put my arms around a stranger, feel another cheek against my own, that person's bone and skin beneath my hands. I had almost forgotten how it felt to hold someone, and I was startled by the feel of fat and veins.

It felt like touching just-plucked chicken, or chops beneath a barrier of butcher's paper. Then there was crisp cotton, moistened silk, the feel of someone else's clothes across my skin. It wasn't sexy or transgressive, being held. I found it terrifying, though I did my best to hide my squeamishness, to separate that animal closeness from everything it threatened to inspire me to feel. The music helped. I closed my eyes and listened, trying to align the complicated motions with the sound. The music made the movement otherworldly, as though I were safely in some magic Elsewhere and had ceased to be. I was not a vulnerable girl-body in the arms of a strange man; I was an archetype who meets another archetype, on a dance floor out of time.

Some say the very name of tango comes from touch, from the Latin *tangere*. It is the quintessential partner dance — the first in history to push the couple close enough together that their heartbeats matched. Waltz and polka were the first to put a man and woman face-to-face, but tango brought them even closer, chest-to-chest and breath-to-breath.

In 1913, during the height of tangomania — the dance's heyday in Paris, Buenos Aires, London, and New York — "civilized" folk were ripe for the audacious closeness of the tango, what a prominent American evangelist had deemed "intolerable for a decent society." Conservatives the whole world over tried to ban it — from legislators to boards of governors to Pope Pius X — though tangomaniacs would swear the dance was not obscene.

Vernon and Irene Castle, ballroom sweethearts of the American stage and silent screen, made their living selling social dance as good clean fun, bowdlerizing jazz rhythms and ragtime for a wider (whiter) audience. Even they tried to neuter tango enough to fit within their program. They (falsely) claimed it was an "old gipsy dance" from Spain — thought formerly "too sensuous" — but corrected and perfected by the Parisians until it "bloomed forth a polished and extremely fascinating dance, which has not had its equal in rhythmical allurement since the days of the Minuet." Done "correctly," tango was "the essence of the modern soul of dancing," commanding "grace, and especially repose." The Castles smoothed away whatever so-called improprieties they could — separating bodies, sterilizing movements — but even their vanilla version of the dance just plain suggested sex.

For my part, I was doing everything I could to willfully ignore whatever sexiness was to be found in Basic tango. My friends and colleagues whistle-hooted every time I mentioned my new avocation. They'd seen the movie version of the dance and spliced me into it, slit skirt and all; or perhaps they'd bought the line from Borges naming it "that reptile from the brothels." But tango has always been more than its prurient reputation. It contains genres, movements, cultures, continents. It is both African and European, yet uniquely Argentine — and carries within it the early story of that nation. A nation built upon a heritage it would rather see obscured.

The first roots of tango, in both name and rhythm, were of Bantu origin; and the creole word *tangó* predates the dance itself, describing drum music, dance motions, and the place where people danced. There was also the Ki-Kongo word *tanga,* for an end-of-mourning celebration, and *tangana,* meaning "to walk that walk." Even *tangere,* from the Latin, would have come to Argentina only indirectly from the Portuguese and Spanish slavers. So either way, the name of tango — whether the moniker direct or root derived — came to Buenos Aires via slave ship. As did its most basic moves.

It was only later, with the influx of European immigration, that these first roots were concealed. Today, the population of Argentina is 97 percent white — or claims to be. The ugly legacy of slavery — and the rich mix of the country's cultural foundation — is glossed over, ignored. If Sarmiento's dream of a white European fatherland succeeded, it is because of all the country has forgotten: The blend of blood and bodies in the outer barrios that made a creole art. The rosters of black dancers, lyricists, composers, poets, *payadores,* and musicians. The guitarists who gave tango its now iconic rhythm. The people we leave out when we call the capital the "Paris of South America" and speak of Argentina as predominantly white. But the Afro-Argentines who gave the world tango ought not be forgotten, nor their continued presence in the art be overlooked.

· · ·

The hybrid tango danced in those first decades was *canyengue,* a word that doesn't translate into English. Literally, in Ki-Kongo it means "melt" — to melt into the music, or your partner, or the dance itself. In *canyengue,* couples danced in Euro-style cheek-to-cheek embrace, but with knees bent and rear ends protruding, projecting stony African "coolness," or *cara fea,* "ugly face," typical of Bantu dances of the time. It was the perfect fusion of Continental intimacy and Bakongo control, the conflagration of *candombe* — danced apart — and couples dancing, plus that contagious *milonga* beat. *Canyengue* became synonymous with both style and state of mind, a bit like "swing" in jazz; if you had to ask, you wouldn't understand. Ironically, it was the European impulse to smooth out tango's African origins that straightened the dancers' backs and brought their pelvises into such scandalous proximity. *Canyengue* gave way to the "fine posture" of *tango liso,* "smoothed-out" tango, and the salon tango of today.

As with jazz, the idea that tango originated in brothels was an exaggeration of the racist upper classes and the media, who did not approve. Tango was found in brothels, sure, but only by coincidence. The millions of men who came by boat to Buenos Aires in the early 1900s — for work, for land — were poor and lonely. Their unslakable thirsts were not for some newfangled partner dance, at least not at first. They queued up for one thing only: to embrace a woman — preferably while lying down. Though, just like jazz in old New Orleans, music was sometimes played to keep the waiting patrons entertained. Men who might not share a language bantered back and forth in tango, sharing their common poverty, their stories, their nostalgia, and their lusts. Men danced with each other because they had no better option. Until, of course, they got upstairs.

And yet the full origins of tango in both Buenos Aires and nearby Montevideo went largely unrecorded, history at that time being loath to speak for those beneath its writers' notice. The sex myth of tango is the genesis that sticks.

The dance is often called a "three-minute love affair." You cuddle into a stranger's chest and take his hand in yours; you wrap your arms around his shoulders. He puts his arm around your waist. You are close enough to feel his breath, and smell his skin and sweat. Your legs will stretch with his. You'll push the full length of you against him, to receive him, and together you will move to music. Rarely would you get so close to someone you did not intend to sleep with. It is fantasy. Every stage of *eros,* from flirtation through intention to discovery, all the way to consummation, resolution, disappointment. This affair, for better or for worse, expires with the song. The partners part, and everyone goes home unscathed.

Most people find this terribly romantic. I, however, had no idea what an affair was supposed to feel like. I had no idea how I was meant to act. All I had were muscle memories of men who didn't seem to want me, men whom I had chosen, as my mum suspected, because of my own deep ambivalence toward sex.

The close embrace for me was but the means to another, less suggestive end. It was not romance; it was a skill to learn, or plural skills: Balance. Patience. Acquiescence. How to lose myself in music — not how to make love standing up. I tried on a leader's body like prosthesis, like a prop. I did as Alfredo had instructed me, and closed my eyes — ignoring their cologne, their hummus breath, their Velcro cheeks. If we each did it right, we ceased to be.

The more I told my mother, the more suspicious she became, as if tango were some sect of forty-something good-for-nothings out to bed her daughter. I opted not to tell her about the time I'd felt a rise in someone's pant leg during class. A fluke — and over before I'd even comprehended what was brushing up against my thigh. I'd ignored it; so could she. I'd send her videos instead, as if to say, "Look, Ma, how beautiful this is!" And she would tell me that it looked like ninjas trying to trip each other.

"I just don't see it," she replied. She was under the impression, bless her heart, that tango was just another distraction thwarting my inevitable path to greatness. When I visited, I played the music for her, the Di Sarli, the Canaro, early Pugliese, the irregular rhythms like a heart under duress.

"Just listen to that, Ma," I said. "The bittersweet, the pain." She shrugged.

"It's kind of creepy," she repeated, in the tone that meant her words contained a lesson. My tendency for reinvention had her perpetually ill at ease. She'd watched me try to parrot normal for too long, and fail. She'd watched me accept deep weirdnesses in others and internalize the blame. She'd watched me disembody, shrink. *You can't just ignore what happened to you, Meghan,* she would say. *It's part of who you are.* It did not seem healthy to her that I allowed myself a body on the dance floor but nowhere else. Then again, she also knew that tango, to me, was all wrapped up in youth and far-off Buenos Aires, and that it made me feel bold and brave. These were perhaps her best ideals, worth nurturing at whatever cost. She, more than anyone, wanted me to find a way out of the valley of my quarter life. "Just be careful, Meg," was all she said.

There wasn't time to dwell on who or what I touched; there was ever more to do. We'd built up to the proper turns: the *molinete* grapevine circle (stepping front, side, back, side) that constitutes a *giro*. The *molinete* takes its name from windmills, children's pinwheels, turnstiles, and you see each in the turn. Either partner does it, sometimes both. Turning around a leader, you feel like the center closing in. When he turns with you—the pair of you like interlocking cogs—it feels centrifugal, as though you're held together only by the fact of turning constantly away.

We moved back to the practice elbows as we learned to turn, then tried again in close embrace. *Switch partners,* the maestro would command, and each follower would make her merry way along to the next body. The close embrace became a constant tactile game. Learning surfaces and textures as they moved, together and apart. Such concentration on my body that I hardly had one anymore. And on these other bodies: no longer strangers, but not yet fully whole. A shirt, with sleeves rolled up. A disembodied forearm. A familiar collar, or the strange plane of a sternum. The vaguest sense of each before the maestro interrupted. *Switch.*

Compared to the embrace, the music required very little of me. I closed my eyes and listened to Di Sarli, sweet Di Sarli, who still dominated class. His music was gallant, chillingly romantic, and patient where so many other tangos seemed to rush. It was steady enough to learn to. A kind of siren song to us beginners. His strings aspired to heights of glory and attained them. If I was having a three-minute love affair with anyone, it was with those strings. They sang together in one sweetly wistful voice. The effect was both heavy and buoyant, like a weighted bunch of flowers.

Tango sometimes felt like that—a mix of sadness and exhilaration. Inflating the balloon of me, then pulling deeper down. High and low. I was lonely going in, then even lonelier. And when I changed my shoes and stumbled back out onto city streets, I felt both that I was exiting an underworld, and that I had flown.

We learned the *sacada* next, a movement that cannot be mastered without complete commitment to the concept of the weight transfer. Learning the *sacada* is partly a diagnostic test to determine whether you are ready for the *gancho* and the other cutesy stuff that follows. The leader leads a step and, as you move with one leg, he interrupts your trailing, weightless leg, displacing it. He has taken your place and you've continued on your path, propelled by the extra energy of his intrusion. If you do it right — if you commit — that free leg starts to fly. You're moved before you have the chance to overthink the movement.

The *sacada* seemed to tie it all together. As though tango, like a heavy-booted force, had stepped into my life, displacing something, filling empty spaces left behind. Knocking through each other's legs, my classmates and I were on the verge of something powerful. It felt as though we'd finally disturbed the sleeping cobra at the core of tango; she was not awake yet, but she stirred.

That night I came home thrilled. "I did my first *sacada!*" I crowed, trying to demonstrate with the refrigerator door as I made myself a sandwich.

"That's great, Biscuit," Peter said, stuffing his hand into a box of cereal. He was not uncaring — just indifferent.

I had, by then, stopped asking him to join me. I didn't need or want him there. Tango class became a wedge between us — this thing we couldn't share. I don't think he felt left behind. My absence was louder, more conspicuous to me. I felt like we were schoolchildren; I was the pal whose family had moved away and, every time I returned for a visit, found that we'd grown imperceptibly apart. But I kept going. Tango was publicly private, like performing. It scratched that same itch: To be myself as someone else. To feel both acknowledged and anonymous. And even though it wasn't glamorous, even though I wasn't very good, it seemed to promise answers to unspoken questions, like an oracle on heels.

I still felt small and harried in the awkward interval after work. I still looked at the eighty-dollar monthly charge and thought it should be saved, or spent more wisely in the name of gender parity. But every week, I forced myself to go. I spent two months of Tuesday evenings in the studio, closing my eyes whenever possible to listen to the hiss and crackle of the old recordings, to let myself be driven forward by the *bandoneón*. Perhaps my fellow acolytes and I had nothing in common but our shared clumsiness, and the simple act of showing up. For fifty minutes, tango held us captive. Maybe our motives differed. Or maybe everybody there was every bit as lost as I was. Maybe the music, in its incurable loneliness, made us all feel less alone.

Chapter Five

SOME WEEKS IN, THE MAESTRO NOTICED ME WAITING OUT-side class doing the Sunday crossword and struck up a conversation. Flattered me. Offered me private lessons in exchange for copyediting his soon-to-be-self-published book. I said yes before I learned the lessons would take place in his living room, which had been converted to a dance studio. *"Horas de vuelo,"* he said, "is all you need. Just flying time." ·

The first email he sent included an invitation to keep warm with him over the weekend. Smiley face. I responded that my boyfriend wouldn't take too kindly to my keeping warm with someone else, smiley face, and thought the subject closed. We continued like that — him perversely, me naïvely — for three months. My mother had warned me young. "People tell you who they are," she said, "within the first five minutes. It's up to you whether to take them at their word."

His book was an adult fairy tale, starring himself as king — part political screed, part romance, part spiritual manifesto. I wanted as much flying time as I could earn, so I spent good portions of my workday rearranging punctuation for him. He said he saw "enormous promise" in me, and would often ask to meet me at the *práctica,* a once-a-week evening practice session at the studio where students not yet ready for the social dance floor cut their social dancing teeth among the more advanced. The vibe was casual, though still intimidating, and the lighting dim. I'd been once, and spent the entire two hours slinking along the wainscoting, waiting, terrified of being asked to dance. With the maestro, I could dance for hours. His leading was coercive, clear. He danced me — like the old *tangueros,* albeit more aggressively. As a teacher, he was good enough to compensate for my mistakes. This made me look much better than I was. For the first time, I felt that I was dancing. Isolated movements started making sense: the triangles formed and re-formed by the feet, the mechanics of the partnered cat walk, the way the turn should flow. I began even to sweat. A rush of air kissed my temples as we stalked the room in long and tiger-muscled strides.

We danced above my level. Because the maestro was ostentatious, he yanked me through advanced sequences as the music moved him. He loved Piazzolla, late Troilo, all the really heavy-handed stuff. When he started holding on too tightly, bystanders began to notice. Suddenly he'd whip my leg to hook behind his and we'd assume that sexy pose you've seen on tango postcards. I hated him for that. I was a beginner and I knew my place. I didn't want my fellow students thinking I was too big for my britches. Or that I was cuckolding my inattentive boyfriend with my tango teacher.

I said nothing. I felt I couldn't — not without upsetting the equilibrium of our exchange. Free lessons, flying time. I took what I was given. Once a week, I'd race to his apartment out in somewhere-between-the-airports Queens for training sessions. He taught me everything he could, including moves I hadn't earned: hooked *ganchos,* stage-worthy lifts and dips. Afterward, he made pierogi.

· · ·

We became close over the course of our three-month exchange. It started innocently enough. I gave him panting, adulatory thanks; he gave me uncomfortable praise. He called me his guru, his best student, and — in a twist of fatherly awkwardness that confused me deeply — his *princesa*. He told me he felt blessed to have me. I told him, and meant it, that I felt the same. He didn't understand my meaning; he called me a tease. And so began the second of many stages of negotiation. My answer to his offers was still no. Did I want to go away together for the weekend? No. Did I want him to take me on an all-expenses-paid vacation somewhere halfway around the world? Well, yes, but firmly: no.

He began referring to his book as "the Baby," which made our interactions even stranger. He said a man had to be very careful not to fall in love with a midwife such as me. He called me gorgeous. He called me kind, intelligent, and good. He alternated between suggestive parlay and sucking what he could from me to help his book. Could I compare him to Orwell, or *The Alchemist,* or Dante Alighieri, perhaps, in an effusive blurb? Would my mother like to write him an online review? Would I, perhaps, like to launch my own publicity campaign? He was a little like the kid you play with who wants to script your make-believe, and is forever trying to mash the plastic of your dolls together in some caricature of sex. You think the storyline is moving one way, and then — *bam* — the clap of doll on doll, cavorting madly in his hands.

I didn't notice this, of course. I saw only a learned man who appeared for all the world to worship me. He spoke six languages — and wrote to me in three. Expansive emails about destiny, both mine and his, preying on my frantic need for fate to unveil something still in store for me that I had not foreseen. Sometimes he wrote about me in third person, his *princesa.* "How beautiful she is," he wrote. "How excited she gets that she is in the Tango, like in a dream." *Oh, how beautiful she is.* The words drowned out my better judgment. It didn't matter to me that he was not the one I wanted saying them. I couldn't understand what I felt then, oscillating between icky and elated; I had no context for it. I wanted his attentions to be innocent — and when they weren't, I tried to sand them down or laugh them off until they were. I wanted to feel desirable, without the fight to fend off his desire. But he was intuitive, excessive, slick. And when it came to Peter, the maestro smelled a rat. Perhaps some part of him did not believe me when I told him I was spoken for. Perhaps I knew I wasn't, really. Perhaps part of me wanted to run my fingers through that idea of fire, to see if it would hurt.

Thrice he tried to kiss me. Thrice he was rebuked. Each time, he stormed away, then sent apologetic missives about how we finally understood each other, and how refreshing it was, for a change, to find a woman who said "no" when she meant "no." For that alone, I should have spat straight in his face. Instead, each time he asked forgiveness, I complied — as I did every time he battered boundaries I had asserted. I accepted his apologies and assumed — at last! — we understood each other.

I rode the E train for an hour each way, to test our truce. He met me at the door in sweatpants and insisted that we dance in socks. He muscled me around him like a lasso, turning, front, side, back, side. I squeezed shut my eyes and spun, and felt the old blind thrill of Buenos Aires, only faster, more acute. Dancing, the treaties held. The worst he ever did was hold a pose one extra beat to admire the figure we made in the mirror.

We danced to the *Essential Leonard Cohen* songbook as much as to anything from the Golden Age, and though the lyrics didn't fit, I began to feel as though the maestro and his studio existed only *'cross the borders of my secret life.* Mum called him my Svengali. He took it as a compliment. Our Grand

Friendship, he said. The perfect team. He accused me later of harboring an archetypal father complex. He was right. "This is something you might want to start working on," he wrote, and warned me against predaceous tango men.

He held my hand once, driving me home. It felt almost paternal, the way he'd laid his palm on mine over the console. He was jabbering about love and Aztec gods and semiology, shouting over the highway din, and driving like a madman into midtown. My limbs were singing from the dancing we'd just done, and the trucks and limos whizzing by were just warm wind blown through the open window. I felt sixteen again, hitchhiking through the north of Argentina on the back bed of a *camión*. I let him hold my hand. Despite the road rage and the unsolicited advances, I told myself that he was harmless, just brutish enough to make me feel alive, but not at risk. If I stopped speaking to him every time he made a trifling pass, I'd lose that. I wanted the channel open, believing we could indeed forge that *gran amistad* without sex or interference that I'd read about in books from bygone days. "It's better this way," I wrote him later, with my dress-up wisdom, "and infinitely less trite." I turned a blind eye from the covert and overt threats of him because he made me feel like I mattered. He made me feel seen.

He had me in the perfect trap — grateful for every crumb of tango he bestowed, constantly apologizing to him for his lechery, and guiltier every day for driving him to it. I told him things I shouldn't have, unintentionally misleading things, like: there was nothing I would rather do than dance with him. Which had the benefit of being true. Tango nights were now the highlight of my week, and he had named himself the gatekeeper. He was the only person I could talk to about tango; he seemed both to know this and exploit it. He was the first person I told when I acquired my red suede shoes. "Good," he'd said. "Shoes mean you're serious." His tone was often professorial, as if to maintain dominance, his mastery of me. Half of me bristled at the implied paternalism, the other reveled in having one more teacher to impress. One more good report card. Proof of my progress, however small.

There is a song, a tango, to explain those first few months of dancing. The secrecy of my double life, and the fragility. "Tu íntimo secreto," another by Di Sarli, became my song. *"La dicha es un castillo con un puente de cristal,"* sings Jorge Durán, amidst a sweet cascade of glory strings. Bliss is a castle with a glass bridge — and of the thousands of us who cross, only two or three will ever make it there. The song asks for surrender: *"entrégate al amor,"* it begs, and I was eager to, having always found my bearings best inside the prettiness of other people's words. The song also cautions, *"tu íntimo secreto a nadie le confíes"*: trust no one with your secret. Dancing was my *íntimo secreto*, rather than some great, clandestine love. I was going to cross that crystal drawbridge into bliss. Svengali was my toll.

After my Basic cycle was complete, he encouraged me to register for his Choreography and Performance class, which would devise and present a routine for tango's rotation in the studio's monthly showcase. When my assigned partner, obdurate and aggressive, quit the workshop after only one rehearsal — a rehearsal at which he'd misjudged the placement of my feet and accidentally sucker-kicked me to the floor — the maestro swooped in to take his place. Should I have been surprised?

This occasioned even more training. More tricky sequences to maim. I lapped it up, high on the dancing, thrilled by my own inexplicable allure. I was improving so much faster than my classmates — because of him, this stroke of luck. But we kept bumping heads against the low ceiling of his persistence. He made another overseas invitation, another loaded declaration. *No*, I told him. *No.*

I told him he could care for me, but must not love me. He

could hold me in his arms only to dance, where I felt nothing but the pure white blur of tango. I knew that we had gone too far, though in my folly couldn't fathom how. I knew, and I did nothing but refuse him and apologize, again. Refuse. Apologize. Refuse. *Pazzo,* I called him. Crazy man. He called me innocent, pristine. "This clean girl with the unpolluted mind." He wanted all or nothing. I should have walked away; instead, I begged him not to shut me out. I begged him for one last shot at platonic virtue, to remain his *gran amiga.* But he kept testing, pushing. Thrusting himself into my psyche with his leather pants and his insistent speech, his hard heels clapping the ground.

The toe-sucking came just after this. We'd finished running through the choreography for the performance. I sat there, stretching, bending over hamstrings, elongating my calves. I took off my practice shoes and rotated tired circles with my ankles. "Here," he said, and took my foot, began massaging. I remember thinking that stopping him might be insulting. He started to peel off my sock. I pulled away. He held on, and pulled me by the foot across the floor. My butt slid easily in yoga pants.

My white fish of a foot was in his lap.

There. I should have stopped it, slapped him, or ventriloquized a ringtone from the cell phone in my purse. I should have run — but I was sure he wouldn't push. A foot rub — generous, benign. He raised it to his lap and kept on rubbing. I tried to speak, defuse the moment with my nervous chatter, found that I could not. He bent down and, in seconds, rested the whole of his lower lip atop my sweaty digits. As if about to play harmonica. Then he started breathing onto them. He lowered the hot cave of his mouth over my foot, and I just sat there, paralyzed, staring mutely at him, determined not to blink. I would not show my revulsion or betray the humid feeling that was surging up my legs in spite of me. My toes were in his mouth.

This was too far; I had let it go too far. I extricated myself and my feet, as politely as I could. I did not stay for post-practice pierogi. I did not let him drive me home. I went and waited for the local E train, sitting on a concrete slab in the empty station, staring at my lap. Nauseated and ashamed. *I told you it was creepy,* nagged my mother's voice inside my head. *I told you to be careful.*

In hindsight, maybe it was funny. Maybe I should have run home to tell Peter that some old cad with half a mullet who'd been trying to nail me for the past three months had just tried to suck my toes. Maybe I should have found it perfectly ridiculous—how thoroughly I'd failed to grasp the situation. How I had stumbled, in my criminal naïveté, perhaps unwittingly encouraged him. But I was mortified. It was the single most erotic moment of my twenties, and it was wrong, all wrong. *A nadie le confíes,* I repeated to myself, and suddenly—ardently—wanted him to disappear into that secret world so I could seal him in with wet cement, just like I'd done with every other shame. Bury it deep and build again. Tell no one. Fortify another castle, crystalline and pure.

It wasn't all my fault, but I was culpable. I had thought that I could talk Svengali out of his infatuation, because I never quite believed him. I didn't see myself as worth the wanting. The awful irony is that, even as I wrested toes away from the maestro, I was writing in my journal how I was not the kind of woman anyone could love. I inspired *pathos, philio,* even *storge,* but never romance, never *eros* or *agape.* And that is what I coveted: the kind of love you closed your eyes for. There was no connection between Svengali's interest, sticky and leering, and my notion of romantic love. If I can explain my woeful missteps, then that is how: I did not take him seriously, in either word or deed.

I couldn't recognize *eros* even when it sucked me on the toes. And I had no idea of the power I might have, the power it must have looked like I was playing with so idly.

I see now how warped it was — and had been from the start. I look back and all I feel are his eyes on me, assessing. Watching me marvel at my progress in the mirror. Deriving some sick pleasure from the way he made me squirm free of his snares. Feeding me just enough of what I didn't know I needed, sensing I was thirsty for it. Preying on my need for fatherly acceptance — and my guilt. Always the guilt.

I wrote to Mum and told her what had happened, how I'd cried myself to sleep, confessing, to her and to myself, that maybe there had been a part of me that had wanted to run away with him — or rather the idea of him. I did want to dance and travel and learn about the planes of astral light and be adored. I wanted this intense, magical friendship, though I hadn't understood it wasn't feasible with a strange man more than twice my age whose primary object was my conquest. "Why is that?" I wrote. "What kind of destructive nitwit behavior is that?" I knew with this last rejection the intensity would fade, and subconsciously, I knew, I had been feeding on it. The possibility that I could still tack wildly in an alternate direction. That I could be wondrous, wild.

"I'm guessing the key word here is magic," Mum wrote back. Magic, to her, was always hard to lose. "This probably isn't the responsible mother thing to say, but I am glad you considered running off." She didn't think I was a nitwit. For the first time, I was just like her. And Svengali was the type of man she might have chosen: worldly, a little deviant, and — lord knows — in her age range. "Here's the question, though," she wrote. "Why do you keep picking men to fulfill you in so many ways your partner of choice doesn't? Why are you settling for so little when the world has so much to offer?" She had too often done the same, she said.

"Meg," she wrote, "don't cry. Live. Don't have guilt that you are being unfair. Where in this pair of men are you seeing anyone being fair to you?" She thought Peter and Svengali were to blame, "a couple of clowns" taking only what they wanted from me without honoring the rest. "You, my darling girl, are only a nitwit in that you value yourself so little.

"Keep dancing," she wrote. "Keep flirting. Hold your head high and give them both a run for their money. You have nothing to prove to anyone. Do what you will, but I am glad you are feeling alive and sexy and vibrant. It's about time, because you are."

I treasure those words now. Back then I could not believe them. Back then I felt only sick remorse. Back then, my stomach twisted at the mere thought of being considered "sexy." I had never meant to flirt, or tease. I didn't even think that I knew how. "A woman has always three parts in her," the maestro had once written to me. "The little girl (that we love so much); the grown up, savvy and sophisticated woman (it's OK); and the asshole part (the bitch, that we all hate)." The insinuation was that, in refusing him, I was playing at the last. I wanted to yell — to flail in his direction with my strangled feminism and my fists. I knew he was a sexist twerp. But I did nothing; I couldn't quite channel the rage. Deep down, I feared he might be right — though not about the sophistication or the spurning bitch. The little girl, I felt, was me: constantly in trouble, constantly confused.

I stopped going out to Queens. Our interactions after classes and rehearsals were perfunctory, curtailed. We both knew this was the end of our grand friendship. Perhaps he was embarrassed too. His motives were coming clear. I was no prodigy. I was an easy mark, the only twenty-something girl in a studio of mid-aged women.

On the night of the performance, I stood at reception, waiting for Svengali, my shoe bag in one hand, my boots still on my feet, as if I planned to run. Another tango teacher came up to the desk. I'd seen him often; he taught intermediate and advanced classes full of pretty girls and ballerinas. His name was Enzo. He was handsome, and still shy of forty. He wore sweater vests and corduroys and carried a rolled-up *New Yorker,* an umbrella, and a scally cap. I assumed that if he knew me, it was only through Svengali's antics at the *práctica.*

"The big night, eh?"

"Such as it is," I groaned.

"Nervous?"

We locked eyes. I told him I was terrified, then promptly disappeared to change my shoes and put on the crimson lipstick Mum had encouraged me to buy for the occasion. The studio was bustling as usual, and indifferent to my nerves. The stakes for these monthly promo nights were low — except for me, suddenly and sorely sure that everyone would see the blunders I had made writ large. There were eight of us performing, four couples dressed in black and red. We danced to "La bordona," the 1949 Pugliese version of a stirring Emilio Balcarce tune. The later interpretation, recorded by Troilo, *"el Pichucho,"* in 1956, is considered the immortal one. But Svengali had chosen the Pugliese, and it was plenty rousing. It was a gallop of a tango — great sprints of tempo that race and slow and stall out into quiet sections like a majestic beast lowering herself to sleep. The strings in "La bordona" play that purebred beast, raring to stretch her gait to breakneck speed, but stifled by her rider's whims for pomp and pageantry.

The song is difficult to dance, especially for beginners, and the maestro erred on the side of vulgar showiness. This wasn't real tango; it was choreography. There was lots of saucy leg-linking and posing, even one section in which the four men and four women broke apart to line dance toward each other, *West Side Story*-style. We bungled the stirring variation at the end with butchered ornaments and sloppy *molinetes*. My ankles quaked, my heart slammed at my ribs, I cringed. But the song came to its famous Pugliese finish, and that was that. Polite applause. I blushed, though not with the customary pleasure of performance. I was now not merely dancing, turning circles blind; I had been blinded.

Peter had come to watch. "Good job, Biscuit!" he said. He looked genuinely baffled, possibly also proud. I neither introduced him to the maestro nor met Enzo's eyes as I quit the room and gathered up my things. I freed my hair from bobby pins, and fled.

Chapter Six

PETER STEERED ME THROUGH THE EVENING CROWD OF HIP-sters smoking outside cocktail bars. The throngs of normal people, ignorant to tango. There was a game on in a sports bar four blocks up. We went in through a wall of noise, sat down, and ordered fried food, foamy beer. I stared, dazed, at the screen, watching the points rack up in each team's square. Modern music thumped through the commercials. I blinked across the table at my boyfriend, his focus squarely on the game. This would have been a good place to give up, to let tango recede. I swallowed my pint and wished the spell would break for good, and let me go. But it did not.

Recently, I found this mantra etched into a notebook from that time: *He visto mi alegría y lo voy a lograr.* Meaning, roughly, *I have seen my joy and I am going after it.* I couldn't let the maestro spoil my *alegría*, however mortified I felt.

I waited a week or two, and then, in penance, sought out a female teacher: well-respected, smug, sadistic Mariela. She taught Pre-Intermediate technique on Monday and Wednesday nights, classes full of still more arduous walking exercises: keeping the body trunk over the leading foot, stepping toe first—sliding, and hovering in the middle of the almost-splits. It was essential training, the mechanics of the all-important walk. *Keep your legs together; let no light between your thighs.* Between steps, always collect the feet together at the ankles. Err on the side of tidiness, precision. These were basics I'd neglected in my hubristic sprint through Svengali's showy sequences.

Mariela taught in a rented space that wasn't quite a studio — more like an empty room hidden in an unmarked building on a side street in the purse district. There was no warmth. Often, there wasn't even music. The class was small and strangely populated: a Bangladeshi banker, a stylish Asian art dealer in a pillbox hat, a potbellied middle-aged white guy named Bill. Again, we didn't speak. Two expert leaders, whom I called her fan club, were on hand to help. They offered no more encouragement than she.

Mariela distributed pieces of paper for each of us to place beneath our feet. In tango, after all, both feet — stepping and trailing — must maintain contact with the floor. Our task was simple: keep the paper underfoot.

"If you lose the paper, you're doing it wrong," she barked, in a voice far too sultry to be shrill, her vowels accentuated in the perfect Argentine liquescence of her speech. She was a lovely human being off the classroom floor.

We stumbled around for twenty minutes, grunting, desperate for success. One by one, we lost our balance and our papers slipped.

"No," she said, pacing the room. "Wrong."

She wasn't even looking at us. She had eyes in her dominatrix bun. Sometimes she'd shake loose her hair, the jet-black waves that hung like shiny meat, and wind it back into a knot. It was too much hair for such a tiny woman. Too much glossy beauty, too much poise. She was petite, maybe five foot three in flats, and I resented her low center of gravity, her incorruptible balance, and her sturdy turns.

She was not the slightest bit impressed with me. I was not

special. I was just another beginner breaking rules, too eager to advance. She seemed terrifically bored with me, with all of us. For the first time, I grasped how onerous it must be for professionals to suffer all these boobs stampeding on their national bequest. The idea of being just another tango tourist gave me a pang of self-reproach.

For the first time, my dedication wavered. I stifled intermittent yawns. The class dragged on in drills that seemed devised to make us look ridiculous. It was possible, I thought, that after all these weeks and fees I'd never get the hang of tango. Not with all the Mondays in the world. What was so effortless for Mariela and her humorless assistants seemed impossible. And she wasn't even wearing tango shoes, but knee-high four-inch-heeled leather boots.

"No. Wrong," she'd repeat, as if exhausted by us, by our failure to achieve. She yawned and checked her watch. "Again."

Her lack of kindness was disheartening, but she was a genius. "Stop," she'd cry, and march into the middle of the room to demonstrate. She made it look so easy; her turns were fluid, gliding—not frantic and halting, as Svengali's had seemed. "Use the floor," she said, her outstretched index finger pointing strongly downward as she pivoted. I noticed she spent more time monitoring our progress than Svengali, and less time preening and twirling in the mirror.

We started another exercise, this time partnered: *ochos*. We formed a circle to simulate the line of dance. Guiding us by the elbows, the leaders drove us around the room, skating our little backwards figure eights while Mariela crossed her arms, patrolled. "Now walk," she said, moving clockwise against the line of dance to catch us in the act of dancing badly. "No," she said, pointing to me. "Wrong."

"Use the heel," she said. "Complete the step." I only imagined the riding crop in her hand.

· · ·

I learned one vital thing from Mariela, which is that one cannot learn to tango overnight. The dance is an indefatigable mistress to whom you must surrender totally. She requires patience and humility and time. In 1920, when a young *porteño* wished to learn, he found himself a mentor at the local *academia,* and prostrated himself at that man's shined-up shoes. Tango wasn't really taught as much as it was inherited. There were no studios. No group class cycle schemes. No syllabi for Basic, levels A–D. The old maestros were just *tangueros* and their pupils pimpled boys, young men with varying degrees of skill and social grace, who learned by trial and error — and example — how to improvise. Since the advent of *canyengue* in the 1890s, apprentice dancers learned by watching, learned by trying, learned by all-important touch. Men practiced with men. A master didn't differentiate between what he danced and what he taught to newer generations at the *práctica.* He simply took those young men in his arms and moved.

I imagine these sessions were similar to class with Mariela, only more hands-on. Learning to lead by following, without the luxury of demonstration. "No. Wrong." The student would be corrected and appropriately shamed. He would work to sweating, work to failure — three hours a day, every day. Slump home with his dance shoes sagging, practicing *enrosques* (tight, leaderly embellished turns) in his underclothes, watching with insouciant sadness as the more experienced dancers strode past on their way to the *milongas,* where tango was danced each night. I see him staring out some back corner window, a sliver cut into the brick, and looking down onto their glossy, lacquered heads, their black crepe suits, white scarves, their polished, pointed shoes. And of course, at all the women he was not allowed to touch.

For generations, tango dancers trained for years before they risked the social dance floor. Honest workers and crime bosses alike would drill like soldiers, until their skills were sure enough to function even underneath the magic spell of the *milonga*. The goal was — then as now — to improvise, and to impress. Even with the white slave trade importing eastern European girls by the hundreds and confining them to brothels and to social clubs, men in the city outnumbered women almost ten to one. Tango was often the only opportunity for men in turn-of-the-century Buenos Aires to hold a real live lady in their arms without having to pay.

A man could, however, purchase tickets — called *latas,* as they were made of tin — and dance with women hired by the *academias* for social dancing. *Tener la lata,* to hold the tin, meant to wait for hours to hand one's ticket over to a certain woman. But he'd have to *learn* to dance with other men. And wait until his maestro deemed him fit for introduction at the dancehalls. Even then, one misstep was enough to banish him. Tango was a privilege, something to be earned.

If only Mariela had been the kind of maestra to take me in her arms and teach me with that surety and care. I longed for her to step in as my gatekeeper, to tutor me until she judged me worthy of the dance. But she remained indifferent. I settled for her biweekly boot camp, accustomed myself to the lack of praise, and tried a little harder every week to keep my paper underfoot.

I took a private lesson with a touring superstar from Buenos Aires. An Adonis with taut brown pectorals and a ponytail. His name was Cesar. It was just the two of us in the rented studio.

"Let's start," he said, laying my right palm on his chest as he began to walk. I tried to slow my nerves, anticipate his steps — show just how pliant and responsive I had learned to be. "Do not be passive," he corrected. "Never only follow." Being pliant and responsive was not enough; he wanted presence. He wanted to feel my weight, resistance in my legs. We did not turn. He barely led an *ocho.* Instead, we walked. He coaxed me to elongate my steps. "Long, like a cat," he said, "a panther." He stopped me in the center of the room. He told me how he had been a dancer since the age of five, and how his father always told him, "Cesar, you must walk." Not once, but "fifty thousand times." "This we must do," he said, to comprehend the dance. *El caminito.* He smiled at me as though I were his little sister, then offered me his arm.

Cesar was equable, relaxed, striding the room in jeans and a sleeveless undershirt. He tucked his hair behind his ear. He sweated, but did not betray the strain. He was the sexiest man I'd ever been in a room with, alone or otherwise, yet there was nothing of seduction there. Beneath my palm, his chest was nothing but a well-made object, as though he were the bust of some forgotten warrior, his skin cool and made of bronze.

He danced. I listened. The afternoon was late; this was his last lesson after hours of teaching. We left the lights off as the sun bled out of Chelsea from the bottom up. Dusk curtained the dusty windows of the studio. The hardwood floor faded gold to grey and shadows clouded in the corners of the mirror. A boom box played the same Di Sarli loop of slow and simple practice tunes.

"It is a conversation," he said, arranging us in practice elbows. This was dancing with a jungle river. My body next to his was soft and reedy; he was a flood I was not strong enough to stand against. I made an effort to remind myself to breathe, to engage my deepest muscles just to stay afloat. To keep my core and cattails strong.

I thought back to dancing with the maestro, how giddy I'd felt being tossed around. It hadn't taken much to topple me—a bit of current, the lascivious attentions of a goatish sixty-something man. How feebly I'd stood my ground. Cesar wanted none of that. He didn't want to dance me. He wanted backtalk, sass. He wanted a response.

"You must always have a secret," he said, and I racked my

brain for one — something better, deeper than the toe-sucking that haunted me. And less deep, perhaps, than buried child-hood shame. None of my girlhood heartbreaks seemed appropriate. But I didn't want my secret to be the mere fact that I didn't have one — that, among all these three-minute love affairs, I was a fraud.

"We both have things to say," he said. "Our betrayals and our broken loves. We tell them to each other with our bodies, but I don't know yours and you will not know mine." We communicate purely what we cannot understand.

He moved us into close embrace; I settled in his arms, where I felt young and sexless. Like a maiden witnessing a tumble in the hay, who stands there dumbly and transfixed, a milk pail in her hand. I bit my lip and danced with extra might. Perhaps my frustration with my skill and with myself would pass for lover's rage. It got darker and we walked again. I stood, pushed back — rather than merely waiting to react.

"Two steps," he said. "And then you cross." His strides were sprint length, superhuman. I labored to match his pace. Hypnotic. I perspired, working latent muscles in my legs — each time pushing harder through the toes, the thighs. My knees bent to keep me rooted to the ground. I did what he did, as they say, backwards and in heels. Got lost in it. We both were drenched in sweat. "Two steps, and cross." The CD skittered to a stop, but we kept going. The room went properly dark.

"Good," he said. "Much better."

We sat in silence as we changed our shoes. It was late April; New York was heating up the oven of its summer sidewalks, but the nights were cool. In the elevator, Cesar told me I had tango in my soul. This was nonsense, but I took it as my missing benediction. More than my hundred dollars' worth. Technique notwithstanding, I felt I'd been anointed. I had magic in me; I didn't need to siphon from the maestro. I just needed to tease it out.

We parted. He went west and I went east, letting the chill air dry my forehead sweat. I pulled on my denim jacket and scribbled scraps of dialogue into my notebook. What Cesar Coelho had said. I wanted to remember how it felt: not being so acquiescent. For the first time in my life, I felt like I could be a woman, not just someone who pretended she could move like one. I contained mysteries, secrets, and unsatiated lusts, though no idea what to do with them.

Chapter Seven

PETER ASSUMED IT WAS A PHASE. WATCHING, AS I CONTIN-
ued to venture out, toting my ever rattier pair of shoes, the
suede rubbed thin and lusterless. Sometimes he'd ask me not
to go. I asked, again, for him to come with me — just one lesson, forty-five minutes of his life — to see my secret world, but
he refused. He wrinkled his face and shook his head with more
fervor than he'd ever felt for me. Likewise I had more desire to
trip away to tango class than I would ever feel for him.

For the next two months, I started frequenting the weekend
prácticas: Saturday mornings and Sunday afternoons. Saturday
mornings were hosted by Mariela in a big, bright midtown studio. There were baskets full of chopped-up bodega croissants,
and coffee fresh on everybody's breath. People were dressed
for dog walks, shopping, lunch dates, or the gym. Everyone
moved a little sleepily, sometimes with the bruise of last night's
makeup visible around the eyes. I went as a stranger, paid my
ten dollars at the door, and waited, as I'd been instructed, to
be asked. I danced with older men, aware now of the privilege
of my youth. I noticed the row of chairs along the wall, and
the line of older women sitting there in flowing pastel skirts
and strappy shoes, waiting for dances. I smiled with contrition
as I took the hand of an approaching upright gentleman who

clutched my waist and drew me to his bony chest. He hoisted us into the walk. This turned out to be dismal. His strides were too upright, mincing, short. Instead of leading a *molinete,* he simply eased me a few inches out of the embrace, cocked his head, and cleared his throat. I took the hint and grapevine-turned my way around him, and then he pulled me back in with a bump of breastplates. I muscled through three songs, then plopped myself down on the bench whence he had plucked me. This was going to require more patience and determination than I'd thought. The bench ladies seemed to smirk in unison in my direction.

Sundays down in SoHo were the same, though I knew a few more people, and got a few more dances that felt worthy of the name. Mariela wasn't shouting from the sidelines to remind me to *use my heel.* It was friendly. Wholesome, day-lit tango. Tango without the risk of sexual misunderstanding. Spring sun streamed in, warm and drowsy, through the open windows; tango strains spilled out onto the street. This was not a phase. It was devotional. A project to which I'd pledged myself whose scope, I knew, exceeded every limit I could see from where I stood. So I went, alone, to *prácticas,* and took my licks. I did my drills, biding my time.

I took a breath and signed up for an Intermediate class cycle with Enzo. There weren't as many ballerinas as I'd thought. He nodded to me as he entered, skulking in with half a smile. He spoke softly, with nothing of Mariela's husky admonitions, or the self-important bluster of Svengali.

"When you take a woman's weight, you have to care for her," he said, describing the embrace. "If you take her off her axis, even for a second," he continued, "do not make her stop before you put her back."

A follower's axis in tango is her line of balance, the single beam of gravity down through her feet. When the leader shifts her weight from one foot to another, her trunk, her axis, comes along. When walking, turning, standing still, she stays on it, held up only by herself. But there are moves and figures that will take her off: *volcadas, colgadas,* and certain other moments wherein two bodies make *la carpa,* a tent, and share a single center. *Apilado* style, which translates to "stacked" or "piled up," is built on this. The partners plant their feet, then lean toward each other, touching torsos, sharing that one point of balance in between them as they dance. That center, whether for a single move or an entire song, requires trust. In tango, it is considered gauche to make a woman lose her balance. Insofar as it is her job to maintain herself, with her core and cattails, so to speak, you mustn't mess with her. You must restore her to her axis if and when you pull her off. These are the negotiations at the heart of the embrace. Afterward, in real life, a follower may be treated like she doesn't matter; but on the tango floor, she does. She must. Without her, close embrace is just a lone man leaning forward into nothing, like a windblown tree.

"*El abrazo.* It's a hug." Enzo demonstrated with a ballerina in the center of the floor. "You hold her well," he told us. "Like you mean it."

He was circling the room now. It was warm, and he'd removed his sweater vest. When he reached me, his cheeks were damp. He smelled like aftershave. With my left hand, I cupped his tricep; with my right, I held his left. His hands were big, calloused, and one horny thumbnail bore a rash. He squeezed my hand, gently, gradually — as you would a plum to test its ripeness. I became aware of him as adult man — the Old World swarthiness, the hulk of him, and his enormous hands. He was young Humphrey Bogart or the memory of some Sicilian grandfather I'd never had. I became aware of myself as adult woman in a way I hadn't dancing with Svengali (disembodied) or with Cesar (statuesque).

He placed his right palm on the hollow of my back to show

me how it ought to feel. He nudged me into close embrace. It no longer felt like handling meat. My arm slipped around his shoulders; my temple came to hover and then rest beside his. We rocked in place, weaving on our separate axes. He shifted my weight from foot to foot.

"Waiting for the train," he whispered. "Waiting for the bus."

Right, left. Left, right. I missed the moment when we started moving: A side step first, and then we walked and paused. Walk. Pause. The wisdom of El Gran Gavito, sage tango maestro of the 1990s, came to me: *La esencia del tango no está en los pasos, sino en las pausas.* The essence of tango isn't in the steps, but in the pauses.

My eyes rolled shut. Just when he had my weight responding, when our walks had synchronized, he took a backwards step that I did not know to expect. I didn't need to know to follow him. I was deep in *la ignorancia sagrada.* My weight was on my right foot, stretched into the floor; it stayed in place. My torso went with Enzo as he stepped back, and my free left leg flew with me, forward into nothing, swept across the space between our feet. Like a face-first trust fall I might have done in acting class, only much less rigid. His chest, which wasn't concave in the slightest, held me up with brute stability, supporting me as he pushed us back upright.

Volcada comes from the verb "to overturn," or capsize. But it feels like weightlessness. I landed softly on my axis and returned to earth.

If there was indeed a moment, this was it. My *precisely when.* Five months into tango classes. For a moment, all the air was taken from me and I couldn't breathe: I felt like a sandbag thrown from heavy shoulders. *This* was all I wanted — for what I now knew to call my axis to be honored, finally. To not be made to lose my balance. To be protected, kept from falling forward into empty space. To be held like someone meant it.

I must have blushed, though not from shame or titillation; this was something pure. The danger of falling forward, the surprise of being steady in my motion, stretched along my spine. The new pleasure of being held. My body hummed and did as it was told. No flinching, no retreating boyfriend, no recoil.

"Nice," Enzo murmured. He squeezed my plum hand gently, one last time, then moved to the next follower. The rest of class could not compare. I didn't mind. I held that information in my body — how close embrace was meant to feel, willing the warm sun radiating through the windows to set it in my cells.

Every time you dance with somebody above your level, you feel this ache. How tango ought to, and might one day, feel. You can follow the unfamiliar when you're led by someone who knows how. And then you've felt it; then it's yours. You're humbled by your own ineptitude, but galvanized. That one dance becomes a talisman. It's what will keep you going — despite the tedium, despite the loneliness, despite the endless list of skills to master. You catch a far-off glint of that glass bridge.

Tango highs are soaring, if sporadic: One good dance, or one good class. One moment when you shut your eyes and fly. Movement matches music and the combination makes your muscles slack. Your mind goes blissfully blank. *Was it worth it?* you will ask yourself, remembering the lows. *All that anguish for three minutes' worth of joy?* Yes, the answer floods up through your limbs. Yes.

Chapter Eight

ALL THE LESSONS IN THE WORLD CAN'T MAKE A TANGO dancer. Only social dancing can. I'd been lying low in group classes and *prácticas,* afraid to show myself in public or make a spectacle of myself at the *milongas.*

"What's a *milonga?*" my mother asked, though she somehow never managed to pronounce it, adding an extra "r," as she often did with words ending in "a."

I explained that a *milonga* was a tango social, the event of dancing. Venues vary, but the hour is late, the lights are dim, the dancers get all gussied up. It's like a monthly, weekly, or — in some cases — nightly tango prom.

"So this is the social part," she said, hopeful.

"Sort of," I said. I still felt like that poor neophyte, peeping from his upstairs window. Undressed and unready for the spectacle of the *milonga.* But as intimidating as the prospect of real social dancing was, it would bring me that much closer to the tango I had seen in Buenos Aires, in the cloistered cavern of that wood-paneled club.

There was a pageantry in tango, a decorum I found oddly reassuring. There were dozens of unwritten rules, most of which I'd learned only by breaking. A gentleman, for example, asks a lady to dance — preferably by the covert gesture of the

cabeceo: eye contact plus arch of eyebrows nets consenting nod
— and their dance is freshly made between them for that music, for approximately nine to fourteen minutes, which equates
to three or four songs, or a *tanda. Tanda* translates to "group"
or "turn" or "series." Between each *tanda,* the curtain, *la cortina,* falls — a shot of non-tango music signaling the dancers to
change partner. You may or may not make polite conversation.
My name is. What do you do? Insert awkward jokes about the
weather, or the DJ, or the news.

Dancing with anyone as long as I had with Svengali, even
at the *práctica,* probably screamed *affair!* to anybody keeping
score. You're meant to dance only a set or two with any given
partner, maximum. Unless you're practice partners or roman-
tically entwined. One party ends the tête-à-tête with "thank
you," and you go your separate ways. A gentleman will sometimes reorient the lady by escorting her to her chair, though
this gentility is rare outside Buenos Aires. A woman who is un-
engaged must sit or stand somewhere and wait until a prospect
meets her gaze.

"Well, *that* hardly seems fair," Mum said, but I wasn't after fairness. The more rules there were for me to follow, the
harder it would be to fall astray. My bigger concern was gin-
ning up the nerve. Despite the potentially oppressive gender
roles, Mum was the one to dare me to my first *milonga.* She was
my champion for taking risks, even those of which she didn't
quite approve — and the more I told her about tango, the less
she did approve. "Wow," she said, "to be a man in tango. Must
be nice."

"Mum."

"No, really. I just sit there and pick someone and then they
do everything I ask them, inch by inch, and then they're supposed to *thank me* for the pleasure?"

"Mum, I swear it isn't like that," I said. Though sometimes,
I realize, it was. Everywhere else, I was a strident feminist. In

tango, I seemed willing to forgive — and far too eager to apologize. As though dancing had no bearing on the real world in which I lived and worked for eighty cents on every dollar and visited the gynecologist. Perhaps I forgave it precisely because it was so easy to condemn. So simply — often cartoonishly — gendered.

"Look," she said. "If you're not going to these mahgondalers, then what's the point?"

I went, very timidly, to the lowest-stakes *milonga* I could find. It happened every Tuesday night at a shabby bar and grill called Lafayette, tucked behind construction on a torn-up Tribeca street. It was frequented by fellow studio-goers, mostly mouth-breathing, arm-squeezing elderly gents, who sat eating lamb kebabs and empanadas, sipping bargain basement wine while waiting for the crowd to coalesce. It started late. I had hours to kill after work, and very nearly about-faced at the door.

I sat at a double-wide row of tables pushed together. Strangers crammed in with me, shoving belongings underneath. Waiters came, encouraging us to start a bar tab. Water wasn't free.

I was still only a few months into dancing, and too nice to reject prospective partners. If an unsavory fellow caught my eye, I'd look down at my feet, go fishing in my purse — anything to derail him. If all men used only the *cabeceo,* a feint down to my ankle strap would work. But beginner leaders often ignored warning signs and sidled up as close as they could get. Sometimes they'd even tap me on the shoulder to ensure they had my full attention before asking the obvious: *Would you like to dance?* Sometimes these men were matter-of-fact and therefore easier to refuse. Other times, high on violins and ceremony, they would almost croon. *May I have the honor of this dance?* I covered my frown to spare their feelings, racking my brain for excuses to say no: I'd already promised the *tanda* to someone else. I was tired. Resting my feet. Waiting for the ladies' room. Or just plain "No, thank you," which should always be enough, though some men took it personally. Half the time I just said yes. I'd learned the hard way at the *prácticas* that if I declined an invitation for one *tanda,* it would be untoward to accept another offer until the next. That *tanda,* however beautiful the music, was a penalty box. And if El Gran Gavito himself materialized suddenly on the heels of some old plonker, my refusal, however laden with regret, would be required.

Or worse, a favorite song would lead the set. Half the time, I think, I accepted less-than-stellar dances just so I wouldn't have to sit out songs I couldn't bear to miss. Like "Poema," recorded by Canaro in 1935. It is a song of sweet goodbye, beginning with thirty seconds of the most delicate violin, tiptoeing across plucked strings and tinkling piano, before descending into a chorus of *bandoneones.* When Roberto Maida starts to sing, he does so quietly, as if he's cradling an injured sparrow with his voice and helping it to fly. The beats are regular, almost elementary. This is tango at its most basic: the theme alternating with each variation, accumulating urgency until the darkness of one section starts to overlap with light. Things get jaunty when the bellows join, then rich and layered once the themes align. It's brooding and bright, legato and staccato, like almost every other tango. And because it's slow and lovely and the *compases* are clear, it's played often for beginners — overplayed. But it's one of those tangos, the ones that stick like woodsmoke in your hair, that bring the whole enterprise of dancing down to quiet sweetness. And every little flourish from the piano or the strings sounds like the twinkle of a cartoon star. The first two thousand times you hear it, it stays with you. Maybe you leave the studio whistling it. Maybe it conjures for you the thing that keeps you coming back. If it plays at a *milonga* while you're sitting for a set, you feel cheated.

I erred on the side of saying yes.

· · ·

When Edward, a Hong Kongese quantitative research analyst who was two inches too short for me, asked me to dance, I didn't turn him down. Everyone in tango has their Tenzing Norgay, the friend they make at base camp who helps them up the peak. Edward was mine. He was agreeable, easy to follow, and comfortable in close embrace. When I made mistakes, he apologized for leading badly. When I followed well, he cooed about how good I was becoming—without any overtones of ownership. Men like Edward are invaluable to a new dancer's self-esteem. Each time you think you've mastered something, some new teacher tells you it's all wrong. Leaders like Edward keep you dancing because they're happy to be patient. And despite our difference in height, he never made me feel ungraceful or too tall. He also never made me feel like a sex object—and I was careful not to give him reason to.

Edward steered me safely through those first *milongas;* we went once or twice a week. We practiced a bit, then parted. With him there to chat with between *tandas,* I was emboldened to ignore the men I knew I should refuse. Without him, I avoided social dancing; it was too daunting to go alone. I was back to logging flight hours, and raving about tango to anyone who'd listen. "I can't tonight; I'm going dancing" was my new refrain.

He took me to see Robin Thomas, famous for teaching beginners, and widely respected as a tango triple threat: DJ, dancer, proselytizer. Robin was the unofficial crown prince of the New York tango scene, and the king of close embrace. Edward, as it turns out, was a Robin Thomas dancer.

We took a class and stayed late for the practice session afterward. As Edward began swishing me around the room, Robin appeared out of nowhere. He was shorter still than Edward and looked a little like a lynx, with ginger hair clipped short around his balding patches. "Where have you been?" he asked Edward, a trace of Northern Irish accent on the "een." Apparently, Edward had been absent from Robin's *milongas.*

Edward apologized, and introduced me. Robin placed his hands on both sides of my head and turned it so my forehead, not my right temple, was touching Edward's cheek. He tugged my left arm farther down toward Edward's kidney and, with that, disappeared. Gone as quickly as he came, working the floor to correct other bumblers in the line of couples practicing.

"Oh, that's very good," breathed Edward, as he began again to heave me through the room. My spinal column shifted, a turning in the orientation of my ribs, as though my bones had changed the shape of my embrace. I felt like a heliotropic vine, tuned to the sunlight at the center of the close embrace. But as my neck adapted to the new and awkward angle, I was aware I looked more elegant that way.

I'd learned more from Robin Thomas in five minutes than I had in months of group instruction. That's why he specializes in beginners. According to him, tango needs "an army of them — yesterday," and he is building one. He's afraid tango will disappear. "It died once," he says, referring to the dark decades of the dance after 1955, once the Golden Age had fizzled out. "Why can't it die again?"

Tango had once before required the enthusiasm of the world to thrive. Back in the days of tangomania, when it looked nothing like the dance I knew. Back when the Argentine oligarchy had denounced it. The dance born of the unclean *arrabales* was a threat. Still, tangomania prevailed abroad. Though it was more or less abandoned by the end of World War I, Paris had given the world a considerable gift in her early appetite for tango — forcing the Argentine elites, by virtue of their own exquisite snobbery, to embrace the dance. Without that first prodigious popularity and the nonstop fervor of the bourgeoisie, tango might never have been recognized as anything but a vulgar dance of lesser castes, and might never have made it past the borders of the outer barrios. Instead, it made a brief but global splash — and stuck, until it was an Argentine obsession. It morphed — out of the styles of the poor, *canyengue, orillero* — into the straighter-backed and smoother style. The music pulled tango poetry out of the realm of impudence and swagger and into wistful sadness — from bawdy humor into heartbreak. By the time Carlos Gardel first sang his soul into "Mi noche triste" in 1917, tango had become the song and dance of pleasure and of pain, of human drama, tragic love. And by the full swing of the Golden Age, it didn't matter whether Europe and the wider world had since moved on; the whole of Buenos Aires danced.

That changed in 1955. The year a military coup unseated Argentine president Juan Perón, outspoken friend of tango and the working classes. We might call his ouster the beginning of the end, though the dance's popular appeal had already begun to wane. *Folklore,* with its simple virtues and pastoral themes, was gaining ground, piped in from the provinces, or brought by migrants coming to the capital for work. Those who benefited from the relative prosperity of the Perón years wished not to linger in the social protest that infused so many tango lyrics. Those who resented Peronism led a middle-class backlash against the poor and brown in favor of all things "white" and "decent," which was to say: not tango. Despite its popular dominance, tango's subversive legacy, and the "dangerous ethnic and racial mixing" it inspired, had always given the oligarchy pause. After all, even the love songs about bad women doing good men wrong could be interpreted as outlets for lyricists to voice their swallowed grievances against the state. When in doubt, blame women for your pain. Folk music was held up as a moralizing antidote to public sin. Tango cafés and dancehalls closed; *orquestas* were whittled down to octets, sextets, trios. Though listening tango flourished, the dance as popular phenomenon fell out of fashion — kept alive only by the older die-hards of the working class. In 1960, RCA destroyed an entire warehouse of its recordings from the fading Golden Age. The music was too maudlin for *porteño* youths, a backward-facing embrace of ancient pain.

Perón won reelection in 1973 and ran a volatile adminis-tration until his death the following year. The military junta that took power next, from 1976 to 1983, did so with the aim of scrubbing Argentina clean of all dissident elements, includ-ing what was left of tango. Artists were blacklisted and im-prisoned, lyrics censored. Meetings of more than three were declared illegal, making social dances dangerous to organize. And radio broadcasters were forced to replace tango with im-ported rock music on the air. This last military junta, some-times known as *el Proceso,* or the National Reorganization Process, did far more damage than merely banishing tango from the civic stage. The regime "disappeared" dissenters by the thousands. It was a time of terror and suspicion — neigh-bors informing on their neighbors, generals ordering civilian deaths, children and adults gone missing, never to be found. The *Guerra Sucia,* or Dirty War, might have eclipsed tango as Argentina's major legacy to the world, had democracy not been reinstated in 1983.

Meanwhile, from safe refuge abroad, Osvaldo Pugliese re-corded instrumental tangos that, in contra-rhythm, counter-point, and complexity, would prefigure the tango music avant-garde. And Astor Piazzolla, disbanding his orchestra and laying aside the *bandoneón,* went off in search of other influences. He drifted in and out of exile, eventually bringing home *Nuevo Tango,* which won him (and tango music as a genre) credibility and international acclaim, though these compositions, how-ever masterful, were almost prohibitively difficult to dance.

Back at home, the dance had all but died. For nearly thirty years, a country plagued by military coups and miserable economics quelled its feet. Tango never disappeared, though it became all but impossible for new converts or young people to learn. Any social dancing happened underground, on perpetual alert for infiltrators out to shut covert *milongas* down. The steadfast *milongueros* who kept the flame alive consider themselves the "lost" tango generation, heroes and resisters of the working class, the outer barrios — guardians of a gilded past.

But then, when tango was but a faded rumor of its former self — diffuse, and more fiction than fact — it was resurrected. The new democratic government of 1984 created the Programa Cultural en Barrios, to encourage war-weary *porteños* to reclaim their public spaces. Then came the big-ticket stage spectaculars. The tango glory days writ large, with dignity and faithfulness, by middle-aged Argentine professionals abroad. *Tango Argentino* and its spin-offs were an astonishing popular success in Paris (yet again) and on Broadway, and the dance came back to roost in Buenos Aires, cradle of the art.

Now, tens of thousands of people dance traditional Argentine tango socially in at least a hundred countries. We are living in the global renaissance of tango. UNESCO-inscribed since 2009, the dance is now a national product, exported like beef. Its commodification encourages traditionalism by way of counterpoint, but also entrepreneurship. A boon to a sluggish economy since the economic crisis of the aughts. Argentina remains the prime source of the dance, and markets tango tourism to foreign pilgrims seeking authenticity. Argentine dancers with limited prospects at home are given a passport out. They tour and teach abroad, and the revival spreads.

But it's a quiet renaissance, and Robin isn't wrong; it did die once. So he works to keep it living — building the army, arming his students with an arsenal of fundamental moves, then sending them out onto the floor. They go forth, unpretentious, briskly musical, and fiercely loyal. In the process, he's won international respect. Within a few months, I would learn to recognize a Robin Thomas leader just by body language: His deftness with the simple turns, his tidy rocking steps in place. His prodigious use of the *ocho cortado,* which neatly puts the couple back together at the cross to segue into other movements — and his careful, comfortable pace.

Then, however, I was just as green, and hoped only to spare myself humiliation. One's first hometown *milongas* are like a first cotillion; you want to make a promising debut. But whatever milestones you have mastered in your group classes — the ability to do an *ocho,* mid-floor, unsupported, on your own, your first *volcada* — become irrelevant in this human eddy of stiletto heels and sweat. The lights are low; the stakes are high. A hundred eyes assess your skills. Leaders wonder whether they will take you for a test spin. Followers watch with malice in their hearts until they determine you aren't competition. You have few friends in this new world, save the good-natured men that you were weaned upon — yet if you dance with those, the better leaders almost certainly will freeze you out. I was beginning to miss the days of exponential learning, the breakneck pace at which I had accumulated my meager string of skills. This new pace was humbler, perhaps, and certainly more thorough. But every time I went out dancing, I found I chafed against the bit.

The weather warmed with summer. Edward and I met at the Seaport Sunday nights to dance. I'd hear the music long before I spotted the *milonga,* just after crossing into the massive square. In the shadow of the tall ship *Peking,* beside a fish shack/cocktail bar, a stretch of dock was cordoned off for tango. I wore flat shoes so my heels would not get stuck between the boards. Dancing there was difficult, and I felt conspicuous in front of the assembled crowd. But there was something old and sweet about that outdoor dancing, those humid July nights that smelled of river, boat exhaust, and calamari. I spent half the time apologizing for my form — *the floor is slippery, my shoes won't pivot when I tell them to, it's crowded here, I haven't danced all week, I'm just not on my game* — but Edward didn't care. Not even when my sole slipped and my full heft fell upon him. "Wooh! Sorry!" I squealed; this became a tic of mine.

A *milonga tanda* started. *Milonga* was not merely the place-name for where one went to dance; it was one of two musical variants to tango, like tango music's boisterous uncle — cheerier, and played in cut time. The other variant is cheeky waltz-time tango *vals*. Both require a different approach to dance than eight-beat tango but remain part of its purview. Same instruments, same basic structure, same crisp end. All three song types are played for social dancing. You dance a *milonga* to a *milonga*, a *vals* to a *vals*, a tango to a tango — all, of course, at a *milonga*. Like most beginners, I was clumsy at adapting tango steps to fit half-time *milonga*, with its *habanera* hop, but Edward, patient as ever, was too busy worrying over his own missteps to judge me for mine.

If I caught one fast footwork sequence out of a proffered ten, a smile would crack across my face in triumph. Beads of sweat dotted my hairline. The thump of my heart synced to the rhythm. My doubts were fading, one *tanda* at a time. I stayed an hour, maybe two, and left the Seaport humming to myself, skipping along the cobblestones to the contagious beat. *Dum bah dum bum. Dum bah dum bum.*

I went home to Peter passed out on the couch. Between work and dancing, I hardly saw him anymore. Sundays, which had previously been reserved for overloaded bagel brunches and movie marathons, were cut short. Weekday evenings, too, had gone. I went to work each morning and sat in my grey cubby-hole, tweaking amateurish graphics for direct mail campaigns, and listening to tango albums on repeat. The nights when I had class, a *práctica,* or a *milonga,* I arrived home after midnight, dropped my purse and clothes into a puddle on the floor, put on pajamas, brushed my teeth, and slipped into bed beside him. Often, we did not touch or speak, and within mere minutes of coming home, I'd have set my alarm and gone to sleep.

I thought about the tango women of the 1940s, who had rebelled against the iron-fisted *marca,* the lead of certain early *milongueros.* Back then, according to Maria Nieves, "the man stood still while the woman pirouetted," bossed around by domineering hand gestures. After their insurrection, the standard of the couple sharing action fifty-fifty first came into fashion. Partners began to dance together, with followers complicit, decisive in the act of improvising. I thought about Nieves as a girl in the forties, barely in her teens, transfixed. She had no teacher, so she danced alone, partnering her broom across the kitchen floor into the small hours of the night.

Part of me was furious at Peter — for never coming with me, for making me do all of this alone. Part of me was grateful for the privacy; I was beginning to think the loneliness would do me good. And part of me felt guilty leaving him behind. As if I knew that every night I danced, the clock wound forward on us, and I outgrew him slowly, tick by tick.

Chapter Nine

TANGO, WITH ALL ITS CODES, WAS LIKE A FUNHOUSE HALL
of mirrors, which split into a million other halls of mirrors in
infinite disorienting directions. Social dancing scared me, but I
had to learn to be surprised — and to surprise myself. *Milongas*
were where technique became expression, and all the things
that I'd been taught turned into tango. Where I could let per-
fectionism go, and improvise.

When Edward got stuck at work one night, I went to Lafayette alone, and sat off in a corner, paging through a magazine
to ward off unwanted invitations. Peter and I were leaving for
vacation the next morning, but I had to dance. I was getting
better by degrees, but ever frustrated by the slowing speed of
my improvement. There simply weren't enough hours, enough
money, for the kind of learning curve I craved. I was desperate
for dances. I wanted my pilot's wings.

Instead, I sat nursing bog water Malbec, probably bottled in
Pennsylvania, feeling silly, clumsy, sorry for myself, and watching as my fingerprints clouded the glass.

"Whatcha readin'?"

The voice was low and slow like late-night radio. My senses
registered him before I could, maroon merino wool, broad

chest, a stubbled cheek, and hints of the same bad Malbec on his breath. Enzo. I flipped shut that week's *New Yorker.*

"Never seen a lady read at a *milonga.*"

Oh no, I thought. I'd missed another rule. Then I noticed, with a pang of warm relief, a creased copy of *Anna Karenina* tucked beneath his arm.

"How's that?" I gestured to the book.

"In-fucking-credible," he answered. "Have you read?" He had a way of omitting the last words of his sentences.

I confessed I hadn't. He recommended that I rectify. We made small talk about Tolstoy and the Russians for a few moments as the *tanda* ended. His voice dropped decibels and octaves to a rakish, interrogatory tone.

"Would you like to dance?"

I fought my impulse to ask *Who, me?* or *Are you sure?* and stuffed my magazine into my bag. He picked his way around the tables, steered us to the floor.

I was nervous. My right palm was sweating in his left, my ankles quivering. I was certain he could feel my heart beat through my meager chest, and not because I was so attracted to him — which, of course, I was — but because he was a teacher. This dance was a challenge, an audition, and a test.

A tango came on, a slow one. I wish I could remember which. Like many leaders, he hummed a few bars to himself, very quietly, mouth closed. For the first time, this did not annoy me. His shoulder blades were strong beneath my arm. His nose was bigger than I'd realized. It released warm gusts of respiration, like a horse on a cold morning. There was something of the stable about his arms as well. I shut my eyes and almost smelled the trampled hay. The other dancers, with their combovers and ruffled dresses, disappeared. The room did too. In its place I imagined walls of wood with hooks and metal instruments and leather straps. It was warm and musky there.

· · ·

There is a moment, learning to follow, when it's simply not enough to shut your eyes and move where you are led. When it is not enough to turn blind circles in the dark. For every movement you interpret properly, every mirror you create by walking in his wake, every step you take into the empty air between you, there is something so much more important. That is standing still. *La esencia del tango* is in the pauses.

I hadn't learned this yet — which is why he held me there. In our impatience to improve, we new followers string ourselves so tight that we are always moving, always second-guessing. In the interests of litheness, listening, we strain ourselves to catch a leader's signals before they're even sent. Our starting bells ring out too soon. I was an untrained colt, braced for the gun — and Enzo made me wait.

My ribcage stilled. The first step was a reflex milliseconds late, as if taken by surprise. I tried to relax, but it was difficult. A new leader is often a little hard to follow. You're not accustomed to his rhythms or his engine quirks. Certain complex steps flow as they should, and others, which are easier, are blundered. "Wooh! Sorry!" I squawked again, and made my best awkward conversation in between the songs.

He was patient. When I didn't get a step, he led it slower, steadier, until my body understood it. My limbs grew heavy, warm and pliant. If I opened my eyes, I was sure the room itself would spin. We danced two *tanda*s before he whispered, "Thank you, that was lovely," in my ear and quit the floor. I steered myself back to the Malbec and my magazine, his breath still on my neck. I didn't want to dance with any of those other men.

I waited until Enzo disappeared into the men's room before I donned street shoes and fled. Like every starry-eyed heroine met with every hairy-chested man who ever graced the pages of a romance novel, I was suddenly undone. Aware, finally, that something remained missing, some void in me that even tango lessons couldn't fill. For the first time since I'd started dancing, I felt that I'd transgressed.

The next evening, Peter and I flew off to the South of France, to his family's summer home. I'd sublet the studio apartment I so rarely slept in, and taken a five-week unpaid furlough from my job. The nonprofit coffers had been grateful to suspend my meager monthly salary; I was grateful to be free. I spent those five weeks listening to Lucienne Boyer and picking lavender, biking to the *plage des naturistes* — a baguette, book, and towel in my basket — and lying naked on the sand. I was learning to read my body like a book full of forbidden knowledge. I'd been to Provence with him before, and lain there on my towel beside his, on that very beach, but this was different. Last year, the nudity meant nothing. I was but one body on a beach with many other bodies. Not even Peter paid me any notice; he was too busy ogling the more nubile of the bathers above the pages of his paperback. I read mine on my stomach, feeling brave, but at so little cost.

This year, however, I felt noticed. Not by Peter, or the hazelnut old *naturistes,* or even the adolescent boys who snuck up from the normal beach to catch a peek. But by the sun, the warm, dry air, the water. I took the heat into my skin as though my cells were thirsty for it. I tanned my pale pink Irish skin to mauve, and only some nights drank enough rosé to find a pair of heels in my suitcase and do *boleos* on the balcony.

Boleo is tangospeak for whip, a by-product of contra-movement and momentum, your free leg cracking fancy in a gesture to the long-forgotten pampas cows. I practiced these — half to test out this new sharpness in me, half as a dare. I tucked one knee tight behind the other and made little tongue-lash circles with it, like the flouncing of a bustled hem. Back *boleo.* I turned forward *ochos* on the terrace tiles and, every so often, changed direction rapidly so one leg crossed in front and licked behind me for the other. Front *boleo*.

I wanted to know if Peter might see me differently in these stilettos in the still-warm night, exercising urges I did not yet understand. If he did, he never said. I didn't ask. Tango had been an escape for me, from drudgery, uncertainty, and painful insecurity; now it was also a weapon I was half-afraid to wield. I wanted it to be the only answer, and it wasn't; there were some things dancing couldn't solve.

Peter and I spent hours together. He played piano; I helped around the garden and the house. We drank cold wine at lunch. Each afternoon, he disappeared into the Internet, where he spent his leisure time — and I into books, where I spent mine. We were good company, good coexisters. Both of us were happier here, in utopian Provence — with each other, with ourselves. Ambition faded into stillness, into the minor errands of provincial life. Cheese, greens, wine, spit-roasted chicken. A day wanted to be lived immediately, like the bread we purchased every morning — and ate by evening, lest it stale. His mother fantasized about a wedding ceremony someday underneath the olive trees in the backyard, so I did too, picturing myself in antique lace, a crown of rosemary and snowdrop flowers in my hair. Sex wasn't everything. What mattered was a family: folks around a table ripping pieces off the same baguette. Bad jokes and grandchildren. Laughing until drunk with it, then doing dishes as a team. Tucking children into cribs.

Peter wanted none of these things. He hated children. Their noise and volatility made his muscles clench. A single wail of a newborn in a restaurant or on a plane was enough to make him wince. I'm not sure he believed in marriage, either, or any of the other things his mother wanted him to want. But he would have settled for them. Such was our affection for each other. I

thought of the Kay Boyle poem "Monody to the Sound of Zithers." *I have wanted other things more than lovers.* Peace, contentment, *to learn by heart things beautiful and slow.* This could be my life. The elements would be my lovers. Clean rain could kiss my eyelids, and the sea could fill my mouth. I could live here, even in the winter when the shops had closed, the crowds had gone, and there was nothing but the cold wind whining off the Alps. I could write books, the secret ambition I'd spoken aloud only to my mother, a dream unlikely and absurd, but that persisted whenever I tried to picture myself as old. Maybe the problem wasn't that I was settling for something less. Maybe "less" was what I needed — to revel in the beauty of the chaste and unembellished, the uncomplicated life.

I was talking myself into it. Uncertain, unconvinced, aware of my own folly. Tango murmured in the background of my indecision, like the sirens and the churn of motor yachts across the gulf. When Peter's folks had gone to bed and things went quiet, I'd play Hugo Díaz on their stereo. Victor Hugo Díaz was a *folklore* musician, a child prodigy at the harmonica, who only began recording tangos five years before his death in 1977. His tangos were all instrumental, with his harmonica substituted for the *bandoneón.* It sometimes feels as though he's scraping music straight out of your chest. It sounds like someone torturing a trumpet. It grimaces at you, squints, and wails. In quieter measures, you can hear his guttural intakes of breath.

I left the porch doors open, went outside, and let his music follow, ripping through the night. While Peter read through his roster of pundits, a gin and tonic underfoot, I lassoed my feet behind me, one knee tucked demurely behind the other, laboring to point my toes. It became my ritual for saying all the things I didn't have the heart to say.

I wrote purple passages in my journal about yearning, about being twenty-five, and looking across the gulf at darkened jetties, and at all those faraway needlepoint stars. I got through all of my detective novels and picked up *Anna Karenina*, which I'd lugged across the ocean in my suitcase and, even as I'd done so, wondered why.

I was relieved to find a woman in those pages more distressed than I. A woman not herself so much as someone else's mother, lover, wife — mercurial and failing at all three. She seemed to storm through the wreckage she wrought of her life on passion only — against unfairness, a man she could not have, the liberty she could not choose. I did not admire her, but her empty places became mine. I sat by the pool, bees humming busily, my feet dangling in the water, and devoured her. With cocktail hours happening behind me, I read, accepting perhaps a Dubonnet on ice, my shoulders bronzing through my sundress.

When I finished, I dashed off an email to Enzo, whose presence I'd felt lurking in the pages. Something like:

e,

> *thank you for the recommendation. I loved her, every word.*
> *my best from the sud de france,*

> > *m**

And then I curled into my corner of the king-sized bed I shared with Peter, a sea between us. That night, I think, he fell asleep above the covers, I below.

Later that summer, Enzo sent a poem. About how he'd watched a tugboat pass on Coney Island that bore a name like mine. And how he sank into the hot Atlantic — how the heat of him, his body, nearly boiled the water — and he imagined how a fevered jet might reach across to me in France. Stunned, I sent one back. It was cheeky and evasive, singsong. Composed while treading seawater, faceup in a shaded cove. I floated, repeating verses to myself to put to paper. The tide swayed and I with it, watching Peter onshore in his sunglasses, eyeing women on the beach. The water buoyed me, cool on my skin, alive. I debated sending what I'd written, but I did — in a single flush of daring, frightened I had opened up a chasm underneath my feet.

We wouldn't speak again for months.

Chapter Ten

SUMMER ENDED. I CAME BACK TO THE CITY BRONZED, TRAN-
quil, and broke. Peter and I decided to move in together; in-
ertia told us it was the thing to do. Perhaps more than that,
it was the debt we felt to each other that compelled us. For
better or worse, we'd linked our lives. We did not blame each
other for the things we lacked. And I'd made room, too much
room, in my heart of late — as if tango had snapped the lines I
tried to live within and I feared hurtling off. I made Peter my
anchor. I wanted him to fill and weigh my heart. Not because
I would have been unfaithful, but because I wished for something more. It was a yearning I couldn't see or speak. A fear
that there was something in me I could not control.

I knew it wasn't my fault that he wasn't happy, but my selfish splashing in the pleasure pits of tango could hardly have
helped. We both needed something big to change. We found
a two-bedroom apartment off Ditmars Avenue in Queens, and
filled it with the contents of my studio. It was the third floor
of a new construction, shoddy, cheap, but full of light. I spent
three days scrubbing sawdust from the corners of the floors
and windowsills, preparing it for us. He bought appliances and
curtain rods, and I hand-drilled brackets into the wall to hold
them. This was to be our home.

I went back to work, and let the weeks notch by. My first boss — erratic, often cruel, but just as often inappropriately generous — had been replaced by a smarmy, ladder-climbing micromanager with a piercing adenoidal drawl. She'd worked her way up from the intern pool and made a mercenary grab for director of development behind my former boss's back. She must have felt her windowed office, overlooking nothing charming, entailed the constant monitoring of her inferiors' every move. There would be no more unpaid furloughs, no more comp time, no more long walks for a Friday morning latte. But we were helping people, every day, and that beat tending bar. I came in every morning with rededication: I took initiative, took careful meeting notes, took precisely fifteen-minute coffee breaks. By afternoon, I sat there in my swivel chair and felt the walls closing in. As if my lungs were empty, but I couldn't take in a full breath of air. I'd spend the final hours of the workday staring at my screen saver until someone came near enough to see. I drank bottles of water just for an excuse to get up, pace down the office hall, and pee.

I stalled in going back to tango. The idea seemed somehow remote to me, a nasty habit I had quit. The more I stayed away, the more I missed it, and the more that made me hesitate. Two months had passed since we'd returned from France. I was sure I'd lost whatever footing I had found before we left. But, I confess, the quality of that last dance with Enzo lingered in my skin, like the trace of water from the gulf half a world away. Sebastián Arce wasn't wrong. Tango is diabolical; it is the marriage of your worse and better natures, in your own body, in the violin and *bandoneón*.

I unpacked my red T-straps from their tote bag. They were rumpled, scarred, and somehow alien to me, despite having been deformed exactly to the contours of my feet. I thought about those long-ago *porteño* man-cubs at the feet of *milonguero* masters — waiting, desperate for a debut at the dancehalls — and my impatience flared. I remembered how it felt to be there in that dark bar behind the wall of scaffolding, unbeknownst to almost everyone in New York City. How it felt to sit and wait to be surprised. I remembered, too, the trepidation. My stomach dropping once I turned the corner and saw another stranger with a telltale shoe bag slipping past the neon signs and through the door. Then the mesmeric lullaby of music, cycling through *tanda* after *tanda,* turning the needle of the line of dance.

I took a deep breath and went back to Lafayette, finding it every bit as dingy and rundown. This time I came alone, and early, to take the pre-*milonga* lesson with Dardo Galletto, Enzo's mentor. At ten dollars a class, these were relatively cheap and entitled you to stick around for proper dancing afterward. I paid my fee and changed my shoes, watching the Argentincs greet one another with dual cheek kisses. Always they seemed to be having a much better time than us *yanquis,* as they called us; perhaps they didn't have to try so hard. For the rest of us, it was an awkward social haven, the illusion of spending time with other human beings — without having to communicate in words.

The class began with all the lights on in the restaurant, with the bartender still polishing and stacking glasses on the bar. Dardo was short, but also ballet strong, and with a schoolboy's innocence against the whorehouse of the world. "Love! Love!" he cried as we circled him, warming up. "You must *show* she that you *love* she." His teaching partner was a goddess, fortysomething and Italian, with all the jewels and bronzy softness to her skin that fortune buys. He called her Bella. She wore party dresses and a different pair of Comme il Fauts each night. These were special boutique Buenos Aires heels, fourinch gold and strappy numbers showcasing her painted toes. Always there were fewer men than women, so she lapped the room with Dardo, leading stragglers. She came to me, her perfume just behind her, and I was struck by a sticky whiff of sweet gardenia. She was elegant, expensive.

"Yes, good," she cooed to me, my face somewhere inside the fortress of her curls. "You do not rush; you wait," she breathed into my neck. I blushed and thanked her. Dardo shouted, "Chaaaaaaange partnerrrrrr!"

I learned from Dardo to find the heaviness in my hips, to really sink my weight into the floor. Tango starts to feel good when you do it right—as satisfying as a slingshot, or a hand held out the window of a moving car to catch the jets of wind. Dancers like Dardo milked the pauses, wound the body spiral tightest, near to breaking, going into turns. For them tango meant to hold and to release. To love everyone you touch for those three minutes, with total equanimity, then let them go. "Yes, *yes!*" our ringleader cried, triumphant. "Do you feel the *love*?!"

I didn't. I kept trying, but I was too tightly wound, and tentative. My hips too narrow, bony, and my body uninformed. What I needed was another maestro—one who wouldn't try to suck my toes. On Edward's suggestion, I started taking private lessons with Michael Nadtochi, former Russian youth champion of ballroom dance. The Great Nadtochi (Mischa to his friends) was one of an armada of tango expats, pros and aspirants, living in the modern *arrabales* of New York—Brooklyn, Inwood, Queens, or in Nadtochi's case, New Jersey. He and his then-partner, Angeles, taught in midtown one day each week, stocking a tiny studio in Koreatown with private students in one-hour segments back to back. They both had studied with El Gran Gavito, *milonguero* legend of the *Forever Tango* cast, and shared a very classic style. She was short and milky-skinned, with hair dyed beetroot red, lipstick to match, and an augmented bust of which she was extremely proud. He was long-legged and wiry, with hair gelled just shy of greasy, but with an air of absolute refinement, like a gentleman of old. When they performed together, she was all sequins and slits, and he wore tailored high-waist suits. A Muscovite Fred Astaire.

As ever, dancing with a teacher, I was nervous. But Nadtochi spoke in soothing registers. *"Tranquila,"* he'd chirp when I apologized for misinterpreting — or some other sin of the feet. He was patient, positive, exacting. There was no false flattery, but when I got a movement right, he let me know it. *"Esa!"* he would hoot, and we'd high-five. Precision was important, but the journey there need not be arduous.

Nadtochi moved like a jungle cat on hefty, silent haunches. He put my palm up to his chiseled abdomen so I could feel the flexing of his core. Then, for one paid hour, we would dance. Weeks passed in something like a training montage: for every session I could afford, I turned up in my mangy red suede heels and rolled-up jeans, or cotton dresses over footless tights. We danced to well-worn tangos, tunes off the beaten practice path. Ángel D'Agostino comes to mind, with his deferent simplicity — something from the days when Ángel Vargas sang for him and together they made *tango de los angeles.* Even with the raw heart of Vargas's voice, D'Agostino's tangos hold a steady pulse, guiding dancers through the dual storms of hopefulness and rue. This was golden music, tunes like dust motes swirling in a patch of yellowed, antique sun, and they made my life lovelier for one expensive hour every week.

To Nadtochi, social dancing was of supreme importance. "Where have you been going?" he demanded. I answered Lafayette. He clicked his tongue. "You mean you haven't been to La Nacional?"

I confessed I hadn't. La Nacional was one of the more intimidating, populous *milongas* in the weekly calendar. It happened every Thursday night, in the performance space above the

Spanish Benevolent Society on Fourteenth Street while, downstairs, men with hard-shell paunches forked up garlic shrimp
from clay dishes, downed rioja and espresso, and screamed at
live-stream *fútbol* games. The *milonga* cost a whopping fourteen dollars — nearly three times the cost of weekend *prácticas*
— which gave you access to a room, a bar, a tin of Altoids, and,
occasionally, an Oreo cookie from a small basket by the cash-
box. When you left, long after midnight, one of the two men
who ran it handed you a rose.

I steeled myself and went one Thursday night after a work
event. It was almost eleven, and the joint was full. I found an
empty chair along the wall, and stuffed my things between its
legs, shoving my purse among three other purses, out of foot
reach. I surveyed the crowd for Enzo, as I often did, but he had
vanished. Nadtochi nodded at me, pleased. "Good to see you!"
he said an hour later, after throwing me his *cabeceo*. "You have
come to the right place." We danced a set, and thanked each
other. It was easy to lose track of hours at a *milonga*. By the time
I took my rose to go power walking east on Fourteenth to the
subway, it was nearly two. The Queens trains were running too
sporadically to wait, so I took the first of many overly expensive
late-night taxi rides across the bridge, slept short and sweet,
and spent a good part of my Friday workday fighting off fatigue.

Under Nadtochi's counsel, I started venturing beyond my comfort zone. There was so much more I hadn't seen. On any given
night, there was at least one place to dance; some nights, there
were three. There was trendy tango, traditionalist tango, tango
for the aged and aging, tango for students, queer tango, tango
to live music, outdoor tango, and alternative tango. I picked
my timid way through each, surveying the topography of op-
tions. My old studio and the Lafayette *milonga* were both C-
list, geared toward an older, less ambitious crowd (had I but
known), but friendlier. Mondays at Lafayette were better at-

tended—more like La Nacional, with its loyal cadre of transplanted *porteños* mingling gaily with their Fernet-Branca and their warm *saludos*. On Mondays there was also Luna, a warmly mixed crowd at a midtown studio, gently shepherded by the enchanted, spider-legged Rebecca Shulman. She half-led a *práctica* in the adjoining room, which many devoted dancers never missed.

Tuesday nights (and Friday and Saturday afternoons), the better older dancers went to TriANGulO, the only tango-only studio in New York, so named for its original triangular location. TriANGulO had a mural painted on its back wall depicting the city tango scene from 2007. Rebecca, Mariela, Robin Thomas—even, I suspect, Svengali—were pictured there in evening gear, plus a host of dancers I had never met, but would be nonetheless surprised to recognize there, months and years later, peering out.

The in crowd—the students and the semi-pros, the tango bums, the teachers, and their hangers-on—spent their Tuesdays at Robin Thomas's Sangria Practica, so named for the communal stockpot of sangria swigged from plastic children's mugs. That same crowd spent Wednesday nights at Tango Café—above a porn shop and an Irish pub on Eighth Avenue, just past the stately post office—which offered alternative music, wine-by-the-box, grapes, and brie.

La Nacional on Thursdays drew a mixed crowd, different every week, depending on the DJ's skill to unify. And on Friday nights, the Ukrainian East Village Restaurant, referred to by the tango cognoscenti as "The Uke," opened up its backroom door. A waiter stood behind a makeshift bar and overcharged for weak mixed drinks and tangy wine, looking bored and mildly offended in his uniform; tango dancers rarely risked upsetting balance with excessive drink. Besides, the ancient floor was pocked and sloped, riddled with sticky patches, and required the full wits of one's feet.

Saturdays rotated monthly. On the first Saturday, Mala Leche, the weekend edition of Tango Café, with an extra room for Twister, gossip, blues. On the second Saturday, the All-Night Milonga, a behemoth that ran through five in the morning and had a designated room for neo-tango electronica. On the third Saturday, Robin Thomas's Nocturne — and I'd begun to notice the pervasiveness of his name brand — the jewel in his New York tango crown, which drew dancers from several states. On the fourth Saturday, finally, a gathering called Practilonga, a relaxed BYOB affair.

Sundays were for the South Street Seaport or the homey, Argentinist *"Milonguita"* La Ideal. Sometimes a group would congregate outside on the Christopher Street Pier, and pass the hat to cover the cost of potluck snacks and portable speakers. It was best on hot days, when the wind swirled up the boardwalk, or at sunset, when the smog above the Hudson River blazed fuchsia and Jersey City started twinkling in the dark.

I still had no idea about the cliques and sub-cliques of the city's tango scene, or the disparate social strata. I bumbled from *milonga* to *milonga,* varying my attendance week by week, avoiding weekend evenings, high-stakes venues, nontraditional music, and the phantom young and hip. But here was an undiscovered country gaping at my feet. A whole wide world in which no one knew me, or my early missteps, and where Svengali was irrelevant. Forgettable. Ignored.

Sometimes I sat for hours, watching without dancing. Sometimes I said yes to strangers, though their leads left much to be desired. Pleased to find myself no longer on the bottom rung of competence, I would thank them after one *tanda* and sit again. Sometimes I said yes out of kindness. Sometimes because I'd learned never to judge a leader by appearance. A frail older gentleman, even one whose suit coat smelled of mothballs, might embrace me with such tender respect, it wouldn't matter if he only paused and walked and paused. He would have tango in him, dignified and deep. Or a new favorite might appear out of nowhere—a stranger with a clear, exhilarating lead—and we would dance so hard we'd collapse laughing, having to catch our breath after each song.

I commuted to work and tango from the last stop on the Astoria line. I went straight home after the drudgery of whirring Xeroxes, the hours wasted in redundant meetings, and when most of my peers were headed out to dinner, I went dancing. I passed Greek patriarchs sipping ouzo and Pellegrino outside corner stores, listening to their wives call children off their bikes and into bed. I ate mostly sandwiches, something small to keep from feeling sluggish on the floor. My purse bulged with my shoes, a book, a canteen full of water. Well after midnight, I'd return by train or taxi, my purse reeking of foot musk and my hair gone limp.

We were on an Old World alley plan, and our apartment had a back balcony that overlooked the balconies of all our neighbors. It was my very own *arrabal*: two-story single-family dwellings packed with generations, porches lined up fence to fence, and ancient mutts slumped in the corners. It had a different feel in the early hours—in that sweet spot between dancing and the morning drudge. All was quiet except the Amtraks rumbling across the ivy-covered Hell Gate Bridge that dwarfed us from above. A bakery on Twenty-seventh Avenue fired its raisin loaves in the wee hours, so the neighborhood would smell of cinnamon and rising yeast. I turned my key in one lock, then the next.

Though I lived there and only there, Peter often preferred to stay at his family's place in midtown. I was alone most of that autumn. I reaccustomed myself to coming home to silent dark, the wall of it, just inside the apartment door, and welcoming the moment when the deadbolt clicked behind me and there was nothing but the hum of power through the wall sockets. The muffled hiss of white noise from the city just beyond the cheap glass of the windowpanes. Sometimes it felt menacing, oppressive. Sometimes a relief.

But I had lived alone once, and remembered how I'd liked it. I'd leave the windows open, pull the curtains shut. I thought of a Billy Collins poem, the one to Plutarch; it is a sonnet about sonnets. Laura says *take off those crazy tights / and come at last to bed.* There was no one telling me to take off mine. I'd set an alarm for early morning and my dreams were disconnected *molinetes,* ill-formed turns.

Tango was becoming my life, to the neglect of all else. Mere months before, I'd felt my loneliest sleeping beside a man who loved me, differently but deeply, with all the semblances of normal early adult life. Now I slept alone. I'd stopped attending acting class entirely, stopped seeing friends for drinks or dinner, stopped thinking much past my next dance. At a *milonga,* I never had to talk about myself. Never had to explain my failures, my abandoned acting project, my strange relationship, my "archetypal father complex," or my childhood. Conversations between *tandas* were rudimentary, and not required. *I live here. I work there. I'm sort of from New England.* I could be anonymous and enigmatic. I could surrender to the music, let it blur my edges, wash myself anew. The men were dance partners; the women were removed. We passed one another with the occasional nod of solidarity. It wasn't the music that connected us, I thought; it was this silent communion. And though I often went whole evenings without speaking to another person, I was not alone.

Chapter Eleven

THAT FALL, I FOUND MY TANGO NICHE. A NEW SUNDAY *milonga* christened RoKo by Robin Thomas and his fellow DJ Ko Tanaka. The space was big, the floor was good, the room was friendly, brightly lit. Its Herald Square location made it easily accessible from outer boroughs and New Jersey. Within a month, it was the largest and most popular weekly *milonga* in the United States. Grand Central Station for the New York tango scene. It made room for everyone, from every crowd, and gave you a sense of end-of-week conclusion, coming home. It gave the city what its tango wheel had lacked: a hub for all its wanton spokes.

The bare "ballroom" had been transformed by long magenta drapes of bulk-bought silk and battery-powered votive candles by the dozen. Patrons ranged in age from eighteen to over eighty, and in economic class from those who volunteered to clean up in exchange for free admission to those who splurged on ten-day tango tours to Buenos Aires. Weak coffee burned all night in a pot next to a plate of thumbprint sandwiches and wafer cookies. Under the warm lights, tango stars in civvies mingled and sometimes even danced with plebes. RoKo was democratic. The tango wolves were tamed. In this upstairs enclave of a midtown dead zone, every Sunday night, people took other, often very different people in their arms and moved to music. Hours disappeared as the lead-footed minute hand spun the clock above the door. There was no posing. No agenda. No drama and no disco balls. Nothing creepy whatsoever. It was ideal, and nothing like a sex club. It was somewhere I could take my mom.

I went to RoKo every week, like church. To get there, I walked north through Herald Square, all converging avenues and neon noise, into the verdant bandage that was Greeley Square. I passed eight-foot billboard beauties in their underclothes, shuttered fast food eateries, and the blond brick behemoth of Macy's flagship store. I navigated the green metal folding chairs and the homeless men and women who had claimed them with their lumping mounds of shopping bags. No matter the temperature, the sidewalks would be wet with spills. I hugged Sixth as it ascended, thinking city life was city life, whether in 1919 Buenos Aires or 2009 New York. There were haves and have-nots. Constant longing, upward striving. Discrimination, poverty, unfairness — so very little ever changed. Some Old World was always vanishing around us.

The turn onto Thirty-sixth Street wasn't special. The corner smelled of pizza and accumulated trash. Businesses and delis were all closed, their metal gates pulled down and padlocked for the night. Outside a historic B-list chophouse, backwaiters and barmen leaned against the brass-handled door and smoked their mid-shift cigarettes, their sullied aprons hanging to their shoes.

Crosstown traffic was always slow that time of night. Vehicles passed in steady eastward waves. From a certain patch of sidewalk, a mere few meters of concrete, it was possible to discern faint strains of tango music from above. If there weren't too many blaring horns, or cars swishing through rain, I'd stop to listen, wondering just how many passed this way each Sunday night, not knowing to look up at building number 29, where on the second floor, six flat glass windows were postered over with an unobtrusive sign, black lettered onto white: *Manhattan Ballroom Dance*. A website and a phone number were printed underneath the silhouettes of waltzing couples. A string of twinkle lights was draped like bunting. How many never noticed the ornately carved façade, its cornices and crests and cornucopia, the unknown birds and urns? Who would bother looking up?

The security guard knew *tangueras* by their shoe bags or their harem pants tucked into boots. He sometimes catnapped on the job, his head propped on his palm. I passed him, called the elevator, rode up, and, when the doors ratcheted wide, stepped into a mass of oscillating dancers bobbing past in counterclockwise lanes. Here, finally, was a secret world worthy of the name.

To Robin, tango was a community — not just an activity that lonely people did together without speaking. He would have been horrified to know how isolated I had been in my first half year of dancing. At RoKo, I began to feel embarrassed by my lack of tango friends. In that great, glowing room, no one else looked quite so unattached. Dancers sat in chatty clumps, made conversation at the snack table. Friends passed around bottles of wine and plastic cups. There was laughter on the floor. For the first time, I entered a *milonga* and felt invigorated, felt like racing in. Apart from Edward, I had yet to make a single friend. But when I saw the tango block party of RoKo, and the rosy, boisterous crowd, I wanted to be part of it; I wanted to be part of them.

I once asked Robin what he thought brought all of us to tango, and what kept us there. His answer was simple: we all just wanted to be held. I thought: that couldn't be. The close embrace had been an obstacle for me, as though it asked for more than I could give. I'd made it this far, hadn't I, in spite of being held? I couldn't believe all the occult mysteries of tango boiled down to a cheap feel. He was quick to qualify, and to agree with me; the tango embrace wasn't sexual. Which was not to say the two don't overlap occasionally. It's like the office water cooler: "After a while," he said, "when you dance tango *a lot,* you end up having only (or mostly) tango dancers as your friends. So who else are you going to hook up *with*?" Rock climbing, he added, was far worse for giving rise to hanky-panky. "You're actually tied to each other," he said, "by rope."

Being held is not the point of tango, but the close embrace is what makes the dance so special. You press your torso against another person's torso; you move together or you do not move at all. The dance won't work without that physical connection, that soldering of sternums, that collusion. To dance well, you must reconcile yourself to this. No matter how your partner holds you, there is that bald fact of being held. The tango embrace is ineluctable — from the Latin *in-,* "not," and *eluctari,* "struggle out." It takes a little getting used to, training yourself to touch and be touched at close range — and to resist the eroticism or revulsion that touch might conjure up. But it will come to feel as comfortable and familiar as a favorite chair, or maybe the embrace of an old lover — warm, and almost drained of pleasure.

Robin Thomas makes a living out of this. "It's really beautiful," he told me, "to see this scientist or physicist who works in a lab all day embrace a woman slowly, sensually, and start moving together . . . to see them finally understand that that exists inside them." And though it may seem overly dramatic: "Not just touching other people. *Talking* to other people. That's the thing these physicists and chemists learn to do. They learn to talk to women." Robin believes through social dancing we are socialized. I wondered for a moment what he thought of me.

Tango, to him, was just another method for communicating with one another. "They could be doing something else," he says. "This physicist could swim with the biologist and it would probably be just as good for them — maybe." But tango was the community he helped create, and one I suddenly longed to be a part of: a water cooler for the many splendid social misfits of the city of New York.

I looked around and saw that he was right. Besides the physicists and engineers and me, there were artists, professors, students, decorators, architects, attorneys, bankers, realtors, and radicals, all mashing themselves together comfortably. Presumably some of us had not been capable of that before we took to tango. And most of us, whether from being held or not, had been irrevocably changed.

A crew of photographers skirted the room taking action shots. Their photos, once uploaded, would spread through social media like a winter cold. People who'd danced together only once would strike up online friendships. Non-dancers had the chance to see their friend or colleague temple-to-temple with someone from a different corner of the world. My dad would call me at my desk midweek when the photos hit, if I'd been tagged in any. "It's awfully cool, Meg," he'd say, then cycle through the other crucial topics in our conversation repertoire: the weather, daily tedium, or how I'd fared with the Sunday puzzle in the *New York Times*.

Maybe it was as simple as Robin said. Maybe all of us were missing something in our outside lives. The scientists and financiers needed a creative outlet. The frustrated artists needed release. The lonely people needed only to be a part of something. You didn't have to broadcast what you lacked. You just had to show up, embrace someone, and dance.

As RoKo came of age in tango, so did I. I started risking conversations on the sidelines, realizing (better late than never) that I didn't have to talk about myself to talk to other people.

I'd make a joke before I reached across the table for a carrot stick or Costco madeleine. I'd compliment a lady's earrings in the restroom. Despite the thousands of people dancing worldwide, tango remains a very minor subculture everywhere but Buenos Aires, Finland, and Berlin. RoKo felt central to me, immense; but just outside it, Herald Square was noisy and indifferent. Maybe 750 people danced tango in that city of 8.245 million, and 29 West Thirty-sixth Street and what happened there on Sunday nights is unknown to all but 0.00009 percent. It seemed prudent to start getting to know a few of them. Perhaps I had been getting to know myself dancing with strangers, stepping from behind the scrim and peeling off the mask. I met them unadorned, and listened to their bodies in the swirling dark to learn about my own. Maybe they didn't need to be strangers any longer for the trick to work.

After a few Sundays under the scarves and twinkle lights, I noticed how easily it came. I cuddled up against these unfamiliar male bodies as though I had been doing it all my life. I had grown accustomed to the heat of someone else's body, to the touch of someone else's palm.

Sometime just after midnight, Robin or Ko would play "La cumparsita," the song that always signals the impending end of a *milonga*. When that was over the fluorescent lights were flipped, and volunteer crews started pulling down the decorations and the tablecloths and pouring coffee down the sink. Robin would play his exit song, *I'm going home, whoa yeah,* all drawn out and bluesy, as people switched their shoes and said goodbye. The affluent donned their fur-lined coats and hailed taxis while the students rushed around the room collecting trash. Our secret world was stripped and sealed for one more week.

Leaving a *milonga* is like stepping off a treadmill. You move differently, as though you're still submerged inside the bathtub echo of the music. As I retraced my steps back west through the shock of neon to the subway, the strains of Robin's song hung in my ears. The pavement braced against my feet, against my throbbing foot bones. Come tomorrow, I would feel my legs filled with concrete. It was half past twelve, a Sunday night. Almost winter: forty-odd degrees and spitting rain. Midtown shuttered and geared for Monday morning. Everywhere, piles of frozen trash. The sidewalk, emptied of Sabretts, a graveyard for umbrellas, their metal carcasses torn and frayed. I waved to other tango dancers as I passed them, the feel of their handprints still in mine.

Tango has a way of taking over, like an invasive vine, until the landscape of your life is changed. For some of the 0.00009 percent, it is a ritual. For some it is a cult, a drug. For me it was a lifeboat off a sinking ocean liner. A postcard mailed backwards to my sixteen-year-old self. The music I had loved before I understood it. The movement I remembered from a few steps in a basement bookstore bar. It was more devotion than escape.

Chapter Twelve

THAT OCTOBER, PETER AND I WENT TO WESTERN MASSA-chusetts on a weekend trip. We went for dinner and, over *crème brûlée* and dregs of wine, we had an honest conversation. Peter had been glaring at a stroller parked beside the table next to us for the best part of an hour. I could feel him balling fists under the table, digging his nails into his palms. He did things like that, to keep from punching walls in frustration. Sometimes, like a mourner, he would tear an eyelash. He was unhappier than I was then. I thought we had been holding each other together all this time; maybe we'd been holding each other back. Stuck in a mesh of our own untended longings, our unmet needs.

I met those eyes, wide, blank, and pale blue. "You really don't want children, do you?"

"Nope," he said.

"Really?" I asked. "Never?"

"Really," he said. "Never. No."

The air was too warm, echoing. I was perspiring slightly in my turtleneck, twisting a triangle of tablecloth between my fingers. Some clipped-wing, flightless bird flapped in my chest.

"And you're never going to want to marry me."

"Not really," he said, honestly apologetic. "No."

I nodded. It stung, the truth I'd been afraid to see for years because he was my family. Hearing it outright, however bracing, I felt free.

"But—" he added. "I will if you want me to." It broke my heart. We could have each gone on like this for years, convinced that staying in our strange relationship meant we could protect the other from all pain.

It was hot and airless and I shook my head. "I think we have to let each other go," I said. "I think it's time."

I thought my saying this would shock him. He just nodded. He looked stricken, but relieved.

He paid the bill. We walked to a whisky bar, where we nursed smoky single malts and talked through the logistics. We wept a little, then went bowling, and stayed up too late laughing, drinking watery domestic beer. It was the most unfettered fun we'd had in months. In the motel, we slept in separate double beds. I spread my arms and took up most of mine.

It was the world's most amicable split. We remained close friends. We even kept our shared apartment, though I bought myself a bed and he resettled his health magazines and free weights in the second bedroom. He still very rarely slept there, but the presence of his mess behind the door was comforting — his toiletries, his winter coat, his scattered gym socks on the floor.

I moved the mattresses alone. This was the final gesture, and would make us both a little sad. Sharing a bed had been the last pretense of our relationship. Now it was the last thing to give up, the thing that made it real.

Our mattress weighed a hundred pounds or so, and nearly flattened me. I heaved it off the bedframe, dragging, pushing, one corner at a time. It thumped flat to the floor. My socks slid as I tried to lift it. I started sweating, wheezing from the effort. I should have waited for Peter to come and help me, but I was impatient. He hadn't been around in days, and my new bed had been delivered. I tried to heft the huge, unwieldy square onto its side, to push it through the bedroom door. It flopped into a lamp, knocking a bookcase, and broke a much-loved framed print into shattered glass. In grappling the thing aright, I stubbed my toes and bruised my arms. The mattress cover tore. The mattress dropped. *"FUCK!"* I screamed, and the word echoed chillingly off the thin boards of the walls and whatever inner bolts held them in place. I found myself hurling frustration at it, at that awkward, senseless bed we'd shared but never really shared, its coils and feathers standing in for Peter. Peter Pan, who would not grow up, and who would never love me in the way I wanted to be loved. Peter, whom I loved so much and had loved for so long, just never in the way I'd wanted to. There were so many nevers there. And so I cursed it, grunting, heaving, swearing. The mattress and the man had blurred and I was angry — suddenly, and mostly at myself. At the two years I had spent unhappy, thinking it would change, that we would find our spark as if by magic and he would be the one. Knowing he would not grow up the way I thought he should — not because he couldn't, but because he didn't want to. Moving his bed, I realized my egotism and my error. He wasn't any better off settling with me than I with him. No matter how depressed he might have been, my staying tethered to him hadn't helped.

Then, just as suddenly, I mourned. That mattress in that moment was my albatross, the weight of all of it on all of me. I cried, loud and ugly, and crumpled like an exhausted child onto the bed. I cried because I loved him, because he loved me just as much, and still we hadn't fixed each other. Now I'd made an even bigger mess. Now I had broken things. I was alone. His mattress smelled of mildew, faintly, and was grimy at the edges. Mine stood upright in my bedroom, brand new and plastic-wrapped. I lay there, surveying the room, the toppled lamp, the shards of glass. I didn't want to be afraid to be alone.

I stood up and I finished it. I toppled mine onto its metal frame, then muscled his around the corner out of sight. Finally the mattresses were moved, the beds were made, and it was done. I sat there on his for a long time before I straightened a stack of dusty bedside books, and left, shutting his door. Some nights he would come in through the nursery window and everything would be just as it was. Some nights he wouldn't. But now one room was his, and one was mine. It felt cruel, though I knew it wasn't. There was a violence in decision, and I had chosen this. We had chosen this. And so the loneliness I'd swallowed and ignored for months rose up as if to pull me under. Without him there, I found that I could name it, finally, and stand before it, heavy as the bed.

Chapter Thirteen

I SPENT MY FIRST FRIDAY EVENING AS A SINGLE GIRL HOME alone with a box of cheddar crackers and a twenty-dollar bottle of wine, watching murder shows. I was on an unfortunate Nietzsche kick at the time, writing things like *the greatest events — they are not our loudest but our stillest hours* in my journal, and thinking about *la pausa,* essence of the tango: in all that forward motion, the ever-present need to pause.

The little silver heart, centerpiece of the Claddagh ring my dad had given me when I was sixteen, just before my trip to Argentina, now tipped away from me and into the unknown. Every time I looked down as I typed, or rummaged in my wallet for my MetroCard, I saw it and felt a not unpleasant chill.

Peter and I charged bravely forward in our new modus vivendi. He'd spend a night or two each week at our apartment, and we'd order takeout, eat on our new couch by television light, and laugh together like we hadn't laughed in months. We retired to our separate rooms, our separate bedside lamps, our privacy. Sometimes we shouted jokes or good nights through the closed doors and the wall. No one else quite understood our new arrangement. "To hell with them!" we said, and cheersed ourselves, both so glad to have the ease between us back. We'd found an honest way to put each other first, and the logistics weren't anybody's business but our own.

I felt like Odin, yanked up by his ankles, hanging headfirst into a brand-new world. Dizzy with the endlessness of what could be now that everything was upside down — resentful that even in this tidal flood of change, some things stayed the stubborn same.

Work was still a wall of grey. Windowless. Whole days spent under the fluorescent light strip in my cubicle, editing solicitation letters. There was so much waste within those forty-hour weeks — time, money, and thought — and I was losing patience with the memoranda and the meetingspeak. I was reading too much Henry Miller — *Tropics* full of mad, banned prose, and all things unabashed — to accept the lack of luster in the business world. To settle, waiting for my life to happen to me — now that I felt it could.

I started printing RoKo photos every week, taping them to my computer monitor until tiny, out-of-focus versions of myself in skirts and heels were circumtangoing the screen. My form was bad, but in my idle moments — conference calls, strategy meetings, oatmeal breaks — I'd gaze at them and see the radiant amateur: her eyes shut, arms around a stranger, smiling to herself. Her haircut shorter, longer, shorter, in a circle. More a flip book than a shrine. Sometimes I could not believe that she was me.

As often as I could afford, I slinked away on lunch breaks to Nadtochi. I wore business casual; he wore track pants. His studio space was rented from an antique furniture dealer, the key to the restroom charmingly affixed to a wire replica of an 1890s ladies' shoe. It had a very Great-Aunt-Mildred's-parlour atmosphere that I equated with the faded grandeur of the Golden Age.

The first twenty minutes of our lessons were for warming up, and often unremarkable. The longer you let lapse between your dances, the more your shoulders tense up to your ears. Your joints and fasciae stiffen, hardening your muscles out of place. Your nerves are citified, your pulse too rapid, and your reflexes too swift. It takes at least a warm-up *tanda* to let go enough to follow, let alone to dance.

Nadtochi led me, slow and steady, back in time. Walk. Turn. Pause. Breathe. Until my heart rate slowed. Until my eyes stayed shut without my squeezing them. Until I couldn't hear the honking and the shouting and the city noise outside. He felt this before I could. He felt my lungs expand against his ribs. He felt my legs grow heavy, enough for him to feel my feet through the floor. When the music no longer sounded as though it had been swallowed back in time, he stopped and I opened my eyes.

The second twenty minutes were for skills: he'd walk me through a movement for two minutes, some kind of *sacada* or *boleo* or *enganche*. In the last, he'd interrupt my step, making space beneath his leg for mine to swing in, then up, then out again into the step or turn. A brief leg wrap, without pausing for effect. *Enganche*, like *gancho*, means "hook," but feels more fluid in its execution, and more concerned with the release than with the catch. Your leg is an arrow drawing back against a bow; the point is in the letting go. He led, on repeat, until my body understood the cadence. Then he'd spend the following eighteen minutes trying to trick me out of preempting the move each time I thought I saw it coming. Testing me, leading me to the very moment of the leg wrap and then shifting gear. He led everything but the move in question, until he could surprise me with it. Until I wasn't moving my leg through the *enganche;* it was moving me.

A good instructor breaks you down until the skills take root in tendons. Following is *not* anticipating; it's receiving. What Nadtochi taught me, in his infinite patience, was to listen, not just hear. To quiet my mind and to surrender my free leg—not stiffly shoot it out before the step was led. Once he felt my body pliant and my muscles tuned, he'd turn the volume up. "Now we just dance," he'd say, blasting Biagi. The pedagogue disappeared and he became a jungle cat again, all sinews — striding, crouching, as the music swirled.

Dancing is like chess, for leaders, but for followers it is a form of meditation. You reach the floor, configure yourself into a pair of arms, and close your eyes. The rest is up to chance and skill. Within this calculus of partner, music, and improvisation, you surrender to the lead. But this is not the same as switching off. You must be absolutely in it. Listening to the void, the music, learning to interpret what you hear. Following is meant to be an active verb, your own unique response to each suggestion.

I was learning to *feel the love* that Dardo swore lived in my hips, and very tenderly to assert myself when I heard something in the music that I wanted to express. This was Nadtochi's doing too. Embellishments were means to make each dance my own. He taught me a handful of these *adornos,* from stolen beats tapped between steps to the shoeshine of my toe along his trouser leg. Each time I tried one out, however roughly — a hidden kick (*amague,* which is like a threat or feint), or the outward flexing of my heel in a turn — he shouted, *"Esa!"* and I beamed. It was no longer enough to follow, to be "danced," Nadtochi taught me. *Dance back,* he would demand of me.

"You see," Gavito used to say, "we are painters. We paint the music with our feet."

The last few minutes of his lessons were a rapid, wordless whirl. I listened with my cartilage, attempting the crude embellishments he'd shown me, feet flicking at the floor like tongues. Wisps of hair were plastered to my temples in a glaze of sweat, both mine and his. My collarbones shone with it; my eyes shone with the dancing. When it was over, we high-fived and made small talk as I changed my shoes and buttoned up my coat. It was the closest I had ever come to feeling like a track athlete or, for that matter, an adult. The one hour a week in which I felt alive — before I went back to the office, slid the eraser across my name under the "Out" column, and eased into my swivel chair.

Chapter Fourteen

I WELCOMED THE FAMILIAR MELANCHOLY CHILL OF FALL. OUR landlord had cheated on a building permit, so our apartment had no heat or cooking gas — for months — and our complaints had long been lost in city red tape. Concerned third parties disapproved of our living situation, for this and all the other reasons. We ignored them. The nights got shorter, darker, cold. Peter brought home an expensive space heater and more take-out and we huddled under blankets in separate corners of the couch. When we needed to, we talked. We talked about the things we had denied ourselves to be together — what he named our missing 33.33 percent. We talked about everything we did and didn't feel, which was mostly free.

As autumn deepened, Peter came home less and less. His room became a door ajar, an unmade bed, a stack of boxes half-unpacked — while mine accumulated bamboo plants and books and all the decorative flourishes I'd missed about myself, living with someone else. Our shared apartment was a comforting idea — continuous, not altogether true. We each kept a tender eye on the other, and gave each other latitude. I made a secret list of wants — to date, to mount a last-ditch, redoubled acting effort, and to daydream of advanced degrees. I was emboldened. I cut my hair. To keep from fidgeting with unripe possibility, I danced.

I turned twenty-six on Thanksgiving that year. Feast day before the long, cold, lonely winter. Peter brought home an espresso machine and a bunch of flowers big enough to fill my bedroom windowsill. The holiday was hard for both of us, a little awkward for his family, but we stormed forward, undeterred. Relegated to the outskirts of this family I'd adopted as my own, I felt again the loss of mine. The scattering: My mother to the south, abandoned to warm weather and her own resilience, working six-day weeks for twelve dollars an hour at a spa and fitness center for the snowbird country club elite. My father drifting in and out of town, from contract job to contract job, and trying to right his own life on the rails. I could not mend what had been broken — on either side of our once invulnerable triangle. I could not make them civil to each other, let alone paste our lives back together, or make them whole again by force. Holidays as an adult, I realized, would always have this tinge of loneliness and mourning. No matter whom I spent them with. But after we were full of turkey and champagne, bone weary from digestion, Peter's family brought out a candle-laden carrot cake and sang. I thought back to something I had overheard his mother say in France. She'd been talking to visiting friends. "Oh, Meg," she'd said. "She's one of us."

I went on a real date. With an actor-chef named Dean who looked like vintage Brando and who took me and my new three-hundred-dollar dress for an extravagant post-birthday tasting dinner. He also kissed me — on the sidewalk, in the taxi back to his place, and on the unmade bed where he had thrown me, physically, upon opening the door. When he yanked my dress off, I asked him — please — not to undress me further, not just yet. He rolled over irately and asked, "Do you have any idea how much that dinner cost?"

The doubts clotted around me. It rained, unseasonably, for a week. I fell asleep to swirls of it howling outside the turret of my bedroom, flooding the backstreets of my *arrabal*. I felt chastened and rebuked, as though the 33.33 percent might just as well elude me.

I settled in for winter out in Queens. Peter and I brought home a Christmas tree, bought from a stoner camped outside the Ditmars Rite Aid with a stock of balsam pines. We lugged it back to our frigid apartment and hung my childhood ornaments from it as we shivered to a soundtrack of Baroque choral hymns. Christmas was our shared favorite holiday; we sat on benches in the park with peppermint lattes, wishing it would snow. It did. I went dancing in it, despite the train delays. By the time I got home from the *milonga,* sloughing up half a foot of snow before me on the unplowed sidewalk, it was three thirty a.m. and the world was white and quiet but for the ice chips flying in my face. I took a deep cold breath that stung my lungs, safe in the stillness of the street, dizzied to think that not a soul knew where I was.

Since the breakup, Dad made sure to phone me daily. He was still coming out of his post-divorce "Well, Meg, it's *your life*" phase of self-imposed neutrality, withholding judgment to an almost absurd degree, but he made himself a reassuring presence on the phone. He'd call my office line to chat minutiae. The five minutes we spent talking about nothing were often the most grounding of my day. If ever I seemed low, he tried to cheer me up. "Think of it this way," he would say. "That son of a bitch Richard Nixon is still dead."

He reverse commuted from wherever he was contracting to spend his weekends in the city with his now steady girl. Whenever he could, he took me out for Friday lunch. Over lattes and salad, he'd ask me about work, and men, and whether we had heat yet, which we didn't. As we neared December, he asked what I might want for Christmas.

I answered without thinking. "Tango lessons."

I couldn't tell then whether he approved. He did. I know now that he bragged about me, his daughter who had infiltrated the New York City tango scene, no matter how unsure she felt about herself. Then, however, he just chuckled, paid for lunch, and sent me money for five lessons with Nadtochi. I went back to work with one eye on the prize of tango prowess and one eye on my LaserJet montage.

Meanwhile, the holiday party season started. Time to think was at a premium. I spent work fund-raisers refilling empty wineglasses and collecting wadded cocktail napkins from would-be major donors, and social evenings singing carols or hovering by the cheese board. For three weeks I ate canapés for dinner, and snuck off to dance as soon as I knew I would not be missed at whichever gathering I fled. I closed most weeknight *milongas,* right down to "La cumparsita." I slept very little, survived on free wine and cookie platters, and pumped every spare hour and resource into tango. By the middle of December, I'd popped a blood vessel in my left eye, like a little badge, a red freckle of delicious excess. I flirted ever closer to the idea of misbehavior, to being rash, or unreliable, or hedonistic. I left my office-ready pumps at home, saving my feet, and pushed the too restrictive woolen pencil skirts back in my closet. I started wearing wide-legged jeans or cotton jersey tango skirts to work. My new look was wholly unprofessional, but spared me a nightly costume change in Starbucks bathrooms.

I sang — for the first time — in a three-woman cabaret, the sort of money-losing passion project dreamed up by a piano player and three not-working actresses. It was our best shot at scraping our way onto a stage, any stage — even one we had to pay for. We called it *The Best Friend, The Ingénue, & The Vamp.* I was the ingénue, and wore a short black dress over new lace underpants and sang ballads about just how much I wanted to be loved. We all teamed up for bawdy group numbers, culminating in a growled collective "You Don't Own Me," asserting our independence from men, and casting agents, and the wide, indifferent world.

We celebrated our modest triumph with another party at the vamp's house on a Saturday in mid-December. She lived in New Jersey, somewhere between Guttenberg and Weehawken, and had filled her house with food and festive cocktail napkins. She'd made gravy in a Crock Pot, trays of meatballs, wedding cookies, and a bourbon champagne punch. We sat around and laughed and drank and made fun of all the men who'd hurt our feelings. We sang along to Eartha Kitt. By half past eight, my breath was thick with roasted garlic, and I felt warm and wobbly from the punch. Tango had wandered from my thoughts, but as we left to catch the bus back to the city, I received a message from Nadtochi. He was going to the All-Night Milonga, and would save a dance or two for me if I was going too.

It was not a date, an overture, or really even any kind of invitation. It was a statement. A summons. The promise of a *tanda,* maybe two — and this time, not out of mere politeness. It meant, or might mean, he thought I might prove worthy of his art. My heart thumped through the fog of food.

I was in nowhere New Jersey. I didn't even have my shoes.

I spent the bus ride back to Port Authority deliberating, half an ear on my companions' conversation, half an eye on Nadtochi's text. If I caught an N train from Times Square and sprinted home first, I might make the *milonga* by eleven thirty. This was the sort of spontaneity I'd acquired. Running out on social obligations, brushing my teeth in panic, rushing for the train. I'd even started wearing eye makeup.

Sure! I punched into my phone, my crossed leg bouncing madly in anticipation.

The All-Night Milonga was on the ninth floor of a Twenty-sixth Street office building, across from the Hill Country BBQ. Entrance cost fifteen dollars and came with paper wristbands. There was a crowded little lobby, changing rooms, a water fountain, and a bar selling vinegary wine in plastic cups. Dancing took place in the blond-floored ballroom, which was so big, thin pillars were needed in the center dancing space to hold the ceiling up. These were vined with twinkle lights and tulle. Tables and chairs were pushed against the walls. There was a cloakroom to the left, and to the right a small and sweaty back room where those inclined danced neo-tango. The closed door bore a handwritten hot pink sign that read *Alternative*. This I would avoid.

I ran into Edward in the cloakroom. Nadtochi wasn't there yet and I was nervous — overfed and garlicky and slightly sodden from the punch. I hung my coat and sat down on the bench beside him to catch up, making far too upbeat conversation, pretending not to scan the dance floor through the doorframe. I knew one person there; I had not come in vain. My nerves abated as we chatted, and I felt nearly normal when he elbowed me.

"Oh, look," he said, "your friend!"

I thought: Edward was my only friend in tango. I had no idea what he meant.

I looked up and Enzo loomed before me in his maroon merino wool. Smirking, one arm on his backpack strap. A heartbeat or two fell out from under me. It had been months, and I had long stopped looking for him first in every ballroom.

"I was wondering when I might run into you," he said, all teeth. His tone felt casually rehearsed. I swallowed, said, "Hi!" with too much held breath in my voice. I leapt to greet him — going for natural, polite, surprised. He placed a grandmotherly peck upon my cheek that zinged down through what would have been my axis, had I felt more rooted to the ground. He still smelled of aftershave.

"May I join you?"

"Of course," I said, and there we were: three on a two-seat bench, my left thigh soldered into Enzo's. The men shook hands across me and exchanged the standard niceties. I laughed, too loud, at someone's not-amusing joke. Enzo patted my knee with one hand, absently, and left it there. He didn't move it as he reached into his backpack with the other hand to brandish red wine in a paper bag.

"A toast?" he asked, with sideways grin, as he began to work the corkscrew.

I nodded, wordless.

"Oh, why not," Edward acquiesced. "But just a splash."

A toast. To nothing. For the sake of toasting. Edward hoisted his plastic cup and took a timid mouthful, then took his leave of us. We sat in speechless silence, sipping, thighs still touching, though the bench had opened up and there was room to separate. He asked questions and I answered them, but they weren't real questions. I wasn't really answering. He put his heavy olive palm down on my knee again and rubbed my spandex leggings nervously. We were talking past each other. Each more focused on the movement of his palm across my leg. How thick that fabric felt between my skin and his hand. The music in the next room seemed impossible, remote. There was no one in the cloakroom but the two of us. Some twenty-five feet beyond, a mirror at the darkened end showed our reflection: red sweater and red sweater dress, very close together on a bench.

He pressed his lips together, let out breath. "When did you get back?"

"Ages ago," I stammered.

"I've been hermiting," he said. "And *la belle France*?"

"She was magnificent."

"I suppose ... to be expected?" It was a painful conversation — not unlike a tango in its rhythm — dark, and full of sudden, heavy pauses. "Wow," he said, and laughed at nothing. I laughed too. The air between us crackled manically. I was giddy with it, leaning against the wall to hide my nervous agitation. To slow my circulation, muster poise. We finished our splash of wine. He tucked the bottle back into his bag.

"Would you like to dance?"

Nadtochi still had not arrived, so I unsheathed my heels and peeled away my winter socks. I wedged in my pale, unpolished feet and buckled the straps across my ankles, hoping to stay my hands from trembling as I did. Enzo laced his as calmly as a kindergarten teacher. He was not the all-business tugging type. There was no rush into the fray. I fumbled with my second buckle tooth, then hopped up, stashed my boots and purse haphazardly beneath the bench. I pretended to watch the dancers through the doorway as I waited for him to lay aside his street shoes. Nearly levitating in anticipation. He took his sweater off and folded it, like a handkerchief, into a perfect square.

We embraced although the song was ending, taking just one step before the resolution, the *chan chan*, then separating. His striped cotton shirt exuded heat. I mumbled something about being rusty, being tipsy, being far too young for him (in tango, let alone in age). Or I was about to, when the *cortina* ended and he pulled me into close embrace and whispered, *"Shhhh."*

We danced three *tandas*, four. Memory fails. There were moments when my feet worked underneath me, flexing, pivoting, when I felt the suede soles of my shoes stretch against the hardwood floor. There were moments when I felt more like a helium balloon, and had no feet, and was in danger of floating into aether. But Enzo had my cord; he reeled me back. There must have been two hundred other people there. Songs began and ended. He did not release my hand between them. He rubbed his calloused thumb along my fingers and my Claddagh, awkwardly, compulsively. He looked at me with big brown camel eyes, as though I were his personal mirage. We must have taken breaks, for wine, for water, for me to retreat into the ladies' changing room and stare down the strange new woman in the mirror, her faint eye shadow, red forehead and cheeks, and sweat strung through her hair. I remember trying not to trip, not to collide with anyone or walk into the walls. I was drunk with desert thirst. For all things warm and dry and winter. I forgot about Nadtochi, forgot why I was there. I was spinning in Di Sarli, in slow motion, dust unsettled in a shaft of light — always falling, not quite landing.

If we stopped dancing, we would lose our balance. We teetered to and from each other, paralyzed. We commented on the *cortinas,* which were unusually circuslike that night and full of haunting harpsichords and horns. We ran out of words. After all, what did we have in common, save dancing and that one book we'd both read? We stood there, anxious, laughing, drugged, our pupils blank and wide. Whenever music started, we would move as if by accident, him stumbling, walking forward into me, and me receiving him. I absorbed the shock of us in my beginner backsteps, still a little too far forward on my toes. Heels up, *relevé.* I scooted my startled game feet in reverse, teasing the hunter. Beckoning. He led sequences I was not advanced enough to follow — not out of ostentation, but because he was no longer in teacher mode. He was just dancing. Honestly, and at his level. I scuffled to keep up. He led *colgadas,* wherein we each moved off our axes for a moment, our feet meeting between us, swinging our centers out and away from each other, like a drinking straw dispenser at a soda counter. Centrifugal. But once I fell away from our center, I was disoriented and unsteady. *Sorry,* I exhaled into his face, my eyes squeezed against our shared cheeksweat. *Mmmm,* was all he said.

"This is a dream," he breathed. "I'm dreaming." I didn't think it was a line.

After one strange xylophone *cortina,* I noticed Nadtochi with a start, dancing in the distance. I caught his eye just over Enzo's shoulder, and smiled by way of explanation. He gave a sagacious nod. But he was on another planet, not the moonstone cavern I was lost in. I shut my eyes and danced with Enzo. Only Enzo. We were sonar tethered. I barely heard the music above the din between us.

We fell from the line of dance into a pair of folding chairs. Empty tables were strewn with half-eaten butter cookies, wadded cocktail napkins, and plastic cups half-full of wine and water. Nadtochi was gone. There were only stragglers now: couples, loners, Argentines drinking Fernet in the corner.

"It's late," he said.

"It is."

We danced another *tanda.* This was the drama hour. Every late *milonga* has one. All violence in the strings. As if the music had grown tired of flirting, maybe even tired of dancing. It sounded like a lady swooning, shouting, her heart sinews strung tough as steak. We'd found a rhythm: pulsing walk, tight rocking turns. I was barely breathing and my arches ached. *Cortina.*

"Shall we?" he asked. I nodded and we tottered off the floor.

It took too long for me to change my shoes; somehow I couldn't get the buckles loose. Someone had turned the lights off in the cloakroom. When I got out to the lobby, I expected he'd have gone. He met me there.

"I have a treat for us," he whispered. We had the elevator to ourselves.

"Close your eyes," he said. "Open your mouth."

I heard the snap of mist, his thumbnail rupturing the rind. The elevator swelled with it. I felt the peeled segment pass my lips. A clementine.

For months, that smell was his. The crispness of it, sweet orange water on the tongue. We staggered out into the street and crossed it, moving away from the *milonga,* into a shadowed patch of sidewalk. He fed me pieces, dropping little petals of the peel into the street. It was after four. We stood in shadows, as if Sixth Avenue weren't just around the corner, waking up. He put the last piece on my tongue and kissed me, which was — even after all that came before it — somehow a surprise.

His sweater smelled of books and shaving cream. My coat smelled of frozen wool. We kissed again; my mouth opened to the warmth of his. He pushed me up against plate glass, cold, his arms around my waist. It felt like an extension of our dancing. I could still feel the bass line of the music in my pulse, and echoes of the melody sawed in my ears. We kissed until that faded into snowy static.

"I don't suppose you'd —"

I was not the kind of girl who went to Jersey City in the dead of night, back to a man's apartment after kissing for an hour up against the windows of Hill Country BBQ. But my body couldn't bear to drift more than an inch beyond his hands, so I said yes. He pulled me by the hand to Sixth, where everything was brighter — dawn was almost breaking — and I waited in Duane Reade for him to buy us fruit juice. We stood for a moment in the fluorescent vestibule, squinting in the harshness of the light.

The taxi was absurd, expensive. In it, we shared the juice. The world was seasick — tunnel, roadway; only we were steady.

"This is crazy," he mumbled between sips, that hand upon my thigh. "This isn't real."

A sleeping street. Dark-windowed row houses. Spindly un-leafed trees. We took four steps down from street level and stood a moment in the cold, the taxi gone, as Enzo fumbled with the lock. There were wet leaves clotted at his feet. Cob-webs. The door opened to the basement level, to a single room crowded with books and mildewed record covers. He called his place disaster; I called it beautiful. A rash of papers in the en-tryway, a scattering of shoes and scarves. A pair of belted trou-sers slung over a chair. Then walls and walls of hardbound art books, hoarded photographs and records. He'd been through fire, then a flood. His books were yellowed, carbon-dusted ref-ugees, well loved. He took the special ones down from shelves and laid them in my open hands. I riffled through them, rever-ent, as he made tea. I sat down on his bed, beneath a wall of pa-perbacks. I ran my fingers gently down their spines, and smiled. He sat down beside me, handed me a mug, and read to me. From Paul Theroux, *The Old Patagonian Express*. The passage where the author reads to old, blind Borges for the first time. I felt old and blind as well, but also very, very young as I gaped up at him. I closed my eyes and let the words wash over me, in sepia.

"*Gradual blindness is not a tragedy,*" Borges was saying to Theroux. "*It's like a slow summer dusk.*" Words swam behind my eyes. Words, I understood. I listened to them in Enzo's voice and heard the way he loved their shapes and quirks, the way he held them in his mouth with wonder. The two men traded an-ecdotes and went dissolving into Kipling, a whirl of iambs and trochees through *the old-grey widow maker* with the *ten-times fingering weed to hold you.* "*How beautiful,*" Borges said. "*You can't say things like that in Spanish.*" I could hear Enzo smiling as he reached the end, where we see a sly cat has chewed the author's sweater sleeve. *"Its eyes were tightly shut,"* he finished, and I opened mine.

He reached over me to replace the Theroux on the shelf above his bed. I shivered. Then he gently took the book I held away. Gently uncrossed my legs. Tilted my chin up with his meat slab hand and kissed me. Morning was becoming blue; light filtered down on us through windows from the street, through dried flower vases, hand-blown glass, all filmed with dust. He laid me on his patchwork bed.

We kissed under the buttered glare of his reading lamp. I sank beneath his weight, into the stable, into ocean weeds. He switched off the lamp. We kicked our feet free of our boots, tangled our legs.

"Is this okay?" he asked, and peeled away each layer of my clothing. My sweater dress, my woolen socks. I nodded.

"And this?" My leggings. Nod.

"This?" He slid cotton straps from either shoulder, buried his stubbled cheek into my neck. I found my body, magnetized, arched upwardly to his. He was a perfect gentleman, almost archival, as though I were wrapped in vellum. I toyed open buttons, freed arms from his sleeves. He pulled his cotton undershirt over his head, pushed off his socks.

"This?" The camisole, over my head. One earring, then the other. He looked down at me, in black lace and a bra, and breathed, *"God damn."* I'd never heard that tone in a man's voice before. My skin was blushing late-night-television blue. If I was afraid of what came next, I didn't want to be.

I touched his smooth and olive skin, and felt my naked arms against the hollow of his back. I helped him with his belt buckle, but didn't dare grope further. I did not know how. I lay there as he undressed, unhooked my bra, and spread across me — his chest, the wide trunks of his legs, the softened leather of his hands. I shivered slightly everywhere we touched.

"Probably too much," he said, his hand beneath a patch of lace, the very last. It was a question.

I mumbled yes, probably so, then nodded my assent and rolled beneath the weight of him — nearly rent in two by my desire to be taken. I closed my eyes. In that vast darkness there was only fullness. I wanted to melt into his skin and to be opened wider, wider, until I became the sea that swallowed him. That held him in my weeds. I wrapped my arms around his neck and tried to match his breathing as it rose and crested, as we panted ourselves, finally, to sleep.

We woke on Sunday afternoon, beneath the overhang of books. He got up, made coffee, sliced a pear. We didn't then and never would know how to talk together. We traded furtive glances, awkward smiles. The sky outside was bright as icicles, but his room was dark. He stood there in his underpants and made us breakfast: English muffins soaked in honey, over-ripened fruit. I sat with a musty sheet wound around my breasts and stared at him with wild eyes and hair. I felt strangely beautiful, naked, in that light, and terribly self-conscious. I made a show of studying the shelf and mumbling my approval when I came to well-worn loves of mine — the Brontës, Abbey, Thoreau, Hesse, Bukowski. He dressed. I dressed. He turned on a hiss of old-time jazz. Come back to bed, I wanted to say. Stay here with me in this cave of quiet. Read to me again. But we had promises to keep. I smoothed the coverlets over his bed and gathered up my things.

We took the train together. Walked there, through cold and concrete Journal Square, glaring like a sheet of ice. Waited on the platform, shifting our weight from foot to foot. We were *waiting for the train* . . . I noted with a smirk. I tried to affect a cool ease with him I didn't feel. We bantered emptily, and sat together watching people read their newspapers or stare into their laps. I hoped that he might hold my hand, but didn't reach for his. Just before my stop he asked my number, which I recited at him over-shoulder as I exited, certain he would never call.

I transferred from the PATH train, sat still and quiet on the N in last night's leggings and my grey wool coat, catching glimpses of myself in the windows, pale and underslept. Daylit Queens went rattling past. The world was vivid, crisp — my body too. I was lit up with something like a fever. *A huge camellia,* in the words of Plath. Hot and dissolving, like *old whore petticoats / to Paradise.* My flesh felt heady and electrified; there was a current thumping in my blood. Flashbacks to the night before lit up my spine, sent scrambled text and flesh and poetry into my brain. Black lace, blue blush of skin, the way he'd put his hot mouth on my neck, and how my edges had dissolved beneath him, the feel of him against a place too deep to name.

If only it had ended there. One night of dancing and a one-night stand. One blue-lit basement scene. A story I told Peter as I turned up, late, and sat beside him at the birthday dinner for a friend. "Did you come home last night, Biscuit?" he asked. "No," I said. "Did you?" He grinned. We passed a heavy plate of spaghetti *pomodoro* back and forth between us and told each other where we'd woken up that morning.

"I had a one-night stand," I whispered to him. *"Me."*

He bumped my fist under the table.

I knew even then. Enzo would never be my boyfriend. He was pushing forty, undermotivated, half-employed. He rented the basement studio in Jersey City, and often left his morning coffee in the pot to rot for days. He drank too much. He was emotionally recondite. And I would come to find — too late — he was a conscience-sick Narcissus, reflected only in his women, and both delighted and repulsed by the results. I was too naïve to see, at first, that he had probably bedded half the New York tango scene, and that he blamed his string of women for his every flaw. I wish I'd understood then what he did and didn't have to give. What I could and couldn't ask him for. Back then, I looked at him and saw every last cliché of the uncageable: the lone wolf whose eyes are always blazing for the exit, the man no single woman could contain. It did not occur to me to try.

He called on Monday. He said, *Thanks for being in my dream.*

I took his lead. I met him at La Nacional that week — snuck in and started dancing, waiting for him to notice me, to say hello. When he asked me, I tried to follow evenly, and failed — too stuck in my own head and wondering whether he would ask me home. He did. I nodded meekly, and we rode the PATH train back toward his mismatched sheets, where I tried once more to follow evenly, and fumbled for his flesh. I waited for him to touch me first. Undress me first. I stared at him, wide-eyed and silent. I waited for his cues. I spoke when spoken to, but otherwise made a beeline for his bed and perched there, tightly geared. I pulled books down off his shelves and flipped through pages. Hoping he would take them from my hands as he had done before. I wanted nothing but to pin him to the sheets and read to him as I undressed him. Read to him and lick his ear. Whisper fragments as I switched off the reading light. These actions seemed impossible to me. My voice felt strangled, and my body roiled, tensed and outwardly inanimate.

We lurched on this way for weeks. I waited for him; he called. We met in darkened wine bars, deserted ones and crowded ones in which we were afraid to talk or had to shout into each other's ear. He asked me to *milongas,* to which he showed up late. I would pretend he wasn't there at first, and he would have to corner me to say hello. He asked me to dance; we danced. He sometimes did and sometimes didn't ask me home. No matter where we were, he touched me first. And then he disappeared, for days.

. . .

That Christmas, Mum was working. It was high season at the country club, and they couldn't spare her. Dad was with his girlfriend and her kids. In the crush of parties, workdays, and late tango nights, I hadn't dwelled much on the season — except to ponder every so often how it used to feel. I'd spent the last three Christmases with Peter's family, the bustle of their company distracting me from feeling anything but merriment. This year, somewhat estranged, I spent so many evenings by myself, walking in the dark between the parties and *milongas*, work and work events, and listening to a constant stream of mournful choral standards on my headphones, on repeat. Missing my family, but not sure, really, if two parents who never spoke still counted as one. Or whether I was lamely missing something that had simply ceased to be. I lay in bed on Sunday afternoons and watched the planes take off, one by one, out of LaGuardia. Then got up and went to RoKo, where the emptiness was easy to defeat. Everything in that bleak midwinter felt encased in ice, but still too beautiful to break.

I went stag to Peter's family Christmas dinner and found myself, hours later, alone and sober on his parents' couch, full of a feast I'd helped to cook and trying not to feel peripheral. Peter had long since fallen asleep beside me on the couch, next to a three-quarters-empty glass of scotch. His parents' tree glowed white and gold and glinted in the windowpanes. I'd overstayed my welcome, but had nowhere else to go; his family had been my family for so long and I didn't want to give them up. Still, I watched Peter's breathing rise and fall and felt like an intruder. I showed myself out into the streets and walked downtown. It was Friday night and yet the city was deserted. There was only one *milonga* open, so that was where I went. Forty-nine blocks south, and six avenues east. I wasn't sure what I was doing at the Uke, picking my way past families celebrating over borscht and blintzes in the dining room, but I paid my entrance to the back, where tango played inapposite to Christmas. My thick wool tights slipped in my shoes, which made me wobble, but it didn't matter. Edward was there. We danced — badly; I was too warm in my turtleneck and couldn't seem to find the flow. After an hour, I went home.

My dancing had somehow gotten tangled up with Enzo — as if he'd taken too much of my weight and robbed the love out of my hips, and I was stuck again inside the tiptoed girl I'd been months before, jittery and passive on the floor.

I was trapped in his *milongas* first, and then the ones he never made it to — when he pled too tired, too weary, or too bored. I watched for him everywhere I went, scanning the entrance, the benches, the leaders prowling the perimeter of the floor. The sight of him emerging from the elevator set off cymbals in my chest. It was a game of wounded predator and skittish, fatalistic prey: awful if he wasn't there, worse when he was. The only power I could claim was to ignore him, but if he was anywhere in sight, I couldn't concentrate, let alone lose myself and dance.

The word *canyengue* came from a Ki-Kongo verb that means "to melt." *Kanienge* (from *mu nyenga*) is the imperative: "Melt into the music!" Melt! As if, from the very heat of it, one could dissolve into the dance. That's how it first had felt. Now I almost dreaded dancing with him. We were not matched in level, and whatever witchery had hummed between us died. I lost my confidence. He was image conscious and impatient, crouched too far down into himself to see the harm his frustration with my beginner weaknesses had wrought. I felt beholden — as if I owed improvement to him, as if two *tandas* were his grudging gift to me, a gift I squandered in my missteps and my nervous lack of ease. *Sorry,* I continually whimpered, miserably, into his ear. I fluttered when we moved, a moth half-tachycardic with the terror. My feet barely touched the ground. Still, I persisted, naïve enough to think that if we only touched our torsos close enough together, we might melt back into that dream.

For months this wore on. We never once discussed the poems we'd sent each other when I was in France, the simmering flirtation we'd stored up for a winter such as this. I never warned him about the drought that came before him, and the damage — how I was not yet the woman he expected me to be. I meant to ask him to be gentle with me, as you would a gift that tumbled, so much more fragile than expected, from its paper wrappings. I rehearsed the words that I would use. *Just be patient,* I would tell him. And explain. Tell him how he made me feel like a hothouse tomato, ripening and red. Tell him other things that I rehearsed, but never said out loud.

It wasn't just the fever stuff. I *liked* him. I liked his skulking boyish weirdness. I liked his brain. The way he read, with reverence, as though words — all words, when read by him — were holy. How he never left the house without a book. How he was alive to art. I liked the music he played — loud and at all hours in his studio. I liked his taste, and how we both tended to dress like paperboys, in corduroys and woolen hats. I liked his adolescent, navel-gazing scowl. I liked the drama of his solitude. The strange and feral, stilted fact of him. He looked like he'd been deeply hurt. I wish I'd asked him how.

The best we ever did was books. We traded war memoirs, modernist tomes, Hemingway, Nicholson Baker, E. B. White. Our solvent currency was this. On New Year's Eve, after we'd managed to meet and kiss at midnight in a special midtown warehouse dance, we missed a PATH by seconds and sat there for an hour on the soiled concrete reading *Breakfast at Tiffany's* from the slim volume in his coat pocket. We sipped from a split of fine champagne until the transit police saw and confiscated it. We didn't care. We sprawled, our legs before us, reading together at the tunnel's maw, warm even in winter.

But when the book was shut, I lost my nerve. I kept my distance at *milongas,* dancing half a floor away from him and shooting furtive glances I did not expect to see returned. When seated across a table from him, I would fiddle with my wineglass, or a coffee cup, looking anywhere but himwards. It was the most confounded lust I'd ever felt; my heart mush thrummed just at the thought of him.

By the time he took my hand, and I his massive shoulder blade, I was transparent. He asked for my weight, for me to sink, solar plexus into hips, and show the love I'd bottled up. But I felt weightless, insubstantial, as if I couldn't access my own force. I was a linen curtain; he was atmospheric pressure. I let myself be flapped and waved. I let him fray me at the hem. Sometimes it felt like he was lunging extra-violently, just to see if I would blow away.

The sex was not much different.

He was as didactic in the bedroom as on the dance floor, but I needed teaching. He was a grown man, at least in form, and he had grown man needs I didn't know enough to meet. I had never really learned to touch a naked male, and I was too consumed with being touched by him to try and learn to touch him back. He never said he was unsatisfied, but then, he didn't have to. We hardly ever spoke. He simply placed my hand on him and sighed.

My mother, libertine that she was, almost approved of the affair — she even used that word, as if to steel me for the inexorable end. She was having her post-divorce liaisons with unbefitting men — why shouldn't I? I told her how he challenged me; how I read faster now to match his pace. How he texted me in prose. But he was just another clown to her, not worthy of my heart.

"Meg. If a man is over forty and has never been married, then there's something wrong with him," she said.

"But, Mum, he isn't forty yet."

"Close enough," she said. I told her she was wrong; it was a generation thing.

"Oh, sweetie, I'm not wrong," she said. "I'm glad he wants to pork you, though. I hate to say that's progress, but it is."

Still, I went to his *milongas*. Sometimes he was there. We danced wide arcs around each other until the dance floor thinned too much for us to keep pretending we weren't waiting for each other. Sometimes he stood me up. Sometimes I sat alone at home in my pajamas and realized I smelled of him. Which is to say of Lever 2000 soap and garlic, musty paperbacks. I confessed to Edward one night, in the back of a shared cab. He was more shocked than I'd expected, given my behavior at the All-Night. "You're talking about Enzo?" he demanded. "You actually slept with that guy?"

"I know," I said, then added lamely, "You wouldn't understand. *I* don't even understand."

I couldn't stop. I'd folded two compulsions into one. Enzo was tango; tango, Enzo. And I was losing both. I kept trying to find my stride, which happened only in Nadtochi's studio, in the stolen sunlight of the workday. But even there, I wasn't dancing back. I kept forgetting to embellish. *"Dále, mujer!"* he goaded. More than once, he asked if I was tired. It's possible he knew, though he referred to Enzo only once, as "that friend of yours." I'd like to think he'd given me the benefit of the doubt. I didn't disabuse him of it.

Enzo was the secret that I danced.

He simmered underneath the last two shows I ever did: an encore reprise performance of the cabaret, and a play Peter and I produced together. *Against Her Better Judgment* was our low-budget swan song. He handled the funding and I wrote the script, adapting six Dorothy Parker short stories, punctuated by a dozen of her poems. I'd grown up on these, reciting even the most caustic barbs at dinner parties so that I might prove a credit to my parents with my nascent erudition. I'd learned a few things from Ms. Parker's playbook about spitefulness and snobbery, what men wanted, and what women never got. The former were a pack of brutes, the latter either hellions or simpering fools. What I'd read with bemused delight in childhood now struck me as sickeningly resonant: Social trappings. Humor awash with bitterness and booze. Predatory or buffoonish men against the sharp-tongued heroines who loved them. There were lessons to be revisited, relearned in her work. A frightening clap of honesty in the droll dynamic she'd exposed. The characters were more gussied up, perhaps, their speeches florid and precise, but not much else had changed since 1931. I, for one, was still waiting by a telephone, bargaining with God and with myself that some or other man might call. *Please, God, let him telephone me now.* That simply wouldn't do.

There were six of us onstage — three women and three men. I found the work discomfiting and personal, the rehearsal process demanding that I pumice over wounds so new I had no strategy to hide them. And see, in stark relief, the ways in which I (often) skirted the pathetic in the name of love. How much I'd given up, and for how little. My costars felt the same. *Good god, I absolutely do this,* we found ourselves lamenting after particularly trying scenes. Cackling, *This idiot is me.* We set ourselves the task of rendering these biting portraits of the sexes both absolutely true and absolutely wrong. For me, at least, it was an act of exorcism. I went into rehearsals raw, to reenact injustices Enzo, or any other cad, had done. Ready to purge myself of my most pitiable behaviors, to bare the blight and kill it off with laughter and applause.

Meanwhile, I flirted with the many facets of Ms. Parker's

personality, as inscribed across her characters. I fake-swilled stage martinis. I hung up who I was with men offstage — timid, frightened, and forlorn — and tried on "kittenish" instead. Racy. Pouty. Scathing. Broad. I left my cast and crew each evening and went straight to tango, though my onstage boldness seemed to vaporize once I passed the borders of the building. I bundled in my grey wool coat and shivered my way downtown to dance.

I didn't know that it would be my last production. I was sure windows were opening. More adaptations. Press clippings. A future company. My director, Max, saw through this. She'd known me since the height of college stardom, and could see the balance shift.

"You don't want this anymore," she said, on a night when we had brawled. She was staying with me, and she'd made me soup, roasted squash and ginger, which I'd declined to eat. I was on my way to a *milonga,* when she thought we should be planning set designs or staging. I fought her, even as I stuffed my shoes into my purse, even as I took half a spoonful from the pot and swooned and wished for just a moment to stay home with her and eat and talk and have that be enough. I bellowed at her; she had no right to tell me what I wanted, what I worked for, what I felt. I shouted at her, sobbed, then went to tango.

"It's okay," she said, much later. "It's okay to walk away."

Max was a good enough director, thankfully, to harness my deep Enzo angst, and play it against the new nubility I had acquired in tango, wringing from me the performance that she needed. She let me kid myself that theatre was my priority, even as we met for dinner meetings three blocks from tango studios, even as I stumbled through rehearsals underslept — though never truly unprepared. I designed the program on my work computer, writing liner notes and balancing the budget spreadsheet between sales meetings. I schlepped to midtown costume shops and thrift stores on my lunch hour. I did not stop dancing. I went on Wednesday nights, and Thursday nights to La Na — late, after rehearsal — and crept home after two. Sometimes I crept back to Jersey City, shivering but barely speaking beside Enzo as we crossed the desolate streets between his place and the PATH station in ghostly Journal Square.

"Keep your wits," Max warned. "You need more you and less men."

I went to RoKo Sunday nights for respite; it was the only place Enzo never went. It took me months to realize he never went because he wasn't good enough. Perhaps he was afraid of looking foolish next to all that talent, too self-concerned to realize he wasn't being judged. The RoKo lights were up too bright for Enzo, with all those young people glowing at 120 watts. Or maybe it was too *nuevo,* and he preferred to linger in the darkened corners of tradition. Either way, it was the only place my dance had not been stained with him.

We spoke only in the prose we passed between us, other people's words. He read Melville into my answering machine, I wrote to him in Plath. I pored through the dog-eared pages of the books he lent me, thinking I might find him there. I never once invited him to my place. He never asked. I did his dishes, folded his discarded pants, tucked his sheets back underneath his mattress. This was what I knew. How I had learned to show my love. We drank tea and herbal *digestifs.* We avoided definitions, conversations. *Whatever this is,* we said, and I would glance away to hide my disappointment.

I knew that if I asked for anything, he would run. I asked for nothing. I had Ms. Parker's mandates in my head: *They don't like you to tell them you're unhappy because of them. If you do, they think you're possessive and exacting. And then they hate you.* To avoid the accusation that our relationship was too much work, I was determined to be no work. Here I was again, with a man I cared for, mutely, and a mutually unmet list of needs.

I knew things were bad, that he was bad for me. That this was no relationship at all. But I wanted him, and had no self-esteem; I thought everything that had gone wrong had been my fault. And the more I thought that, the more I thought we could be salvaged, and give each other what we'd been withholding, consciously or otherwise. My buried feline abandon. His accountability. I wanted him, but I was still afraid that if I reached for him, he'd cringe. That he would pull away and I'd be left to stumble in the emptiness between us. It always felt like an audition. I watched his gaze narrow — weighing me — and shrank.

Then I performed for him. Singing half-veiled love songs to him in the cabaret, acting out the relevant Parker parables from the black box firetrap we'd rented on West Seventy-seventh Street. Both times, he showed up late; I begged stage managers to hold the house. He watched and said it was the first time he could understand me. I whispered, he said, in a mumbling geisha voice with him, but was a booming, wailing, fearless bawd on-stage. After a Friday night performance, my hair still abounce with curls, he fêted me with cava and *moules frites*. I beamed across the bistro table in my greasepaint, thinking that he finally understood. Thinking I had won.

Mum flew up for the show as well. "Against *my* better judgment," she snorted, braving the February cold despite her vow never to set foot in another Northeast winter. She bought herself a down parka with a fur-lined hood at T.J.Maxx, which she would never wear again. She took me to the Algonquin afterward, for twenty-dollar cocktails, which we drank on leather plush chairs, twenty feet from our beloved Round Table. We took tourist pictures underneath the painted homage to the Vicious Circle, with Ms. Parker sneering at us from beneath her wide-brimmed hat.

She told me it was the first time she had seen me that way

—meaning sexy. Luscious and assured. That I had carried myself, spoken, and moved with a certain upright womanly maturity. "I know it's acting and everything, Meg, but you were a grown woman up there." Whatever Enzo was doing to me, she thought, had loosened something, dislodged some long-lost piece.

It was over before it ever started. In adjective form, *kanienge* means "worn-out" or "tired." Done. Melted, but *by* something —time, music, or something worse. Enzo had melted me. And I had given him too much room. Room to let him love me if he ever wanted to, *if I were only sweet enough*. Despite the progress I had made in character, beyond the fourth wall I made very little noise. I took up very little space. I ate and ordered daintily. I waited for my cues. "Eat!" "Talk!" he'd say, as frustrated as I was with my diffidence. But I just stared at him, unblinking.

He needed space. *I'm freaking out,* he wrote. *I'll call you in ten days.* When he did, I didn't answer. *We should talk,* his message said. Sure that he was ending it, I went meekly to the slaughter. I stood flipping pages in a SoHo bookstore waiting for him. He marched me to a sidewalk bar, damp from a day of rain. We ordered tea and tiny glasses of Cynar. He ordered dinner, and we didn't speak until he took two bites.

"I don't do things halfway," he said. "And what we've been doing . . ." He trailed off.

"Is basically book club," I offered. "With semiweekly sex."

He laughed, startled by my candor. I laughed too, and stared into my iron teapot, touching my fingers to the scalding belly of it. It was too hot to hold, and yet the warmth was mooring. Relationships were hard for him. He hadn't been with anyone in eleven years, he said. "I'm still not sure I can." But he wanted to make an honest go of it with me. My patience had redeemed us both. "I want to try and embrace this," he said. "For real."

"That's . . . not what I expected you to say," I stammered.

"Me neither." He smirked, and just then, it was spring. I laughed again, and kissed his bitter liqueur lips. I did not go home with him that night. He put me in a cab at Houston Street, and I flew across the Queensboro Bridge, back to my turret, giddy with my luck. I imagined cooking for him. Lighting candles around my bookshelves, setting a big red bottle out to breathe. Bob Dylan B-sides on the stereo. The windows open to the dewy *arrabal* outside.

Three days later, he needed space again.

If only he had never called. If only I'd been gutsy — as he had seen me be onstage — or managed to share with him what he'd unlocked inside me. Instead, I was heartsick all the time, unable to ask anything of him, touch him, or reciprocate. Unable to throw my arms around him even when he presented me with an offering of first editions, treasures from a rare book store. And trying, always, to convince him just how undifficult I was by letting him dictate the terms.

Here, too, I was following; I wasn't dancing back.

He was cruel at the end. The last day of our affair was May Day, a Saturday freakishly warm, spent at the beach. It was a marathon of an attempt: picnic, swimming, racing horses, beer. We did what he thought couples ought to do. On the Long Island Railroad on the way back home, we read *Mockingbird Wish Me Luck*. A Bukowski new to both of us. We took turns thumbing the pages, murmuring into each other's ears, pretending the words did not apply to us. By the time we ordered midnight omelets in a diner on Fourteenth Street, all was lost. I was the mockingbird alive inside his tomcat mouth, *wings fanned* and *feathers parted like a woman's legs.* He took me back to Jersey one last time. I hung my grey bikini in his shower to dry.

He made love very tenderly that night, barely mussing the

sheets beneath us. He did all the things a man in love was supposed to do; he touched my face, looked deep into my eyes, and met his lips to mine with so much care that, for the first time ever, I made noise. A little whimper of a moan.

Monday he called — the cat calling the bird, *to bargain it to another place.*

"I tried," he said. "God knows I tried."

No, I said. I could initiate. I could speak louder. Be louder.

"I've been pretty shitty to you," he said. "And you've just let me."

I argued. *And the bird was no longer mocking, / it was asking, it was praying.* There were things I'd never thought to need, and things I never knew were mine to give. Things I felt I hadn't said. Did he not feel it there? Roiling and subterranean and possible? Did he not feel it too? He did, he said. Of course he did. Our tremendous connection, as he called it. "That's what makes this so hard."

Later, he would accuse me of not meeting him in the middle, never realizing I was only waiting for the middle to stop shifting underfoot. Still, there were moments worth remembering: the night we saw John Hammond dwarf a thirty-five-foot stage, warm cans of Guinness smuggled in our coats. The night we shared charred octopus at a table strewn with rose petals — our accidental Valentine. The night we kissed under an awning in the rain. *"My god,"* he'd breathed, "that *mouth.*" But then he'd put me in a cab and hadn't called again for days.

We both knew it wasn't working, that it would not work. Though I did beg.

"Sometimes you just have to say no," he said, after one interminable pause. "I'm saying no."

Chapter Fifteen

IT WAS HARDER THAN I THOUGHT. *THIS HURTS LIKE HELL,* I wrote to Mum, from bed, through tears, at seven the next morning. She sent back my horoscope for that day: *Life can't bring you the sublime gift it has for you until you interrupt your pursuit of a mediocre gift.* Was Enzo a mediocre gift? I knew that I would miss him, fiercely—miss swimming with him through all those pretty words, miss sitting with him in the dim and dank while gruff men sang sad songs. I wanted to be somebody's great love; maybe I had wanted to be his. This ending felt like goat song, tragedy. I went to work that morning with Eliza Bennet in my head: I was humbled, I was grieved. I repented, though I hardly knew of what.

We had a few awful encounters after that. Choked conversations on street corners at three in the morning, post-*milonga*, sanitation trucks beeping, blowing dust up in our faces. All the things we'd never said we shouted at each other, finally. I was, once more, for a moment, the woman he'd so recently unleashed onstage. Then I gave up and played dead in his teeth.

We met a month later to make peace. We saw a Goddard film. He felt clammy next to me, with a stale brownie on a paper napkin, spilling his tea onto his hand. Only then I noticed he was balding slightly, back to front. Maybe he was *kanienge* too. The film ended and I gave him his Bukowski volume back, a handwritten letter hidden in the poems, thanking him for "thawing" me. I would like to think he did more good than harm. I signed it, *yours for a winter and a half.*

Edward said, "I told you so. Good riddance!"

Peter expressed relief. "He's not even good-looking, Biscuit."

Still, I thirsted for him, for the possibility of him, or who I was with him, or maybe simply who I was. I hadn't been myself with Enzo, but I'd come closer, somehow, to something true and taciturn in all that heat. He had been my flowering. I consoled myself with Ferlinghetti: *Yet I have slept with beauty / in my own weird way. / and I have made a hungry scene or two / with beauty in my bed.* That felt like something real.

I had muddled sex and tango into one pulpy cocktail. It was a rookie error, a mistake I vowed never to make again. I had fallen victim to the very cliché I myself had sworn did not exist. I'd slid my fishnet thigh up someone else's pinstriped trouser leg. Who would now believe me when I insisted tango wasn't sexual? I no longer had an answer for my mother, or for anybody else.

The circles under my eyes had grown pale and deep as tile grout. I stayed up far too late and danced, even more than usual, and staggered my way through the workweek. Enzo had told me I was young and beautiful, that boys would come break down my doors, but I did not believe him. Didn't want to. I went on a strange date with a man who asked me with distaste, "Why are you so serious all the time?" then tried to muscle his way into my bed. I sent him home and took a boiling shower until I felt the fear recede. I didn't want him. I would rather be alone.

Enzo became a phantom. A memory of stumbled, apologetic *tandas* and awkward glasses of prosecco. For months, he haunted my *milongas;* every dark-haired man his height was him. Sometimes it really was—standing with his back against the bar, and glaring at me through the Boschlike sea of bodies. *Like a leopard, I watch,* he said. And so did I.

In an attempt to cheer me up, my father sent me a pair of Elvis earrings he'd found at a flea market. Such was his code: all humanity filed neatly between the twin poles of "that rat bastard Nixon" and "the King." Elvis beamed out at me from each of two mismatched enamel squares. The only charm I'd need.

Peter came home, armed with take-out once again, and sat me on the couch and made me laugh. He had a new girlfriend, who hated the idea of me, but he came anyway. "I wanted to make sure you weren't lonely," he said, and we spent the evening watching doctor shows and rummaging for junk food in the pantry shelves.

I filled my calendar, tried doing some non-tango things. Movies, the symphony, parties thrown by friends. I met a cinematographer at a party for a friend of friends who talked to me for hours about Aristotle and taught me to say "rosy-fingered dawn" in Greek. He kissed me, right there in someone's kitchen, and then asked, "Where did you come from? You are nothing like the girls your age."

I didn't want him either. He asked to see me the next evening; I declined. Instead, I cooked and ate an elaborate three-course solo dinner, filling the apartment with the scent of sautéed garlic and tomatoes, only for myself. I was finding an axis, finally, off the dance floor.

I was one year into tango, not counting the months I'd spent away, in France and after, and still astonished by how much there was to learn. I'd moved up a weight class, to a pair of gold and lavender heels with open toes. I went to RoKo every week and sat and danced and sat again, wallflower hopeful, on the pleather couches. I watched the expert dancers, their movements as simple and elegant as drapery cascading to a puddle on the floor. I wanted that, the heavy-rooted sureness in their steps, the lightning quickness of their ankles, the stillness of their heads. Even when the dreamy cloud had lifted, and it all went back to foot muscles and tedium, I still wanted nothing more than tango. Certainly not more dates. Not even acting, which I had stopped entirely, relieved. I stopped other things, too, that interfered with dancing: drinking, eating onions, sleep. I lived by tango rules. The cubicle computer screen collage spilled off onto the wall.

I would use the dance to lick my wounds. The best revenge on Enzo, after all, was to surpass him, to dance until he disappeared.

Nadtochi, whether he knew or not, was helping to rebuild my tango mettle.

"I have a student," he said one afternoon, when we had finished our lesson. "He says he tries to *cabeceo* you. Are you not paying close enough attention?"

Obviously, I was not. The man in question was a tax attorney in his fifties — though you'd hardly know to look at him. He stood six foot one in dancing shoes, with a grey hairline fighting through a helmet of black dye. I'd seen him at La Nacional, looking, very seriously, over my head. He had a sort of sternness to him I'd found intimidating, some pseudo-dignified *milonga* game face I hoped I didn't have. It had not occurred to me that he'd been waiting for my eye contact to initiate the eyebrow nod.

I finally caught his *cabeceo* and we danced. As I recall, it was a *vals*, sugary, in 6/8 time. He was every bit as serious as I had feared. He met me, scowling, on the floor and offered me his arm. I took a deep breath, lunged up on my metatarsal bones, and settled into his taut chest. He was a little stiff, but I could feel how much he cared—about the angle of his arm, about my comfort, about the swing set rhythm of the *vals*. His dance was very elegant, if rigid, and full of careful turns. We bobbed together for that *tanda* and the tango *tanda* on its heels. When we were finished, he paid me a respectful compliment. His "thank you" was sincere.

His name was Marty Nussbaum, and we started practicing together once he emailed me his tango bible, a manifesto outlined in a six-page pdf. It was divided into testaments, old and new, describing his triumvirate: Gustavo Naveira, the Rabbi-Buddha; Mariano "Chicho" Frumboli, Patron Saint of Rhythm; and Sebastián Arce, their gracefully begotten poet son. The holy scriptures, as he called them, included in-depth technical analysis and video. Genealogy and creation myth. A story of how the tango world began.

It was a formal invitation: to be his "third alternate" practice partner. He signed it:

The rabbit hole is at your feet, Alice. Welcome to my world.

Abrazos,
Martin

I ate. I grew enormous. I dove in. Here, finally, was a proper initiation to the guild. Here was a man who had devoted his entire life to tango, a man whom I would never want to sleep with, and who, I hoped, would never try to sleep with me. A tango nerd. A pal. I locked my pace in step with his obsession. We met on Tuesday nights at Robin Thomas's Sangria Practica. While the cool kids chatted in their natural habitat, dancing in their flashy shoes, we were in the corner in our practice flats, doing drills that he'd devised from workshops past. We'd work for an hour or two, and then he'd walk me to my train. He was solicitous, and kind.

. . .

In the beginning, we spoke only of tango, which was fine with me. Marty was more obsessed with dancing than anyone I'd yet met. He'd married young, for love, had two boys, and divorced. He was Jewish, except as applied to shellfish. He'd started dancing with a woman he was dating, and kept dancing long after she left. If tango were a tar pit, Marty fell in splashing, then went breaststroking away. He'd sunk, gleefully, into the sticky blackness to the ruin of his former life. He'd advanced in his career just far enough to land a private office where, behind closed doors, he spent his workdays poring over tango clips. He rarely took a lunch break. He swam laps at the gym each day to limber up. And danced. For a while he was so desperate for good *tandas* that he would analyze the odds, comparing Facebook event numbers on any given night, applying counterweights and probabilities: floor quality, entrance price, proximity to his favorite late-night snacks (which seemed to center on falafel joints and spirulina shakes). He was about a decade into dancing when I met him, and just as underslept. He failed to find the bags under my eyes impressive.

"I'm a *milonguero,*" he said, "with a day job." Balance was not among his skills.

I went from being his third alternate to his go-to gal, mostly because I was young and game and patient, and, like him, had no interest in talking about anything but tango. And since he was my only practice partner, I relished the extra time. I didn't mind not mastering the moves he'd taught himself from YouTube. I was indefatigable, determined, as if every hour I spent there helped me dance my way back to the light. The more I stretched and strived with Marty, the more ascetic my pursuit, and the less I feared that tango was to blame for all the soreness in my heart.

"What's your tango story?" he asked one night, while we stretched our quads.

"My what?"

"Your root."

I thought about making the joke I'd made during the cabaret — about how I'd had to take up tango dancing just to get a grown man to put his arms around me, but that no longer felt appropriate, so I answered, "It was a New Year's resolution."

"Nice," he said.

Otherwise, he was all business. Fanatically focused. Frustrated if it wasn't going well — and high on purely manic joy if it was. He'd land a fourth *sacada* — an extremely difficult displacement move requiring a freakish pivot backstep into my forward step. Or he'd lead me through one: an over-rotated clockwise swivel, away from him, then backwards into the embrace to break his forward step, our hips in opposite directions — and however shambolic it had been, he'd crow as though we'd struck uranium. He had all the enthusiasm of a ten-year-old with his first remote control car, still unsure how to wield it. He did not take bathroom breaks or stop for water. When I did, he'd rub his fingers together in a display of fiendish over-eagerness until I returned. He was anxious to keep going until the lights were flipped, until the studio proprietor came to kick us out.

Except for *valses* — our mutual respite. Whenever those Biagi 6/8 meters played, we made a pact never to practice, just to dance. He'd drop his shoulders, take my waist, and we would both remember, suddenly, to breathe. To smile. Marty was different then, stately, turning steadily as a painted pony on a carousel. I closed my eyes, relaxed my arms, and turned with him, as the *bandoneones* and piano chased the strings around in laps.

Marty and I were token squares among the tango hipsters who had built the Robin Thomas empire. While I'd been frittering around the more obscure *milongas*, lusting after Enzo, they'd been in Olympic training. The men wore wide-legged trousers

then. The girls wore tube tops, short shorts, harem pants, and handmade plastic jewelry. Their shoes were purple, leopard, glitter green. I felt like a grey crayon in the midst of all their cheer. They did not abandon friends for tango; they tangoed with their friends. And afterward, they did not retreat to separate corners; they congregated, chatting, keeping Robin company while he spun the tunes. They drank sangria out of cartoon cups. They were my tango idols.

I envied almost everything about them. Dancing, they smiled wryly into each other's cheeks. There was no "tango face" there, no customary glower. They played. The boys tried out all sorts of moves, but archly, with a sense of humor — and with delighted expletives when those moves went awry. The girls embellished with the music. This was grace — elastic, buoyant, heretical grace: effortless *ganchos;* never over-led, *boleos* slicing unsuspecting air; *sacadas* like hot spoons through hard ice cream. They sweated under the pinkish lights of Dance Manhattan, stretching their long muscles, gossiping and sharing laughs. Their *práctica* felt like secondary school; they were the cool kids leaning against their lockers, smoking in the halls. They weren't mean, but they were better dancers.

They all knew Marty, though they rarely danced with him. He didn't care. He followed Robin for his music, and as long as there were competent dancers along the fringe who would accept him for a *tanda,* he was pleased.

Marty taught me everything he knew. His tango world was so much broader than the one in which I had been bumbling. It was academic, and inspired discipline, analysis, endless drills. To be good at this, one had to study — and, ever the eager pupil, I was happy to immerse myself in tango school.

Though, traditionally, tango was danced in close embrace, temple to cheek and chest to chest, this is not the only way to dance. The tango I'd been doing was traditionalist, what some might call *salon* or *milonguero* style: nothing too big or too fancy for the crowded social dance floor. I'd thus far avoided open embrace, where the follower pulls back and holds the leader's bicep, and there is space enough to balance a good-sized beach ball in between them. I still equated "open" with "alternative," the province of the weirdos who danced only in the dank back room of the *milonga* with that hand-lettered neon poster board guarding the door. It was always darker, sweatier in there, furtive and metallic like a naughty video. I thought they had a fog machine; I was afraid to look. "Alternative" dancers danced to "alternative" music, which usually meant electronica. It failed to move me. It felt thin, without the texture of the rhythms lacing under and above the *bandoneón,* and there was too much air between the couple, too much negative space. The embrace was wide and planar, the hand contact vulgar and impersonal. I called it "pizza hands," the palm held flat to steer a lady like a waiter would a cocktail tray. These dancers looked around the room or at their shoes — not at each other as on tango posters. But the looking — any looking — was all wrong.

I'd learned dancing with my eyes shut, and had no desire to open them. So when Marty stepped away and offered me his bicep as our point of contact, sliding his arm across my back until he held me only by my scapula, I warned him off.

"Marty Nussbaum," I said. "I don't do *nuevo.*"

"I know you think you don't," he said. "But you'll just have to learn."

He sent me video upon video of Gustavo Naveira dancing with his second wife and partner, Giselle Ann — attached to emails full of complicated verbal pyrotechnics to describe the movement, which was more playful, more musical, and *tighter* than anything I had seen before. This tango was smart, athletic. All things were possible in this dance of planetary orbits, two bodies in black silk spinning out and magnetizing back together in concentric circles on the floor. Gustavo and Giselle finished each other's tango sentences and did so with an equality I'd never seen before.

I let Marty lead me farther down the rabbit warren, to Gustavo, godfather of *"nuevo."* What I would learn — what I had failed to realize — was that I had been dancing by Gustavo's rules all along.

To understand, I had to reel back to Buenos Aires in the aftermath of *el Proceso.* The city ravaged by inequity, with her grand old bones intact, but not much holding them together. Just before the shiny world bank skyscrapers pushed the poor and brown-skinned past the city limits — and this time not to *arrabales* but to outright slums. Growing numbers of Argentines had begun to emigrate — to Spain, to Italy, to the United States — for opportunity. Newcomers arrived from nearby countries in the Southern Cone, carving out their places in the immigrant city of old. After decades of turmoil and terror, *porteños* once again began to fill their streets. This was the backdrop for the tango renaissance: The music as beloved as ever — its brightest blooms preserved in hundreds of recordings from the Golden Age. The dance as love-worn as the pattern on an antique rug beneath the dust and tread of time. The people finally unafraid.

Gustavo taught his first classes at the Programa Cultural headquarters in the city center, with his first wife, Olga Besio. Students poured in by the hundreds. A four-week trial class became a five-year gig, and a pair of stars were launched. Gustavo quit his economics studies and went pro, leading the newest tango surge. Meanwhile, the neighborhood centers began to offer tango classes of their own. *Milongueros* reappeared. Old barrio clubs reopened. Social dancing was collectively reclaimed. The soul of tango was reborn first and foremost where it had always lived — in the clubs and cafés and *academias* of the capital.

When the high-gloss stage productions hit abroad and started touring, foreigners by the thousands caught a glimpse of real tango and, just like I had been, were suddenly possessed with mad desire to crawl past the proscenium into *that dance.* Pilgrims swarmed south and joined the throngs of aspirants, clamoring to learn. And so the paradox of modern tango: How to teach an improvised tradition. How to replicate a cultural context that no longer exists.

Ethnographers dogged the surviving *milonguero* masters to catalogue and canonize their every step. They published tomes of surgical directions — how to orchestrate a figure, how to take a step — complete with photographs of elderly dancers demonstrating in unprepossessing shoes. I read these books and hardly recognize the dance I love, though I understand the debt that tango owes to them for preserving the endangered language of the Golden Age.

New teachers found they could accommodate the floods of students by teaching them *el paso básico,* the basic step, the pattern Alfredo had taught me in my schoolgirl months in Buenos Aires. Eight steps: a box. A cross, a resolution. It was something that could be replicated, drilled. A teacher would call out the numbers, one to eight. All other movements — the *ocho, molinetes,* the *volcada* — were accessed by this grid, choreographed and sculpted from the cross and meant to lead back into it. (*On the gentleman's Two, he takes a second side step, leads her to pivot into backward* ochos . . . *come together at the Four, cross, and resolution.*) Only by this roadmap through the bramble could any sense be made.

But it was academic. Empty. Students might learn how to replicate a figure, but they would not learn how to follow or to lead. They would not learn how to improvise, the molten core tenet of tango. They learned to mimic, not to dance.

Gustavo changed all that.

· · ·

By the mid-nineties, while researchers were still sitting with their pencils dissecting the embellishments of aging *milongueros,* Gustavo started getting restless. Asking questions. Rewriting the rules. He founded the "laboratory" at Cochabamba 444, and in so doing, albeit with deep respect, set free the art of tango from its well-guarded nursing home.

His methods — and the methods of his investigation group — Fabián Salas, Pablo Verón, and Chicho, Marty's Patron Saint of Rhythm — are called *"nuevo"* tango, though it was never really new. Gustavo and his cohort spent a decade breaking down the dance. Disassembling the machine. Dancing among the bolts and springs until they made more sense apart than they had made together. They talked and danced for hours, days, as so many had before them in the *academias,* all those years ago. They went looking for the underlying structure that would help them inventory *all that could be done* in tango.

They were looking for the hidden hinge, the string that holds the pearls. They found it in the turn, the *giro,* which Fabián says "opened all the doors at once." The *giro.* The geometry was planetary: The man around the woman. The woman around the man. The pair around the room. *There are no steps in tango.* Which is to say, there are but three: front, back, and open (side) — with everything connected by the constant invitation of the turn. There was no more talk of "figures," no more mention of the *básico,* the eight-count box. There was no roadmap; there weren't even roads. There was nothing but a common compass and a game of choice: directions, turns, and crosses. Closed and open. Gustavo had wanted to contribute something truly new to tango, something extraordinary, and he did, just with materials already piled in the corners of the shop.

"The 'basic step' doesn't exist, number 1 doesn't exist, number 8 doesn't exist," Fabián said. "There are *no numbers* . . . this is what you have: you have three steps to each side; you mix a bunch of combinations and this is all you can do." The cipher broken, they developed a technical language still in all but universal use today, a tango pedagogy broad enough to accommodate new blood and new ambition, while honoring all that came before. Like so many partner dances of the early twentieth century, tango was born to express the content of its music. Good dancing was not the primary motive — until, suddenly, it was. Now it is a question only of dancing. The dance is growing, changing, renovating; the dancehall music hasn't changed in sixty years. To me, that anachronism had been part of tango's magic. A *milonga* often felt like a museum — full of majesty, genteel confinement, time.

The "alternative" tango I disliked so much had simply stretched Gustavo's methods too far. Even Gustavo condemned it, saying it was missing something critical; it was "athletic but not sensuous, excited but not thoughtful, self-congratulatory, but not tango." It was "dull." Real tango held so much more within it — beyond anatomy and music, beyond a rigid diagram of feet. And real tango is what Marty and I spent so many hours trying to achieve.

Open embrace, at first, felt ostentatious. I was embarrassed by it, dancing two feet from my partner, all my movements naked and exposed. After an initial evaluation of ginger little figure eights and *molinetes,* stark and shaky, Marty diagnosed my skills as weak. He said this with a keen glint in his eye, as though I were a new, rewarding project. And he was right: My movements were feeble out there, floating on their own. My pivots weren't grounded as they should be — firmly, like a pestle into stone. My turns were not centripetal enough; if I wasn't held fast to a leader, I'd fly off into space instead of gravitating, turning ever into the embrace. And finally, devastatingly, for all the work I'd done, my balance wasn't very good. I wobbled when I shouldn't, foot to core, and leaned when I ought to have

been standing cattails-tall. It seemed I'd made the *other* error
followers so often make, mistaking close embrace for over-
sharing equilibrium. Which is to say, in learning to be held, I'd
gone a bit too far: relying on the leader for my bearings as I
shut my eyes and let the ballroom whistle past. No wonder I
had felt so thin and friable with Enzo. So relieved to have my
weight accepted, my embrace and footing honored, I'd given
far too much away.

The old *milongueros* didn't say only *"la baila,"* as in "dance
her;" they also said *"la lleva como dormida"*: "carry her as if
she were asleep." I had been letting myself be danced *como
dormida,* letting the leader carry me instead of moving on my
own. But Marty didn't want a sleepwalker; he wanted a practice partner. So he swung me out — arms' length — and made
me open up. This new technique required a different kind of
standing on two feet: self-sufficient and unwavering. Learning
to own the movement rather than let myself be swept along. I
remembered exercises I'd glossed over from Mariela's classes
with a pang of recognition, and started running through a
checklist for my dancing posture like the guidelines of a golf
swing. I felt first for my foot placement, pressing each of three
points into the ground — metatarsal, metatarsal, heel. In each
step, I collected at my ankles, making a tidy passing *V.* I honored the lanes and tracks of legs, careful to space my feet at
distances and angles that would align our movements in the
proper, pleasing triangles. I used my heel — for power and
control. And I listened for the lead, as carefully as if I'd had
my eyes closed and the lead were Braille. With my eyes open,
heeding my own unaided axis, I found I listened even harder.
Each weight transfer from foot to foot was a buoy in the blind
channel through my leader's mind — a way of understanding,
without speaking, how I needed to move next. I began to claim
my balance everywhere I could. Active in my every muscle in
the dance.

We tested my progress by dancing extra-slow. In open, this felt almost clinical. Where before, following had been pure obliterative reverie, now it was a strange cooperative construction. *You carry this board over here; I'll bring the nails. Here's the hammer; I'll duck while you swing.* When we came to joints in the dance that were particularly insecure — the mid-steps of the turn, the landing after a *sacada* — we'd stop entirely, to see if I would waver or hold strong. The technique got more complicated, but so did the concept of connection. The push and pull and give and take, feeling the whole of someone else's body working through the pressure of the palms. There was elasticity between the lead and follow that I hadn't understood. *Tango nuevo,* I realized, just refers to everything that has happened in the dance since 1983. The term does not describe a style. Just one more era in the evolution of an art that feeds on innovation — challenge, originality, one-upmanship — and has done since its earliest days. In the 1940s it was Petróleo and El Negro Lavandina who "rethought" the dance — inventing steps, refining others, even stealing the *enrosque* from ballet's pirouette. A banker and a bricklayer had forever changed the face of tango. Now it was Gustavo's turn.

Traditionalists sneered; they called him *el payaso.* Clown. But he was building on this noble tradition. Decrypting the vast creative possibility in tango, and finding a way to teach it to new generations. Gustavo made it so that every student, once she understood the string, could wire her own pearls as she pleased.

Chapter Sixteen

WHILE I WAS HONING MY BALANCE ON THE DANCE FLOOR, the rest of my life was seesaw-tipping into flux. I'd made my cautious peace with theatre, leaving behind the moldy black boxes, the constant threat of flopping. I missed the bond, the sense of purpose, more than I missed performing. I felt the emptiness of no rehearsal schedule, all those weeknight evenings gaping free. I danced to fill the hole.

I caught an early summer cold from lack of sleep but didn't take a sick day. I hadn't taken one in months; we didn't get many to take. That morning, my snide supervisor stormed into my cubicle and demanded, "What is wrong with you? I feel like you're always getting sick."

That may have been true. I was perpetually run down by stress — mostly of my own invention. I found myself swallowing the apology that would have been my usual response. The *I know! I'm so sorry! I can assure you that my work won't suffer.* I couldn't bring myself to say the words. I looked up at her from my juiced kale and shrugged.

"Clearly you need to start taking better care of yourself," she simpered.

I thought I was. So my staple diet of cheese crackers and PB&J was supplemented only on non-tango nights. So I ran on five hours of sleep or less, and sat through work undead. So every spare cent went to tango. It was physical — exercise! — and therefore must be good for me. It was also mostly sober, so abstemious. And other people were present, so it qualified as socializing, too. I did not miss acting. I did not miss sex. I rarely saw my family, and I barely kept up with my friends. Tango had me by the hair.

Mum came to visit, likely to check up on me, after the melting of that winter. And though I couldn't get her to RoKo, I managed to drag her to La Nacional, for a laugh. We went in and paid our fee. I introduced her to the organizers, offered her an Oreo, which she declined. We sat at the bar, with flutes of cheap prosecco, and I watched her watch the social underworld that had consumed her daughter.

"Which one is Enzo?" she hissed.

"Shhh!" I said. "He's not here."

"Too bad," she said.

We swiveled on our stools so she could see the dancing. I thought, for a second, that she might finally understand — this secret world of mine. The thing that had untamed me, that was to blame for my anomalous behavior, not to mention my affair with a man eleven years my senior. I thought all this would make her proud; she might say I'd finally found the savage playground of my twenties, where she was sure all young women belonged.

"Well, what do you think?" I asked, hoping she would relish all these people, from different classes, different countries, doing this enchanting thing together on a Thursday night. She crossed her legs and clutched her bag and pursed her lips. She stared at the concentric wheels of the line of dance, at the sea of drab New Yorkers, as she called them, bobbing around the room in black.

"It's all very dreary."

"But less creepy than you thought?" I asked.

"Meghan," she said. "Honestly." And rolled her eyes.

I looked around, and tried to see it her way. The median age was probably north of fifty. Everyone was sober. No one smiled. And no one, I noticed, was particularly good. I thought tango was this delicious thing I did, this wild, narcotic enterprise. But I also saw how old and staid and stilted it must seem to an outsider. It didn't look like any fun. There was something beautiful and universal that anyone could grasp, but — to look at it — there was also something equally preposterous, and deeply weird. A bunch of unsmiling people with their eyes closed in a bright room looking sad.

Marty was there. In an effort to normalize the evening for her, I introduced them. I could see her sizing up his G-Star jeans and Lycra shirt, his vaguely skunk-like coif. He smiled like a caricature of himself.

"I take it back, Meghan," she said when he'd been lassoed by a lady's *cabeceo*. "This would be a very sad sex club indeed."

Nadtochi arrived, and greeted us, and asked if he could borrow me for a dance. I followed him into the mêlée, started swirling, shut my eyes. *This*, I thought. *This, at least, she'll see.* Nadtochi, of course, danced beautifully. When the song had ended, and I opened my eyes, I looked to her for approbation and found she wasn't on her barstool where I'd left her. I did a quick scan of the café tables, but she wasn't sitting anywhere.

Marty. He'd swooped in, led her to the floor for a penny lesson, and was just then bent over, doing something to her feet. I cringed. My mother was not cut out to follow anything, least of all him. And there she was, in the middle of the line of dance, with Marty trying to strong-arm her into ceding control of either leg. Stiletto heels went lashing past her shins. Clumsy leaders knocked into the pair of them, mid-floor. Marty was trying to show her his version of *waiting for the bus*. I finished the *tanda* with half an eye on her, in case she tripped him. When it was over, she wince-smiled, shook Marty's hand, and glared at me until we gathered up our bags and left. As if on cue, an arm shot through her path, holding a rose. She took it with a snort.

"Look at you!" I said, safely in a cab. "A dance with Marty!"

"He's very nice," she said, turning to me, "but I will not be dancing tango with him. Or anybody else. Ever again."

I gave up forcing her to try to see what I saw in the dance. She didn't have to get it. No one did. I didn't need approval anymore. Or benediction. My dance was not the dance she saw. It was the unseen cambium and sap that grew the tree; all she could know was bark and branches. She saw the outward flagrancy of touch; I saw something simpler, and good. Borges wrote, *"What was once orgiastic devilry is now just another way of walking."* It had become as natural to me as air, and every bit as clean. With Marty, I unsexed my tango. The whole enterprise was pure again. He called me "the Kid." He'd rattle on to me as though he'd only just discovered speaking — about women, tango, vitamins. It hardly mattered; I just rattled back. We spoke or wrote each other daily. I made a rule he dubbed "the Flaherty," or "the Code of the Kid," in which there were three kinds of tango partners: A's for social dancing, B's for romance, and C's for practicing. A C could be an A sometimes, but not a B. And B's made lousy C's; the mere attempt would ruin A and B both. One must not conflate the three. It was a very elaborate, emotionally stunted way of saying, Marty, dear, avuncular . . . please don't blur these lines. And, ever respectful of my wishes, he never did.

We remained a solid A and C. After Enzo, the sex morass of tango was now so obvious to me. I opened my eyes over my protector's shoulder and saw the couplings I'd so studiously ignored: the pairings-off, the sharky men who angled toward the lonely women. I had told myself, my mother, and anyone else who'd listen that tango wasn't like that. Now I had perfect evidence that it was. I was perfect evidence that it was. I confessed to Marty, archbishop of my tango, how I had broken my own rules. He was less concerned with the fact of my transgression than with my poor taste in transgressors.

"You did *what* with *whom?*" he demanded.

We were having a post-practice snack: a tuna wrap for him, a pack of cookies and a cardboard-carton milk for me. "Have you had these juice smoothies?" he interrupted — pulling one off a refrigerated shelf. "All fruit, very good for you."

"*Te absolvo,*" he said. "It happens to the best of us. Remind me to tell you a story sometime . . ." He chose a smoothie from the case and made his way toward the cash register. I followed. We paid and stepped into the summer night.

"But seriously, kid, *Enzo?*"

I nodded and hung my head, contrite.

Marty and I met at Robin's every week, making perfect asses of ourselves. We stretched like athletes, spotted each other, tried *soltada* sequences with gravity-defying *ganchos* we'd witnessed only on the Internet. To pull off what he asked of me, all I needed was an axis. To stand still and sturdy on my own two unsupplanted feet. The rest was brain play: I turned off what Enzo had turned on and danced, my thighs together and my intellect engaged. We spoke in shorthand — parried, sparred. As my footing improved, I challenged him as often as I could — to lead better, stretch further — until we were very nearly tango equals. Until his quest became my quest. Until he was as true as Galahad — and I as clean of heart.

Marty worked harder at his dancing than any leader in New York — five to seven nights a week. He danced for hours without stopping. He made agendas for his practice sessions, studied up beforehand, crammed an overflowing list of skills to master into every hour. "Let's get this Gustavo back *sacada,* then we'll try it to the other side!" he'd say. Somewhere along the way, I had become his *only* practice partner, which made me feel more valued than any employer ever had. He sent me daily emails, with links to videos. *Look at the amazing over-rotated ocho into her front step at 1:14–1:29. You should watch her feet in the cadena sequence starting at 2:41.* He anatomized each millisecond for me: *Okay, at :04–:06, he does left/right/left as quick-quick-slow. The left gives an impulse intention that differs slightly from the prior causal lefts that pivot . . .* and on, and on.

He planned elaborate and expensive engagements for us with his holy trinity: *Okay, now I'm going lunatico. Absolutely freaking out. While I was away Gustavo opened Registration for Fest part 2 — seminar in Boulder limited to 25 couples, September 7–12, and posted dates for NYC!!! YIKES!!! We can spend a week in Boulder and learn to do GyG colgadas!!! 16 hours of colgadas and volcadas! Building them step by step, inside out, backwards and forwards, both sides, every attack angle, upside down. He works them into phrases. And then the weekend with MORE workshops with GyG and the next generation. Everything is 10% off if we register by August. How is your credit card balance doing? Let's break the bank wide open!*

Our execution often fell short of our eagerness. In the interest of mastery, I suffered bruises, stubs, and bony knee wounds to the shin — a product of his exuberance. A *gancho* gone wrong, after all, is really just a kick. But we were an unlikely team, loyal to each other and committed to the craft. Together we postulated, theorized; we built a creed. And we took care of each other, made each other optimistic — as though dancing could erase whatever ailed us in the world.

By midsummer we were lifelong friends. His constant emails weren't always about tango; sometimes he'd send me treatises on relationships, on his sons' achievements or his mother's failing health. More often I got rants of varying length on the seafood he'd consumed that weekend, or the date he went on with an out-of-towner, or his effusive sentiments regarding Springsteen and Neil Young. I wrote him about my horrid boss, my fluorescent dungeon of an office, my disintegrated family. We earned each other's friendship. Talking about dancing made it possible to talk about everything else. He sent me what he thought was a George Eliot quotation once, but was in fact from Dinah Maria Mulock Craik: *Oh the comfort, the inexpressible comfort of feeling safe with a person, having neither to weigh thoughts nor measure words, but pouring them all out, just as they are, chaff and grain together, certain that a faithful hand will take and sift them, keep what is worth keeping, and with a breath of kindness blow the rest away.* I declined to correct him. We were each other's faithful hand.

Marty is a good soul, through and through. If there is a tango heaven, he has already secured a berth. There is a purity to his quest. He spends a lot of time alone, content to pace the room until he finds a partner. When we met, all I wanted was to be as strong in solitude as he was, as steadfast in my searching. I wanted to be a *milonguera* with a day job, just like him. And Marty is fearless — a little stiff sometimes, but always in pursuit of greatness.

He listens to his partner, to the music. Sometimes one (or both) will get the better of him, and he'll go schoolboy bounding down the line of dance, driving his partner up and down in harried three-point turns. I once heard someone call him Foghorn Leghorn. He does have a bit of the stretched rooster about him: tall and beaky, always lanking about knee-first, scouting the yard for followers, but — whatever points we lost in coolness for our partnership were well worth losing. He steered me straight, looked after me. He told me whom to emulate, whom to avoid. He kept one eye on me, no matter where he stood or danced (he never sat), ready to swoop in at a moment's notice to save me from a backbreaker, or an overly effusive older gent who liked to dance with me because his height precisely matched that of my breasts. Marty would defend me from the clutchers and the cruel. If I said, "Marty, I need to dance," he'd be there.

"Anything for the Kid," he'd say.

Chapter Seventeen

I MIGHT HAVE BEEN CONTENT TO LIVE THAT WAY FOR YEARS — trudging through life, living through dance. Coming home to an empty place that wasn't quite my own. Wasting daylight hours at an unsatisfying job, and nights in hot pursuit of tango. Pressing my body into male bodies by the dozens; touching, yes, but never being forced to feel. And hiding, boldly, in oblivion.

But I was weary — from lack of sleep, from sweet surrender, and from a total want of drive for anything but dancing. My job had the potential to be bearable, but wasn't. I'd twice been promoted out of the cold-calling pits, and most of what I did was project-oriented or creative. My overall purpose was to raise money to help people. But any satisfaction was negated by the megalomaniacs running the place, who gave me responsibility — far beyond my pay — but no authority. Who said, "You are the help. The help move boxes. You don't make decisions." And then expected me to put out fires. Their fires. My boss routinely threatened her employees' jobs, including mine, as we were leaving every other Friday afternoon because she liked reminding us she could. I'd run out of ambition. I got through daily projects, but spent the remainder of my workdays writing back and forth with Marty about tango theory — and scratching slyly in my journal.

"What do you want to be when you grow up?" my mother asked. "Because it's getting a little late to start figuring that out."

"I have no idea," I said, which wasn't true. I did know; I was just too timorous to admit wanting to write. I'd wanted that since I was small, and found no better solace than in books, but was perennially convinced I wasn't good enough. That still seemed true. Besides, I thought a person was allotted only one pipe dream per life, and I had used mine up with acting.

At home, Peter's girlfriend launched a doomed campaign to rid me from his life. It wouldn't be successful, but it kept him occupied and anxious. We saw each other less and less. At this point I lived alone, and he paid half the rent. I didn't sleep. I'd come home after work at six sometimes and nap. When I awoke, sheet-printed and disoriented, I'd make myself a sandwich, then set off into the dark with dancing shoes wedged in my purse.

New York had gotten summer hot and loud. I tramped daily through the exhaust breath of buses and the heavy scent of summer sewage and of pee. Sometimes it was electrifying. Like living in the center of the world. Other times it was too much, and the city was a huge hand pressing on my chest. Rattling home over the bridge one night, my taxi speeding down the luge-like outer lane, I felt calamitously alive, and young, and possible, but also like I might careen into the black water below and not be missed. I was tired, maybe, of the anonymity. Of the riot-paced unknown.

My mother intervened. She'd seen me charge off to New York City full of dreams, squeak out a living waiting tables, and eventually give up everything but tango. The city was a dream destroyer, she said. She didn't want to watch me sink.

"Come to Florida," she said. I heard the offer: quit the job, relinquish the apartment you cannot afford alone, stop living in the shadow of your absent ex. "Come live with me." Restart. Live somewhere where daily life is not so insurmountable. Sip cocktails on the Intracoastal. Put your tired feet into the tepid pool.

"It doesn't have to be so hard," she said. We could help each other. We could make it easier.

Divorce had been her dream destroyer. She'd always thought she'd have a family when she grew up, and that's what she had lost. But she had made her way back into the workforce, back into the dating pool. She'd lost weight, dyed her hair seashell blond, painted her nails. She was still divorced, and broke, and by herself; not much could change those facts. She still woke in choking panic in the middle of the night. She was the happiest she'd been in years, but it was effortful, and she was not immune to loneliness. Neither was I, no matter what I told myself or how often I danced.

I was standing outside the New York Public Library branch on Mulberry Street, an iced coffee melting in one hand, my cell phone in the other. I was overdue back at my desk. The humid breeze that slid across me felt like something she had sent, a different kind of warmth than the exhaust from SoHo's glossy cars. I'd given New York five labored years. Maybe it was time to let her go.

"I could apply to graduate school," I muttered quietly. "For writing."

That small admission startled me, but to Mum it was inevitable. Befitting. Overdue. Perhaps, I thought, instead of living underneath the prose of others, no matter how immortal, I'd find that I had something real to say. That I could build a life with my own words. I was in no way sure, but suddenly, on that sticky street, I wanted very much to try.

"Bravo," she said.

"Brava," I mumbled.

"Don't be such a little asshole, Meghan," she laugh-snorted. "I'm American."

"Sorry."

"Surely you can do that from down here," she said.

I felt resistance, then relief. I sat down on an empty stoop and thought through my routines, removing subway rides and rent checks, deleting fire trucks and blaring horns. That there was life in other places I was ready to concede. Then I remembered tango. My heart sagged in my arms. "But tango is here," I said. "And tango's all I've got."

My mother, clothes-ironer, sense-talker, hair-holder of my youth, said only, "I know, honey, but you need more than that."

Her certainty by far outmatched my own. In the months between decision and execution, I tried to shut my ears against the private chorus of my second thoughts, but I could not. Leaving felt at once too easy and impossible. I gave three months' tentative notice, as though I still might change my mind. I talked to Peter, who was then in France, to ponder whether we could break our lease. We were still pondering when our slumlord landlord moved an old plaid couch he'd found out on the street into the basement of our building. Within two weeks, bedbugs had marched upstairs and underneath our door and tunneled into our new blue couch, into my brand-new single-woman bed. Two weeks after that, my office suffered an unrelated infestation. The city was conspiring to kick me out.

Peter paid for our possessions to be piled into a fumigation truck. One Friday afternoon in late July, I watched the movers throw my things in boxes and heave those boxes two by two downstairs. I closed the door behind me, shut the keys inside the mailbox, shouldered a single disinfected duffel bag, and left. Behind me: my street, the loaded truck, and my beloved *arrabal*. Above me: one last Amtrak thundering across the Hell Gate Bridge. The life that I'd attempted there so easily undone.

The threat of rain gave way to a reality of rain. I tried to call my mother, to tell her I had done it, but my cell phone battery was dead. I rode the empty N train to Manhattan, watching Astoria vanish behind me in the tunnel underneath the river. I could almost hear the snapping of steel cables, the ties that held me to the city breaking, and the giddy vastness of the void.

Chapter Eighteen

THE PLAN WAS THIS: MUM WOULD SPEND AUGUST WITH HER cousin on the Cape and fetch me on her way back down the coast. I had one month left, and vowed to spend it dancing. One last fling with tango and New York — my Carnival — before I had to give up both for Lenten abstinence.

I danced through "La cumparsita" almost every night. It is perhaps the best-known, most played tango of all time, and every time it's heard it marks an ending. The name translates to "the little parade," as it was once a simple march for carnival in Montevideo. The martial *rum PUM pum pum . . . bah deedle dah dum* drags you to your feet in search of one last partner, to rejoin the line of dance for one last lap. Astor Piazzolla denounced it as *"lo más espantosamente pobre del mundo"* — the most frightfully poor tango in the world — though he went on to record four different versions. Juan d'Arienzo, *"El Rey del Compás"* (King of the Beat), recorded six. There were dozens of recordings, and I learned each one. The song became a knowing friend, a temper to match my every mood. There was that first gramophone crackle of the Firpo version, De Caro's strange cats-crying cartoon strings, Troilo's brooding, piano-plonking romance, and Di Sarli's heavy dream. Varela had taken a beautiful, though melodramatic, stab at it, as had

Hugo Díaz. I was partial to the later D'Arienzo arrangements because they were best to dance. By midsummer I knew the song by heart, and could identify it, whichever version, within the first two beats.

It seemed only fitting to use it as my farewell anthem. To drain the dregs of each *milonga* before returning to the guest room Peter's family had so generously offered me. I had nowhere to be in daylight, so I took my time, wandering through Manhattan in the wee hours, high on dancing, whistling tangos to myself, and basking in the late-night wind across my legs.

As my days reeled in the chaos of ending and beginning, tango remained calm. I found balance only on the dance floor, only in my new mail order Comme il Fauts: black suede with seven-centimeter heels and open toes. In tango, at least, I felt the floor beneath me. I'd reached a state of priestess peace — preferring to withdraw into enigma rather than to try and right the details of my capsized life. Each dance was cosseted in darkness, like an ancient poem of death where that was nothing to be feared. My eyes sank to a close. A soft curtain fell. Behind it, there was only music, and I moved through air.

I never got particularly good. My curves were flat, my feet too big, and I never quite acquired the necessary haughtiness, nor the paranormal powers of the tango witch. I could not dance a leader into madness. But I was friendly and enthusiastic and I put my heart in every step. Leaders often figured me for a midwestern farm girl. I laughed too much, made nervous jokes, and generally lacked the flair for the dramatic that any really bewitching follower ought to have. I was a four-door Volvo among Ferrari coupes. I grinned and waved to leaders as I passed them. I still squealed "Wooh! Sorry!" every time I flubbed a step. I broke decorum in *cortinas*. I was the earnest girl, without a stitch of tango cool, but still I'd finally found my place around the Robin Thomas water cooler.

Tango was like a running dinner party at a massive table, and I was the guest who slunk in late and didn't linger once dessert was cleared. If I didn't make it one night, I knew they'd welcome me the next. And not just Marty — everyone. The cool kids turned out to be less exclusive than I had assumed. I danced with my tango betters — even on days when I was dancing like an old appliance. I started making conversation between dances, getting to know the architects and interior decorators, the bioethicists and engineers. I met photographers and poets, chemists, models, flame swallowers, telephone technicians, an activist, an acrobat, a yoga teacher, two costume designers, a neurologist, investment bankers, writers, chamber violinists, and a Balanchine ballerina. I met women who had walked away from their careers, renouncing partnerships and pensions, just because they loved the dance and life was short. I told them I was jobless, drifting, with all my worldly things in storage. They told me I was brave.

I started to refine my tastes, in close and open. It was no longer a question of wanting to dance each *tanda* until the night was over, to suck as much tango from the carcass as I could. Leaders felt distinct, depending on their musicality, how long they stretched their strides, how smooth they were in turns, their flexibility. The lanky, long-haired cool kids were the best for rhythmic softness and their gentle, rapid twists. The sturdy, broader-chested men were often best for slow songs because they milked each *sostenuto* in the strings and made me feel that I was floating, balanced on the wide pillow of their embrace. Certain men had power, others pluck. Still others refinement. And, for those nine to fourteen minutes, I was different with each. I learned to sit somewhere strategic, to look for the right eye when the music turned a certain way.

It didn't always work — and I was never very bold about it. No matter how my stare bore toward a leader between *tan-*

das, without eye contact there could be no *cabeceo.* The men had the advantage here. They sat less, hunted more, had more control over their whens and whoms. They sought out favorite partners for breakneck *milonga tandas,* saccharine sweetheart *valses,* drama tangos, and the restive, rhythmic ones requiring spunk. I began to notice how unprincipled these predilections were. Some men looked to me to dance Di Sarli, and I stretched longer, danced more wistfully, and laid my arm across their backs with extra tenderness. Some men beelined to me for toe-tappers with a pulsing, driving, syncopated beat; I grinned the whole way through those dances, stealing beats with little stamps and *piques* on the floor, squeezing their hand in praise whenever we made some particularly playful moment in the margins of the tune — a feat of timing, temperaments in sync.

Good dancers changed their personalities to suit the *tanda.* Those unearthly tango highs depended on your luck in landing the right pairing at the right time. My shorthand for sorting leaders into categories — dreamboats, backbreakers, clutchers, broncos, chicken hawks — was not unique. You met so many people dancing tango whom you remembered only by a flash of color in their clothing, or this tactical report: His lead was firm. His hand was limp. He felt like *this.*

The men trade notes as well. Enzo once danced with Guillermina Quiroga, a tango *fantasía* goddess, and compared her to a Lamborghini. *You barely have time to fasten your seat belt and she's off.* Other women are more like tanks, which can be a compliment. I'd been called a feather, a siren, a soothing wind, a refrigerator, and a water buffalo.

After eighteen months of dancing, I was finally beginning to understand the mechanics of improvisation at the heart of tango. How the leader moves first, in anticipation of the music, and at the same time — fractions of a second before stepping — tells the lady where to go. He sends infinitesimal impulses, which she has milliseconds to interpret: muscles tightening in his torso or his legs, a half-extended invitation. She moves and he moves with her, already preparing what comes next. Only the couple's outer works are visible in tango — legs moved, shapes made, figures drawn — just as a clock's hands belie the intricacy of its operation. The inner work of cogs and weights remains unseen.

The leader also has to steer. It is important not to collide with anyone or stand on toes, not to kick anyone or dance into the furniture. And, should a lady skewer some unfortunate with her stiletto, the gentleman who led her takes responsibility. Her eyes were closed in close embrace.

The follower, in exchange for accident insurance and protection, bestows on him her trust. But this, I'd come to realize, was not as patriarchal as it seemed. There was so much more within that clock than I had thought. The dance, for all it sounds like *man say, woman do,* is not an act of domination. The best leaders speak of leading how the follower wishes to be led. This mystified me. I had so far believed my preferences were immaterial, and that the leader had complete imaginative control. "How can you tell," I asked one of the cool kids between *tandas,* "what a follower wants?" I raised a skeptic eyebrow. We were having one of those tango-typical half conversations where both people have one eye angling through the milling crowd for *cabeceos.*

"You can always tell," he said. He made a point of dancing to a partner's level — meeting her where she was comfortable, but also listening for how she liked to move. "Some ladies want a lot of time in the *parada,*" he said, referring to the move that interrupts her *ochos.* The leader inserts a foot into her path, halting her elliptic figure eight, and she is stopped (*parada*). What happens next is usually up to her. She can stall, embellish, flirt, demur, or shine her shoe up the leader's inseam. She can also whisk herself over the doorstop and continue dancing.

Ladies' choice. The leader waits, his foot outstretched, until she crosses over.

I was a speedy threshold crosser. Maybe I gave my leader's foot a little tap or nuzzle just before I made the leap, but I was too self-conscious to milk the moment, to leave any real feeling there. I was still convinced that every impulse was a test with one right answer. That there were no choices I would have to make, except to riddle out and execute whatever any given leader asked of me. That the object was to disappear.

I was on the verge of understanding. That my style, my preferences, my physiology factored in. That I, the follower, had power. As Cesar Coelho had told me, the dance was conversation. A circle of anticipation. The leader led, but that lead meant nothing if not executed, and I controlled the execution. The choice, whether to accept what he proposed, was always mine.

I started dancing with a man I'll call the Mogul, who drove a fancy car and owned a meat processing plant outside the city. He smelled strongly of soap and pungent just-for-men shampoo. Despite his chin-length curls and slightly tasteless shirts unbuttoned sternum deep, he was empirically good-looking, tanned and chiseled. Because he often wore nylon athletic pants to the *milongas,* he had a bottom-heavy swagger when he walked the room and a slight rustle when he danced — which was like warm gin over ice. I'd had a *tanda* with him months before and flubbed it. So when he fixed me in his *cabeceo* one quiet Sunday night at RoKo, I had to glance behind me to make sure he wasn't eyeing someone else.

His hand was soft. His well-gelled hair had hardened into strands that tickled as I pressed my forehead to his cheek. We danced to late-era Pugliese, all dramatic flounces and Borgesian knife jabs of *bandoneón*. All very virile. I was embarrassed by the way it made me feel: electric, lithe, important. Not skittish and frangible as I had felt with Enzo. The Mogul took huge forward steps — lunging, pushing, martial steps I had to run with. I had no trouble keeping up. I flexed my knees and bore down into the floor.

We stalked laps around the other couples. I was breathless after. He made little clichéd *mmm* sounds in my ear, and toyed with my fingers briefly as we broke apart. Many men did this; it's not always suggestive. I noticed he was slightly deaf and slurred a bit. We each did the standard *cortina* trick of looking vaguely at separate corners of the room, waving our eyes past the other's like a searchlight until it seemed too awkward not to speak. I spoke. He stared back blankly as if he hadn't understood. Then he smiled, slow and broad. He was the kind of handsome man that tango made much handsomer.

We danced another song, and broke apart. "Wow," he said. "You are a beautiful dancer." I blushed and thanked him.

"No, really," he said. "Just lovely."

As we finished the *tanda,* I noticed the compliment had unlocked an unusual and reckless radiance in me. I danced with a kind of confident abandon I had never felt before, striding, pushing, stretching. This heady music had always been my least favorite. With the Mogul it was different. Capacious and invigorating. I felt powerful, and liked it. We danced another, thanked each other, parted, and I strode away with a swagger in my hips I'd only seen on television.

He was older than I thought he was and used to getting what he wanted. For some reason I could not then comprehend, that included me. *Meet me at the Black & White Ball,* he texted, referring to the expensive summer benefit *milonga* I had planned to skip. *I will pay for you.* Or: *I know you have dinner plans, but come dance with me after. Just wear a dress and bring your shoes.* He befuddled me. He opened doors and steered me through them, his lion's paw at my lower back. He exuded sex, but didn't seem to want a thing from me but dances. Some-

times he drove me home from the *milonga*, revving his auto-
matic engine, skipping traffic lights, and blasting Héctor Varela's late-fifties histrionic tango hits. I was still playing a role
— adult female in possession of herself — and so at every turn I
acted as though in control, which I was not.

He was the sort of man who filled his loft apartment with
expensive things, modern furniture and works of art, and
scolded me for treading shoes across his white wool rug. He
was always late, distracted, thumbing through his BlackBerry,
skipping through the tuner on his radio. But he seemed lonely
to me in that obnoxious car, its engine purring. Lonely in that
austere and kitchenless apartment, without a woman or a pet.

He was a Leo, into horoscopes and proud of it, and so I
came to think of him as leonine. Sometimes he looked at me as
though he might devour me, but he never did. He often drove
me home, and we'd spend hours in stilted conversation, always
with the engine running, until he'd lean over with a warm and
lingering brush of lip across the corner of my mouth to say
good night. There were no other intimations. I accepted his
invitations, and his offer of a freelance job designing marketing materials for his line of deli meats. We met for pre-*milonga*
meals to discuss promotional brochures. I almost dared him
to seduce me — thinking, if he did, that I could cease being
the guileless girl that Enzo hadn't wanted. But he did not. He
bought me an (illustrated) anniversary copy of *The Elements
of Style*, a gift that might have been construed as romantic —
the gift of grammar! — had I not had four copies already on my
shelves at home.

One night he took me to a beach-themed rave on Governors
Island. It was, not surprisingly, my first such party, but I feigned
ease among the glow sticks and the fake palm trees and shirt-
less frat boys from Long Island. I drank a shot I never would
have ordered for myself, and tried to act my age. We picked our
way through patchy sand, trying not to spill our draft Peronis

in their plastic cups, and swayed together. Our tight *canyen-gue* rock steps modulated into dancing I would have to classify as dirty. I shut out everything but the trancelike beat, my eyes hard on his chest, my body unrestrained. He pulled me close, ostensibly to protect me from the brutish moshing, and I thought perhaps I felt his hands threaten to part the fabric of my sundress, a halter fastened at the neck. But the beats came thumping to a close, the coeds scattered, and we rode the ferry back like teenagers on an awkward date.

In many ways, he was extraneous. I was drunk with tango, not with him. He was a coveted leader I was lucky to score dances with. When he came slinking into RoKo, I could feel a dozen fellow followers tune their forks to him. But I knew that he would ask. I knew his hair-flipped head-cock *cabeceo*. I knew the music he would choose. I also knew, or hoped, he'd save me for the end, for when the strings went mad. So I avoided him for hours until they did.

I preferred to dance with lighter leaders early in the evening, the ones who made me feel like we were water spiders dimpling a river. Coquettish, I ignored him. I felt his eyes on me, but made him do the work. My toes were pulsing and my face was ruddy with the dance of other men. He was an afterthought. He didn't matter to me off the dance floor. But I let him linger; I let him tell me things like "I can't get over how we danced last night, how beautiful it was," how he'd been replaying moments in his head all day. In his version of me, the frightened schoolgirl made way for a new warrior queen. I liked that woman, and the Mogul brought her out in me. He was the tango equivalent of a martini in the early afternoon: he made me feel warm and buzzing, highly competent, and slightly slurred. Invincible. Within an hour or two, the effects wore off. But then again, the clock was ticking—and, with just one month left, I couldn't lose.

Chapter Nineteen

TWO WEEKS BEFORE MY IMMINENT DEPARTURE, MARTY IN-
vited me to my first tango festival. Four days and five nights in
Baltimore at Tango Element, the premier annual event in East
Coast tango. He'd registered us for ten seminars, six hours of
super-advanced classes daily, followed by *prácticas, milongas,*
all-night *milongas,* after-hours *milongas,* and performances by
visiting teachers, the best of the very best. We would split our
time between Chicho and Sebastián, the base of Marty's holy
trinity, and come home glowing from the white heat of their
haloes.

Festivals are unique to tango of the modern age, and there
are hundreds of them. Dancers congregate in some distant hotel, most sharing rooms, two *tangueros* to a double bed, with
some in sleeping bags or cots. The cafés sell out of bagels and
bananas and cannot brew the coffee fast enough. The lobby
couches and the halls are thick with dancers, and all the ballroom carpets are overlaid with rented wooden floors. For one
long weekend, there is nothing more important in the world
than dancing tango.

It goes like this: Coffee, sweatpants, dance shoes, hairbrush. Class for seven hours. *Práctica.* Stretch. Moan. Fall
facedown on bed then roll off groaning to the shower. Cotton

dress, mascara, splash of scent. Leave everything in room but heels and entrance wristband, pinned to skirt hem. Walk unladen through convention hotel halls and into swirling mass of dancers in a Gothic ballroom. Dance, and time submits. Dance until dawn glows cobalt through the giant windows. Pry your throbbing, sodden feet from shoe straps. Plod barefoot down marble floors. Elevator, key card, click shut of heavy door. No lights. Slip dress from shoulders to the floor. Toothbrush, hairbrush, bed. Sleep if you can. Wake to the bleating of clock radio alarms, and begin again.

Baltimore changed everything. I danced thirteen hours a day, class after class and *tanda* after *tanda,* rotating between heels and floppy ballet practice slippers. My feet went sore, then throbbing numb. I removed my ankle straps like turkey trussing, their imprint lashed into my skin. I danced until my toes blistered, until it hurt to stop.

At the opening *milonga,* traffic on the floor was four lanes thick. The wooden squares were tacky underfoot, making it difficult to pivot, and a step dead center would make each one sag. Dancers tangoed forth, undeterred. They kicked and spun and threw *boleos,* showing off. Leaders collided with other leaders, and followers occasionally lanced a passing dancer with their heels.

Sebastián was sufficiently annoyed by this lack of floorcraft that he scrapped his advanced lesson plan the next day and taught us dance floor etiquette instead. Sebastián is a bit of a prima donna. He has a reedy voice and a lustrous pouf of curls, often shellacked into a ponytail or other dapper do. His partner, Mariana Montes, is a sculpted blonde with hard-line cheeks and nose, straight hair, a pancake abdomen. They are showy dancers, capable of all the twirls and leaps and spins that impress theatregoers, yet their devotion to their art is visible in every aspect of their dance. They can embrace each other in a fluorescent room, in sweatpants, take three steps, and make a stranger cry.

For them to find us lacking was a condemnation. Sternly, they herded us onto the very edges of the dance boards and demonstrated tidy two-step sequences that could be done while waiting for the line of dance to come unclogged. Sebastián lectured us on proper entrance to the floor, traffic codes, the steps that he considered inappropriate for busy *milongas*. And that night, he assured us, he'd be watching.

The next day was the same. "This cannot be," he said. "This simply cannot be." The third day he yelled. How dare we desecrate his temple with such disrespect. How dare we presume to dance at levels higher than our own. We were amateurs and butchers. Where was our respect?

"You think you can do what we do," he bellowed. "You cannot. You haven't *put the time.*"

It was as if he'd slapped us with the unfair truth. None of us trained seven hours daily. None of us performed. But we saw his smooth fourth *sacadas,* the high-kick flash of Mariana's heels, and we wanted all of it. We were impatient. Covetous. We wanted Herculean tango polish without twelve labors' worth of toil.

Marty and I bounced between Sebastián's lectures and Chicho's anti-lectures. Chicho is a genius, but he is not a man of words. He would agree with Sebastián regarding floorcraft and respect, but the populist in him offers all his latest moves to every class, regardless of their commitment to the art. He'd studied first with Doctors Salas and Naveira at the Cochabamba *laboratorio,* and then eclipsed them. Gustavo once called Chicho "absolutely the best dancer I ever saw" and used to joke with Fabián, "We have to get him to really join us in this work, or else we have to break his legs!"

Chicho is the most advanced tango there is. He and his

partner Juana have invented new *colgadas* where their bodies bloom out like the petals of a drooping tulip, nearly to the ground. Their feet meet in the center, like the pistil. He supports her at that daredevil angle only by her hand—then she throws in a front *boleo* to accentuate the empty space between them. In certain back *boleos,* Juana tips precariously to one side, her torso almost parallel to the floor as she whips her leg behind her. And then there are the spins—unorthodox breaches of embrace that flow into owlish over-rotated *ganchos* and *sacadas* as they pretzel through their turns. The moves were too advanced for nearly everyone, but the gauntlet of them had Marty flapping limbs in mad impatience.

Chicho leads extremely quietly. Most good leaders do. You cannot see the information being passed within the couple. This is how spectators miss most of the artistry and *work* of tango, and why, perhaps, all that's left to untrained eyes is sex and legs. But Chicho's quiet is unearthly quiet. There is no showiness in him, no broadcasting, no strain. His lead is silent, blank, as casual as a shrug, yet it upends the orbit of the dance.

Then there is tiny, freckled, red-haired Juana, substantiating what we cannot see. The effect of them is mystifying. He shifts a fraction of an inch and she flies off in all directions, her little feet vertical in her extension, like a cartoon deer. They dance like a *bandoneón,* pulling apart to come together, always elastic, always with exquisite tension in the air between them, yet also gliding, effortless. We took the neat blueprints of what they did and scribbled over them with crude attempts.

At the end of every lesson, Chicho stacked us into marching lines behind him and started rolling through the sequence he'd just taught, marking each step with a number. *One,* he said, leading Juana to a funny backward cross. *Two,* an off-axis rare *boleo. Three,* some inventive riff on the *sentada,* where the lady lifts and perches on a proffered knee. *Sacada. Four,* resolve and back to cross. It went on longer than I thought

Marty's memory could take. Then he upped the ante; the final moments of any Chicho class often culminate in this frantic drill: the same sequence repeated to match his virtuosic timing and his speed. Marty loved it. We couldn't manage any one component of the sequence well, but we could flail through the motions. "Kid, who *cares?!*" he'd snap, and try to plug steps in by proxy, hurling me harriedly through each. What was important to him was to keep the pace, the breakneck devil pace of Chicho. Twenty couples stamped through complex moves, arms flying, feet pounding the floor, and Chicho held the center, stomping out the numbers, marking time. When the music cut, he shrugged off our obsequious applause and sent us out.

Marty and I separated each night for the *milongas,* which I spent mostly by myself, seining for dances or sulking in the coffee line. Festivals can be quite solitary. There is a lot of late-night mental silence to contend with, and the usual insecurities — waiting to be asked by strangers, the fear of messing up — are complicated here. Within the general mass merriment of tango festivals — the simple folk coming to meet new people and take exciting classes and buy new shoes from traveling boutiques — a more serious event transpires among the tango royalty. There ought to be a separate cordoned entrance and a secret handshake for the upper echelons. They all sit at the same tables, dressed to effortful perfection, and uniformly glowing from their dancing. Even if some of them might dance with you back home, the odds aren't with you here.

Below the A-listers — the teachers, DJs, visiting superstars, and itinerant career *tangueros* — are the solid mid-list dancers of the region, your local equivalents. You won't know who they are at first. You must not appear too eager or accept strange invitations willy-nilly. You have to be selective. Trouble is, they'll be selective back. There are too many beavers out there whomping tails across the dance floor. It is important to be generous, and dance occasionally with beginners, but with all the seeing and being seen that goes on at festivals, the stakes are extra-high. The vetting process for potential partners can be exhausting. New leaders will not invite you until they see you dance — and if you're dancing badly (or bearing up against the bad dancing of the individual you're dancing with), you have to sit. You have to project poise in solitude, and dignity in attitude. No *tanda* will be worth your begging for it.

The Mogul was there as well, but on the prowl. I saw him lurking as I skirted the edges of the massive parquet floor. I, too, scanned the crowd. It was my counter-*cabeceo*, bringing out the conqueror in me. By the early hours, I'd be settled in the arms of strangers, careless, swirling. Subsumed, and rooted by the crowd. Di Sarli echoed down my legs and up the rafters. And up above us were the teachers, seated at the big round table on the dais, watching us watch them. This was tango at its purest: students at the feet of masters, a genteel hierarchy, a common cause.

Every midnight, the throng parted for one pair of teachers to take the center ballroom floor. We'd scatter to find seats for the performance as the DJ cued up songs: a tango or two first, then a *milonga* or a *vals*. A professional couple must be fluent and impressive in all three, to prove their versatility. After the festival, videos labeled by the couple, the song, and when and where they danced go viral among the tangoscenti. Theories spin from close readings of these clips, about the evolution of particular technique and trends versus the overall development of the dance. Performances give tango dancers something to aspire to, something to remind us of the magic binding us to tango.

Every couple was distinctive. Sebastián and Mariana threw in the usual leaps and Broadway spins, flashing around the

ballroom, glittering in black sequins and silk. Their performances were surgical and sharp, every aspect perfect in its execution. When I watched them dance, I understood: I could
not do what they did.

Pablo Rodríguez and Noelia Hurtado danced gently, in a
way that constantly suggested circles. He hunched over her
and she fit snugly in. Like so many professionals, she was petite even in her four-inch heels, and seemed to overflow with
golden Botticelli curls and curves that spilled from her bod-
ice, which was twisted sideways by the end of all their spinning. Their dance was liquid, spherical, full of tensile turns and
wide-arc *lapices*.

Two lanky boys from Buenos Aires, Martin and Maurizio,
were the only same-sex couple there. They wore beige jackets, white shirts, skinny ties, and danced a set of shifting leads
powerfully asserted. Their dance was sharp, full of low kicks
and rapid-fire *ganchos*, and seemed to come straight out of the
old *academias*.

Silvina Valz was next, with short and snappy Oliver
Kolker, who was then her spouse. I'd seen her once before, a
few months earlier, on her own. She'd performed with Ciko,
co-proprietor of Tango Café. Ciko was a free spirit who had
walked away from a career in architecture to become one of
the loveliest followers in the States. The faerie queene of tango,
dressed in white. Silvina wore a fitted pantsuit and a blouse
with ruffled cuffs, her long hair bunned into a sleek and geo-
metric mass. She led three songs. Combined with Ciko's flowing hair and quiet whimsy, the effect was mesmerizing. I remembered thinking that Silvina Valz led better than any man
I'd ever seen.

I didn't know much about her, save that she radiated depth
— a dark star, pulsing — and she was beloved. She did not ad-
vertise herself the way most teachers and performers did. She
did not troll for accolades. But when she showed up anywhere,

the tango world stood at attention. I had no sense of where she lived. She was the nomad sage of New York, Paris, Buenos Aires. A daughter of the Golden Age. She'd learned the old way, from the ancient *milongueros,* by fitting herself inside their arms and following, by drinking *cafecitos* in their company, red wine late into the night. She'd left Argentina at the age of twenty and moved to Paris to become a dancer. She'd studied biokinetics, Feldenkrais, Alexander, modern dance, flamenco, and ballet, sought mentors for herself in poetry and philosophy, in thought and dance. Then she'd met Gustavo, the last teacher she studied with before becoming one herself.

Silvina was petite and filbert brown, with one long, straight rope of hair she twisted and moved from shoulder to shoulder whenever she was idle. She was neither wispy nor coquettish, though she was every inch a woman — thighs to eyes. When she danced with Oliver, whom she outmatched, her legs sliced out from underneath her slinky backless dress as though she herself had flayed the fabric into strips while dancing. I caught glimpses of the power and the muscle underneath her creamy skin as she flew by. Part elite athlete, part meteor. They danced a showstopping *milonga* to Canaro's "La milonga de Buenos Aires," a song that might as well have been written for Silvina herself. It's a joyful, melismatic romp with an exceptionally fast-sung second verse extolling the virtues of a particular *porteña,* the *flor de Buenos Aires.* More than any other woman I had ever seen in dancing shoes, Silvina seemed to have that dignity of the *porteñita primorosa,* granddaughter of the beauty of the past.

I'd seen her that morning as well, stepping out of the lobby elevator as we stepped in. She had her long rope of hair tucked low, tied at her neck. She was wearing gym gear — black shorts and shirt and sneakers, headphones. She smiled dimly at those she recognized, fiddled with her phone. The crowd parted in deference as she passed. I wondered how she had the energy to teach, dance, and perform all weekend and still go down to face the treadmill in the windowless hotel gym. Her body was everything mine was not — muscled and curvaceous, brimming with abundance. Soft where I was boned. And mighty, despite her litheness. She moved like a *grande dame* and a dictator, ladylike and lordly all at once. Every step was masterful, and strong. I'd heard stories of her showing up to the *milongas* in a pair of chino shorts. As if opting out of the tango costume theatre of allure. As if withholding the unembarrassed sexuality in her for a more private sphere. Silvina concealed nothing, but was very clearly not for public consumption all the same.

During their next dance, Silvina overtook the lead mid-song. This time she led in four-inch strappy heels, pushing forward with force enough to guide her husband through the intricate footwork. She betrayed no strain. Beaming, she drove him up and down the floor. She embellished, threw in a playful hop; the crowd went mad. And her *enrosques,* the involute in-place spirals that are a leader's most impressive bit of flair, outshone his by several carats. I'd envied other dancers' talents, their sensuality and power, but what I wanted from Silvina was her unimpeachable integrity. Her self-possession, her unrestrained uniqueness on the floor. And her immovability — the fierce fidelity to who she was.

Chicho and Juana were saved for Sunday night, the final performance of the festival. He wore a simple suit and silver dancing sneakers, she a gold and gauzy dress. They looked like gods: the long-haired rebel with his sparkling Artemis. They strode into the center space. We cleared the floor as we had for all the others, forming a cross-legged circle at the edge. They embraced just before the music cued, then started dancing, slow and understated. I looked on with awe.

It's rare to watch a tango couple as a pair. Followers follow the ladies' footwork; leaders watch the men. Chicho and Juana were different. He piloted; she flew. But the mechanics were invisible. There was only the indistinguishable border — where his dark sleeves met her bare arms, where his leg whipped through air with her *boleo*. It was so intimate, I felt like an intruder. Juana kept her eyes closed or averted, and spun atop her perfect feet like the tiny ballerina in a music box.

It is often said that so-and-so is *on* the music, so-and-so is *in* the music, but Chicho simply *was* the music. He danced to beats and off-beats, to all the tiny and forgotten flashes of instruments half-hidden by the orchestration. Saying, *this is how this song wants to be danced.* Sometimes he didn't dance at all, just stood there holding her. Even his stillness danced. His body spoke the song: the pain, the joy, the longing. *This is in here,* he seemed to say — with a back cross or with a subtle, errant turn into a trifle of piano. *There is also this,* he danced, *and this.*

We clamored for them, pounding our fists and Comme il Fauts into the floor, whooping. Don't stop. Never stop. One more song. A two-song encore is considered standard. Chicho and Juana were asked for five.

When the performance ended, we hobbled stiff-kneed to our feet. The tinny tunes resumed. Men found willing partners; mortal couples took the floor. I was in a stupor, but I caught the Mogul's *cabeceo* and met him on the southwest corner of the line of dance. I took his shoulder and his hand, and he my back. I inhaled his soap and gel. And something deep within me clicked.

I stretched out, channeled all the power in my limbs. I danced frustration, longing, my impatience with myself and with the world. I dove headfirst into my forward steps. I was an engine, several-cylindered, expensive. My foot was on the gas. He merely steered.

It was the closest I had ever come to open conversation with an adult man. And there were no words spoken. *There are things,* I danced. *Things that I feel, things that I need.* I needed him to hold me, but not so tight that I would not be free. I needed him to take my hand, my waist, my weight. I needed to close my eyes and feel my way through what existed nowhere else but in that dark, blind dark. I needed trust, for him to keep me safe for those three minutes. I needed him to listen, move me where I wanted to be moved. To talk to me in terms that I could understand, in limbs, in sound. I needed him to be a vessel. I needed our *tanda,* our embrace, to bear the weight of all my longing, all my pain. My strange and winding route to sureness. My betrayals and my broken loves. *It is a conversation,* Cesar said. He could say anything he wanted in return, and I would listen. But what was said we'd keep, each to ourselves; our secrets were too personal to specify. *I do not know yours and you will not know mine.*

In the third song of the *tanda,* the strings kicked in, tough and taut. My feet were bloodied, calloused, and my legs leaden and sore. My body was impossibly fatigued, but I belonged inside it, and inside that dance. He was archetype and effigy; he could have been anyone. He led, which is to say proposed, and I accepted, answering back — *loud* like I had never been with Enzo. I slowed our pace to pivot, grimacing, as the orchestra drew out a dissonance, suspending resolution, and I held us there. *Parada.* I had complete dominion as I waited to release us with my forward step. I felt a sudden rush of blood; he felt it too. He adjusted, reinforced his arm around my back. He held on tighter than he needed to, but not too tight. That was the boundary I claimed. Another silly *mmm* escaped his lips. I could have whispered anything I wanted into his deaf ear.

This is here in me, I said. *This too.* Watching Chicho and Juana had taught me how to say this in movement, how to find it with the song. And Silvina had taught me to aspire to power.

Chapter Twenty

WE DROVE HOME THROUGH THE NIGHT AND I MOURNED every darkened mile that dragged me back to dawn, the city skyline, and the imminence of endings — the festival, the summer, my endeavor in New York. I slept through most of Monday, hoping I might wake up back in Baltimore instead, with time permanently paused. I had only ten days left.

I wandered through midtown as if on shore leave, trying to elude the feeling of finality and vertigo. I danced because it was the only thing that mattered, the only thing my heavy limbs could understand. I had no responsibilities, to anyone. It was the kind of life my mother called "fantasy land," but Baltimore had shown me just how deep that fantasy could delve. There was no end to the rabbit hole. If I let it, tango could replace all other solace and eclipse the unlived future. I had the sudden and deranged desire to dive still deeper, to train until my body could approximate even a fraction of the perfection I had witnessed at the festival. I wanted to know what it would feel like to need nothing else.

At the Mogul's urging, I was added to the guest list of a summer tango ball in a penthouse overlooking Central Park. He did not ask if I would be his date, but wrote to tell me when I should arrive and, please, to save him the Varela *tanda*, "Historia de un amor."

I showed up in a backless cotton jersey dress — a bold *cielo* blue — and white high heels I'd worn once in a play and left at Peter's place. I drank champagne. The Mogul and I air-kissed, then made awkward conversation, overlooking all the oaks and elms and horse-drawn carriages below. I tried to pretend that this was not my first penthouse soirée. When we weren't dancing, we did not have much to say.

Marty was there; we shared a *vals* or two, and remarked upon the white-tailed waiters and the bankers and the models on the terrace. To Marty, the Mogul was the Gatsby of the tango world — even though the penthouse we were in belonged to someone else. He found the opulence worthy of awe, as though it must contain a riddle.

I was no Daisy; I only dreamt of being loved that way. And if I were, I would disdain the more pragmatic choice of wiser women. I was the kind of girl who *stayed in Mississippi*, as Dylan sang, *a day too long*. But I looked hard at the Mogul through that champagne lens and dared to wish.

I'm not sure what I was even wishing for. When one is unattached in tango, the heat sometimes goes haywire and the *what if* sparks: *What if this make-believe were real?* It can infuse the dance with urgent, artificial longing. But, with the possible exception of Gustavo and Giselle, tango partnerships, romantic and professional, broke up as frequently as not. Hence my ABCs — or, as Marty called them, the Code of the Kid — and all my attempts to demagnetize the dance. I'd long since closed myself to the *what if.* But maybe with the Mogul, I was giving in.

The dark wood ballroom was unfinished for occasions such as this. There were tea lights along the windowsill, and one long bench with velvet cushions. The plate glass wall looked down onto the black heart of the park, Manhattan twinkling at the edges. And when Varela played — because he had made sure to play it — the Mogul came to claim his dance. This, despite the lavish setting and the awkward small talk, was the same.

The party dwindled, packing up around us. When we left, he put his jacket around my shoulders and walked me back to Peter's parents' building. He led me chastely to a café on the corner. We chattered, then we kissed. For the second time that year, I felt the cool of shop windows against my back. I remember feeling vindicated; this man *did* want me — at least enough to pin me up against Café Europa in the wee hours of a Friday. I cannot remember how it felt — lips, a vague curtain of hair? What there was between us wasn't courtship; it was one long game of who-would-touch-the-other-first, and I had won. I said good night and went upstairs alone.

I sat down on my borrowed bed, clicked on the light, kicked off the heels. I had nothing to say. No lines of other people's pretty words, and none of mine. He had given me no fever. I liked my body just as well when it was here, by itself, as when with his. A fire flickered somewhere, but it hadn't touched me. I was alone — the door closed and the walls impassive. I didn't want him there.

Marty, however, was convinced it was the romance of the century. A proper tango fairy tale progressing through each stage of courtly love.

"Kid," he said. "I've never seen him quite like this. I predict a Christmas wedding at the Plaza! A ring from Tiffany! You won't have long to wait for a surprise in that little teal blue box." In another life, perhaps, I might have been Marty's Daisy, not the Mogul's. Even so, the former assumed that everything the latter built must be for me.

It was a pleasant fantasy. And though I'd found my footing on the dance floor, I was otherwise still lonely, still so passive, and I didn't know enough to know better. I was still keen to have my choices made for me, and keener still to be in love. Befuddled by my contradictory desires. The Mogul was a man straight from the pages of a glossy magazine. I couldn't imagine why I shouldn't want him. He was suave and self-assured and seemed like an adult. He liked curry, Canaro, sailing, art. He could wear a linen shirt unironically. He looked tanned even in winter. And if he found me sexy, then that must mean I was.

He gave me confidence when I needed confidence. Boldness when I needed boldness. I was penniless and scared. A flop of an actress and an adult with some Hail Mary wish to be a writer. New York had bested me, but I still didn't want to quit. I needed a reason, besides tango, to want to stay — and Marty's fantasy of Gatsby gave me one. If the Mogul wanted me, then that meant *someone* did. I just had to want him back.

Mum arrived the following afternoon, her Hyundai loaded to the rearview mirror with all her summer kit. I'd come to her with everything — skinned knees, Sapphic love tales, socialist ideals, the string of men who wouldn't touch me, the few who had. Now this: my confusion over a man some twenty years my senior.

"I think maybe I am in love with him?" I asked.

"Oh, you are not," she answered. "Trust me, Meghan. He is a mirage." *If a man is over forty and has not been married yet, there's something wrong with him.* "Don't waste your heart."

I begged her to stay the weekend before taking me away; she agreed. We called it our farewell celebration tour. We drank fizzy wine, took photographs in dusky parks. Saturday night, the Mogul took us out to dinner: thirty-dollar fish on Madison Avenue with cold white wine and *panna cotta*. We sat out on the sidewalk in the path of limousines and downtown buses, in a hot cloud of exhaust. I played the role of grown-up woman deftly, as I had with Peter — toying with my stem glass, ankles crossed, proper fork in proper hand. He asked permission to take me dancing after dinner. Mum agreed.

At the *milonga*, we danced three *tandas* before he told me he was tired. "Will you stay with me tonight?" he asked. It felt like victory. And so he took me home — back to his cavernous apartment with the pillared sculptures and the cat door for an ex's long-gone pet. I tiptoed across his precious rug. I still didn't know that I could simply ask: *What do you want from me? Why are we here?*

We kissed again, this time for hours, until our lips were chapped. There was no music. Lights were on. I didn't know that I could say: *I changed my mind. Please take me home.* He removed my dress, my underthings. My nakedness was gradual, and faraway. I'd gone somehow numb. It didn't feel as good as dancing with him had. It didn't feel like any kind of dream. It was gratifying, perhaps, to be touched, but I was limp in all but brain. I wanted him. I maybe didn't want him. Still, I let him unwrap me anyway, in the darkness that was not so dark because New York at night is never quite.

I lay there on white sheets, among white pillows, a beige platform in the middle of what felt like emptiness. Naked in a circle of lemony light, the vents and workings of the building humming, desolate, inside the night. The wheeze of city noise outside. It felt like pretend, going through the motions. Stretching limbs and easing out of garments, feigning an eagerness I didn't feel. He began to kiss me, and the little noises of that effort echoed, silly, against bare walls. I tried to fake the shiver I had felt with Enzo, how his mouth had branded me wherever he had touched. But I felt cool here, like fish flesh, in the open. Damp wherever he had kissed me. Clammy under central air. Aware, perhaps, of my own silence. I was thinking, spiraling; I wasn't dancing back.

We didn't speak. Time contorted, too far between the shores of day and dawn. My mouth and throat went dry. I wanted to stop, or sleep, or ask for water. He moaned every now and then, which seemed to magnify my silence. We were tentative with each other, sluggish and restrained. He mumbled something about how beautiful this was, and I saw that he was reveling, that he was pleased.

I had not forgotten what it felt like to be touched. I'd simply never learned. It was easy, too easy, to confuse the proximity of close embrace with real intimacy, to mistake sex for substance. And because the Mogul seemed like such a gentleman, I fell for it. With Enzo I had *known* at least that I was prey; the Mogul lured me into thinking that we stalked each other. I misinterpreted his practiced caution, his big display of trust, for real feeling. But his game had simply been to wait, to taunt his quarry, to delay the kill. In "unsexing" my tango, I'd stifled my desires — along with the notion that I might even have such things. But here they'd flared and spiked and reared themselves under the false pretense of real affection. All for some fantasy of being greatly loved.

And here I was: a body, skin stretched over bones, being kissed in full and hollow places. Anesthetic. I had to force myself to stay in focus, not to float away. He stared into my eyes with such intensity I almost laughed. His gaze was glassy, shallow — tidewater. Had I seduced him? Or had he merely let me think I had, so the responsibility would be mine to bear? *You asked for this,* I thought. Either way, it all felt drained of meaning. It was sweaty and a little sour and, in the morning, we were nothing but two naked strangers, emptied of surprise.

He took me for lunch. I stumbled through the heat of midday Sunday, moving slowly, as if through a wall of dense fatigue. I still did not know how he felt. Nor did I ask. The food was crisp and tasteless. I wanted to get back, to ask my mother why I couldn't feel. Why his face across the table seemed so unappealing, unfamiliar. And yet how much I needed him to reach for me, to keep up the display of care, the chivalry, the charade of our closeness. He did not. I knew this wasn't eye-shut love, but I was too embarrassed to admit it. I couldn't reconcile what little I felt with what I thought I'd wanted, what was here chewing before me. The man I thought he was, the man he seemed to be.

"How was it?" Mum asked when I returned.

I lied. I still don't quite know why. She would, of course, have understood, and freed me of him. "So wonderful," I said instead. "We kissed for hours."

If she sensed my emptiness, she didn't press. She repacked her overnight bag. I gathered my pile of possessions, shut them in a suitcase. We ate one last pricey midtown meal, sitting out on Seventh Avenue sipping our Sangiovese without speaking.

"You're not really going out again?" she asked as I tucked her into my guest room bed and dressed for one last RoKo.

"Of course I am!" I chirped, shoe bag in hand.

She couldn't understand how one more *milonga* could be so damned important. Hadn't I danced all weekend? Hadn't I had enough?

"It's *RoKo*," I pleaded.

"You'd better be ready to leave at eight a.m."

"Of course!" I chirped again, and not without with a pang of guilt. Trying to outrun the sinking, used-up feeling from the night before.

"I know you love it, Beanie," she said, as she watched me go. She said again what she'd been telling me for months: "But you need more than that to make a life."

RoKo had a rueful glow that night. The songs were sweeter, the bulk-bought cookies fresher. People with whom I'd barely spoken suddenly were abandoned friends. I did not know whether I would see the Mogul; I had left that up to chance. "I'll only bother going if you will be there," he'd said, "probably late." I hadn't bothered to confirm. Those hours were mine. I danced long and hard and lost myself in the embrace of leaders who were no longer strangers. That practice went much deeper than anything the night before. I knew now how their arms felt, how their limbs moved, the precise pressure of their palms. I knew who I was with each of them. Or at least, I knew the version of myself I played for the duration of each song. My feet pointed and flexed. I stood on one leg as the other whipped around me like a windsock. Free. My heart lurched at the end of every *tanda,* as if the dance itself were unwilling to let me leave. Tango was kudzu, and tsunami, the quiet center of my storm. I thought: how peaceful it might be to stay, to drown.

With each dance, the time before me dwindled. A year in Florida became six months, became a month or two. "I'm coming back," I said to anyone who'd listen. "I won't be gone that long."

When the Mogul arrived, late and harried, he barely had time to hang his leather jacket on the rack before Robin cried out, "Last *tanda!*" and the dancers scrambled into pairs.

"You're not really going," he murmured in my ear.

"I'm coming back," I said, again. For my own benefit as much as his.

"Good," he whispered, and we danced, but it was nothing special. I was tired; he had not warmed up. We got better as the relentless *tanda* powered on. There weren't many dancers left, and volunteers were already switching off the plastic votives, stacking them in boxes. We found a rhythm, slatting together in our habitual embrace. It was less fraught, less electric than it had been before. But there remained the satisfying stretch, the push and pull, the dynamic surging through our steps. This was still the something I would leave behind, I thought, the thing worth coming back to, tepid as it felt.

"La cumparsita" tolled its awful bells. That night, I believe it was Rodríguez whose little parade would march me home.

I felt, in panic, the weight of that last song. My final anthem. It wasn't what I might have wished for; Rodríguez's version clocks in at a mere two minutes and forty-five seconds, and moves fast — too fast for someone wishing the *milonga* would go on forever. It tripped merrily along with splashes of piano, surging choruses of strings, and, always, that constant threat of ending. Of conclusion. I wanted to leave everything I felt there on the half-empty floor — the confusion and the doubts — but the song would not be overstuffed. It came choking to a halt and that was that. *Chan chan.* Lights flipped and magenta curtains pulled. The Mogul lingered like a valet while I said good-byes and put away my shoes, then drove me the twenty blocks I would have preferred to walk. I felt like screaming. *This was a mistake* — him, not him. Leaving, staying. Everything.

"Don't be long," he said, and bussed me chastely on the corner of my mouth.

I slipped upstairs and into bed beside my mother, snoring quietly, her alarm set for seven. I couldn't sleep, so I watched her. She'd laid her traveling clothes out on a chair beside our bags, ready to take me south, to sanctuary, to a place I might consider home.

Chapter Twenty-One

WE HIT THE HIGHWAY, A STRETCH OF TAR THAT FADED across two days' drive to grey, then flattened out under the stretched Florida sky—parched seashell, dried-up-starfish white. I brooded in the front seat, overwhelmed and unaccustomed to the lack of jagged skyline. When we pulled into her condominium complex, a hulking apartment building on the Intracoastal Waterway, I expected to feel different. I did not.

She'd tried as best as she could to replicate our former home, hanging pictures as she'd always hung them, arranging knickknacks on the shelves. My room was her storage room, where all abandoned paperbacks and projects were crammed in with orphaned electronics and the family photos she found too difficult to see. All my grade-school yearbooks and journals were there, too, staring at me from the bookshelf. In my continual desire to reinvent myself over the years, I had torn out nearly all the pages. What my mother could preserve, she did: evidence of little lonely me trying very hard to seem like someone else. The full force of my newest failure settled in. I was just another twenty-something moving back in with a parent because she couldn't make it on her own.

. . .

As if that weren't bad enough, I noted a gradual inflammation in my nether parts. When this became unbearable, I asked my mother for an appointment with her gynecologist. *I'm sure it's nothing,* we both said, but it was not. I'd never had a cold sore, but apparently the Mogul had, and I'd contracted his. There'd been no symptoms; he'd had no idea that sun blisters from years ago lay dormant in the skin inside his mouth. Yet there I was in Florida, a few days later, furious and terrified in a paper gown.

I cried for one week straight.

First of all, it hurt like hell and lasted days. Then came the avalanche of shame. Even my mother started crying, mourning my *little unspoiled perfect body.* She stroked my hair and ferried me to the pharmacy for medication, called in sick to work. She installed me on the couch in her pajamas and we drank echinacea tea and went through television series after television series.

I ranted bitterly. It wasn't fair. I'd been so careful. I'd had so few affairs, it seemed impossible to have ended up with this affliction in so ladylike a place. Worse still, I'd held in me the thought of being tainted all my life, a certainty I carried, like an inward graft. Now, here was the proof, the wound made visible, the flaming sore.

"My poor baby," she repeated and repeated, even as she reassured me it was not my fault, and — just as she had said when I was seven — that I'd done nothing wrong. "So what," she said. "This happened and the world won't end." But I was unconvinced. The shame I'd felt for years had flared — irrevocable, conspicuous — between my legs. I could no longer mask it, damp it down. Everything I'd ever feared about myself was coming true.

I felt a bowel-deep chill, though I was in the tropics, reading novels poolside, drinking wine in palm frond gardens with my mother and her friends. It was coming into Season in the biosphere; a steady stream of transplants flew in from New Jersey, Boston, and New York. Old white people, rich and middle class, arrived in droves, filling the air-conditioned eateries, the outdoor tiki bars, the parking lots and indoor shopping malls. This was my break from all I'd left behind. This slow and shallow pace. No strings attached, just time to write, to breathe, to wear bright-colored sundresses, hibiscus flowers in my hair. My mother had done so much to give me this Room of My Own to turn my life around, and I was wasting it. I'd given up. I had nothing to say.

I lost whole days on the Internet, convincing myself of ghastly complications. I had a couple of awful conversations with the Mogul — all his ardor gone — who tried for days to tell me I must be mistaken, that there was no way I had ended up with cold sores on my undercarriage because of him. "You must have been with someone else," he said. I hadn't. "It must be you," he said. It wasn't. I had to call him twice for final confirmation of his hastily procured results, just to be sure. "Oh, right, yes," he said. "As it appears, I did have that."

My mother thought that this development, and the Mogul's absurd apathy, would make me change my mind and stay forever. His "please come back soon, please come back now" refrain faded to silence. The bare fact of my lesions had rocked something in him he could not confront. I came to hate him for this, for his lack of character. He was not worth returning for, and yet, if I was sullied now, then so was he — and who would have me now if he would not? I throbbed with indecision. The emptiness I felt, and the infection, were too much to bear if both had been for nothing. I'd ruined everything, I thought, and had to set things right.

I called my dad. I'm not sure why; this was not the sort of thing a daughter was supposed to share with her father, but he'd called me twice without response and we were close enough for him to know before I told him when something was wrong. I knew I couldn't face his voice without confessing. Without blurting out, through tears, the sorry state of me. "Just tell him," my mother said. "It will be just fine. You'll see."

"But what if he doesn't want me anymore either?" I'd been trying for so long to be his perfect little girl — squeaky clean in atonement for the stain of my first childhood. This new defilement felt like punishment deferred. The uncles catching up to me, the icy speculums of state examiners, the past clawing me back. We had avoided mention of my tender parts for years. We both preferred to think of me pristine. What if this time, this truth, made me too ugly to keep?

"Oh, Meg, that's *all*?" he asked. "You had me really worried."

"So you don't love me less?" I sobbed.

"I will never love you any less," he said. And then, to cheer me up, "Look on the bright side. At least that rat bastard Nixon is still dead."

I cried a few days more, and then resolved to face my situation with a sense of humor. At this I was sometimes more and sometimes less successful. I started cracking jokes at my anatomy's expense. So did my mother. Every conversation was an opportunity for puns. I was so thankful for her then. We made a batch of margaritas, and we laughed and clutched our sides and cried. "Well, Meg," she concluded — and we howled over this one — "Marty was right. The Mogul *did* give you a surprise present in a box. It just wasn't from Tiffany!"

We fell into a routine. I drove her to work at seven every morning, in my bathrobe, then came back to brew coffee in her two-cup pot and sit out on her balcony, looking across the water as it heated with the day. I sat there, staring at my laptop, until it got too hot, then went inside, down to the pool, or to the supermarket. I stared dumbly at the pages of my GRE math study guide, overwhelmed by all the algebra I had forgotten, the precalculus I'd never learned. Each afternoon when Mum came home, she asked about my progress.

"Get much writing done?" she'd say, and flick on a reality television show she'd previously recorded. I'd mumble something about process and the muse, knowing I was fooling no one, least of all myself. This dream felt just as silly as the others had. I started dropping hints about returning to New York. She wasn't pleased. We were supposed to take these months to help each other. She didn't understand what could have changed my mind — the Mogul (now *non grata* in her house), or the dance, or maybe just the city with its talons deeply dug. I didn't understand it either, but I'd already decided to abandon her. I'd already decided to go back.

I should get a job, she said. People were hiring for the Season. She said it every other day, and every other day made me repeat: I wasn't staying through the winter.

"You're really going back for that clown?" she would ask.

"It has nothing to do with him," I'd spit. I couldn't say for sure what it did have to do with, but being there, with her, felt cowardly.

My body stung and ached and itched in hidden places and the shame muddled my head. When I couldn't write or stand to feel — when I didn't know what to make of this or that, or him, or me — (which was most of the time), I cooked. Dinner was an unmade thing that could be made, something I could get right, and a way to show my gratitude. I crafted sprigs of herbs and fish fillets into something finite, which saved me chasing question marks around the room. Or dwelling on the hot stab of my humiliation. We ate most nights on the balcony, listening to the frogs. And almost every night, I fell asleep into disaster dreams: helicopters crashing overhead and buses falling from the sky. A semi driving off a building to erupt in flames below. I ran from fires and billowing explosions, sprinting atop a train that moved too slowly to outrun the burning city at my back.

I dreamt of perils and projectiles. Sailboats crashing into pontoon planes. And lovers who left me howling in the hallways while they danced with everyone but me.

Two weeks passed. I started doing intense vinyasa yoga, curling my legs under my hips, stretching my bones. The studio was half a mile from my mother's place. I sped there in her car, her Leonard Cohen CD blasting, just to catch an hour of movement. It was a sorry substitute for tango, but in that world of parking lots and manmade lakes, the torpor threatened. I could sit on her balcony and turn to concrete, like the rest of Florida, or I could move. Whether to keep tethered to my body, to relieve the pain, or to shake loose the stubborn words lodged in my head, I chose to move. I filled my pockets full of prana. I became a pigeon queen.

Weekends, we went out. We put on eye shadow and sandals, painted nails, and drove around through nights of outsized restaurants and uplit water features. She knew everyone. She'd rebuilt her life here. I had demolished mine. I felt that all my hopes were spoiling in her fruit basket.

How absurdly passive I was then, and how I seemed to strive in all the wrong directions. It had to do with acting, maybe. I had been real onstage, the most myself when playing someone else. Offstage, I'd been acting all my life — playing the well-adjusted woman, sexually assured. Playing the girlfriend, young professional. The city girl. Playing all the parts I feared I wasn't, and everything I wanted to be. Playing *tanguera*. Maybe if I stopped trying to be normal, trying to be everybody else, I might be capable of saying something true. What was it I was constantly escaping from, into tango, into theatre? My notebook began to fill, and not with what I'd planned to write — a series of acerbic anecdotes of waitressing, in hopes that those six years were not a total waste — but with childhood scenes.

My tone shifted, from snarky affect to bewildered girl. The sores began to heal. I'd write, then drive to yoga, where the room was dark and warm, and through a haze of sweat and incense, find myself sobbing quietly onto my mat. We'd cycle into *natarajasana*. Dancer's pose. I'd kick my leg behind me, up and back and up, and feel honest. Like a dancer. Inviolable, as I reached forward into air.

Mum drove me one evening, charitably, to the Jupiter School of Ballroom Dance for a *milonga* tucked into a strip mall on West Indiantown Road. There were seven people left when we arrived, at an hour I'd assumed was fashionable. They didn't charge an entrance fee. Mum sat beside me in one of the many empty seats along the floor, her purse on her lap, as I took my Comme il Fauts out of their silken sack. Buckling the straps, I wobbled like a five-year-old on Mommy's heels. I hadn't danced in weeks.

I sat shyly, chatting with her, my face turned out of *cabeceo* range.

"Well?" Mum asked, jiggling her foot.

"Well what?"

"Shouldn't you get to it?"

I wasn't sure why I was there. Except perhaps to test myself: to dunk my toe back in the open sea and listen for its call. Maybe the dance had lost its magic; I needed to know.

A *milonga tanda* started, and a lanky Cuban boy approached. Stuck out his open palm. I nodded and stood up. We started moving. He could have burped or stepped on me or galloped across my exposed toes and I would not have cared. I heard the *DUM bah dum bum* thump of the *milonga* bass line and my body whirred back into equilibrium. He was not advanced, but I was rusty and he wanted to fly, to pivot fast and *viborita*, twisting down the dance floor like a drunken snake.

He sped us down the empty stretch of room along the mirrors. I thrust my disassociated hips and cheated into turns, all technique gone.

Mum sat and watched, legs crossed, hands folded on her purse, making conversation with the dwindlers.

"That's my daughter," I heard her say. "She tango dances in New York."

They called last *tanda,* and the boy and I hauled each other through three slow, sappy tangos. Our dance was awful, but I grinned into his cheek and knew that she could see. We made it through the Di Sarli "cumparsita" before I undid my buckles and went home.

I got back that night to an email from Marty, eagerly anticipating my return. *Everything's gonna be alright, kid,* he wrote. *You'll see.* For him, there was still a green light blinking in the dark across the sound. But I did not agree. If there were indeed a beacon on the pier, that beacon was the dance itself, which made no promises of ever moving within reach, but which was always there, beckoning and beautiful. Whatever deficits there were in me, I could disown them. Even in that unsatisfying backroom dance, I knew this was the missing link.

One afternoon, while Mum was still at work, I bought my one-way ticket back — exactly one month to the day. I knew that it would break her heart. I knew that it was selfish of me. She needed company, support. It was wrong to go, but also wrong to stay. I was too unsettled, too humiliated. I'd been beaten. Flunked my life and run away. Here was my second chance. Besides that, it was autumn. I couldn't think in all that heat, in all that ferny green and postcard blue, when elsewhere everything was dying.

I had three hundred dollars to my name, a suitcase full of summer clothes, two pairs of jeans, my ratty tango shoes. A laptop and a pair of yoga pants. A notebook and a coffee mug.

Everything else was locked in storage and I could not afford a place to put it, or a truck to get it out. I needed nothing else. I'd been propped up by so much kindness — from Peter, Marty, from my mother — I wasn't sure how I would ever pay it back.

But I had chosen this. This *quilombo* — Argentine slang for a hot, holy mess — that needed fixing. I wanted Marty to be right, and was resolved. I could be autonomous. I could be brave. The city would do her worst, but I could try again — this time with no attachments. With a heart empty to all but tango. I would use the very thing that had dismantled me to patch myself together. This time not with the abandon of addiction, but intent.

Mum was my ballast — I leaned against her. But there, I was a barnacle on her life. I couldn't see myself except through her. She was too close. It didn't matter whether she was right or wrong. I had to stop pretending to be anybody else.

Chapter Twenty-Two

AT FIVE O'CLOCK ON A FRIDAY NIGHT, THE FIRST DAY OF October, my plane descended through a layer of clouds like dunes of sugar over East Islip into the airport, grey and blustery. I had checked one bag. I rode a shuttle bus into Manhattan, watching outer Queens fade into inner Queens, watching dark descend as we drove into midtown, watching all the windows light up, yellow against black. The city was indifferent to me and my return. I hit the pavement, matching pace, determined to be equally indifferent. I never wanted to own anything or risk loving anyone ever again.

Peter's doorman greeted me. Everyone was out. I piled my things back in the corner of the guest room I'd abandoned one month earlier, laid my toothbrush on the lip of the same sink, then went to meet a friend for dinner in a bistro in Hell's Kitchen.

"What am I doing here?" I asked her.

She asked about my plan. I answered, "Strictly speaking, I don't have one yet."

We finished our *pommes frites* and our wine.

"It's on me," she said, snatching the leather wallet of the check away. "You're unemployed."

Strictly speaking, I had no money, no apartment, no job, and no plan. But the night was warm for early autumn. The steady traffic crawling up Eighth Avenue, a blur of white fading to red, and all the sounds and smells combined to soothe me after weeks of quiet, uplit palms, and stately strip malls. There were no other voices in my head. Not Mum. Not anyone. I loved New York for making me anonymous again. For being loud and open late. I walked along the south edge of the park to take my laptop in for servicing well after midnight, then back with a hot chocolate in a paper cup that I had bought from a bodega and that had burned my tongue.

I slept deeply in my borrowed bed, and in the morning stuffed a dress and heels into my purse to catch the commuter rail from Penn Station to New Jersey. It was day two of the Princeton Tango Festival. Marty would be there. The Mogul would be there. A whole host of friends and strangers were there already, dancing without me. It didn't matter that the last train back that night left well before the *milonga* would be over, and the first one Sunday morning not for hours afterward. It didn't matter that I hadn't danced all month, not since that one night in Jupiter. I put on my Elvis earrings and rattled across the river with a bagel in my lap.

The sky was day-after-a-disaster blue, and even the industrial ugliness of Newark sparkled underneath it. Everything had crashed around me, except tango. After the Plague of Locusts and the Plague of Boils, as I had come to call the bedbugs and the sores, respectively, dancing was the thing no one could take away from me. The thing I couldn't lose or break or make a mess of.

The afternoon *práctica* was held on the Princeton campus in a big-windowed room, the kind with dust motes filtering through long shafts of light: spacious, sunny, and as warm a reintroduction to tango as I could have hoped for. I greeted acquaintances, then sat cross-legged chatting near the DJ table, nursing a coffee and pulling my hair back into pigtails. I accepted someone's *cabeceo*. I was rusty and he didn't mind. He took me gently through remembered movements, to familiar sleepy practice tunes. I bobbed between leaders, limbs creaking, until Marty turned up. "Kid!" he cried, and dropped his backpack to the floor beside his black leather sneakers. We embraced. We were no longer practice partners. He'd wanted to search out the holy grail of tango, his Giselle — the woman who'd be game for all of it, A, B, and C — and I had realized that practicing with one person only was no way to discover how I wanted to dance. But I hugged his taut and bony torso gratefully. I stretched up to meet him on my tiptoes and we waltzed. With Marty and me it was always *valses;* the rhythm and the whimsy touched us both so deeply, we could dance like that for hours.

That afternoon I danced with as many leaders as would have me, apologizing for my rustiness, reminding everyone I hadn't danced in weeks. They all just shook their heads as if to say, *Shh, we're dancing now. You're fine.* Three hours passed; the sun began to sink, casting the campus into pale autumn evening grey.

Marty and his new attempt at ABC let me borrow their hotel room shower, where I steamed myself to lobster pink and changed for the *milonga.* The three of us went for an Italian dinner. One glass of red for courage — *por las dudas.* One bowl of hot tomato soup with bread. Marty ordered half the seafood menu: grilled octopus, a crab cake, *cioppino,* pizza with *fra diavolo* shrimp. We drank strong espresso, and passed around a tin of mints. I decanted ice water into a bottle in my purse. We went for thick, rich cocoa at a shoebox ice cream store and walked to the *milonga,* past well-coiffed·Princeton kids in Top-Siders and salmon chinos who ignored the strains of violin wafting from the Mathey College common room. Perhaps they never heard them. Inside, the vault was filled with tango, up to its darkest ogives. The chandeliers were lit above a hundred couples twisting in a reassuring loop.

When the Mogul entered, Marty and I were dancing to Caló, something quiet and sustained. "He's here," said Marty, and my heart began to beat so hard that Marty asked if I should sit. "I'm fine," I said, battening my eyelids down and re-draping my arm across his shoulders. But I wasn't fine. I was agitated. I was angry. Half of me thought that if I saw him, everything would turn brittle and clear. The other half was keen to punch him in the sculpted chin. He was not the shining knight of Marty's romantic imagination; he never had been. He was just another selfish man who didn't want me, but who'd tricked me somehow into wanting him, and left me with a wound.

He shuffled over in his parachutist's pants.

"Dance?" he mumbled. I nodded meekly in return, but it was awkward, strained. Our balance never intersected; our beats were off by half a blink. I was so mad at him — and more so at myself for dancing with him. We slumped across the floor, walking, turning, like two wagon wheels out of sync. In the *cortina*, I waited silently, eyes right at him, for the contrition I thought I was owed.

The lights came up for the performance. We took seats atop a giant carpet roll and waited as the featured dancers did their encores. The Mogul neither looked at me nor spoke. It took me one more *tanda*, three more songs, to understand I didn't trust him — not even to lead. Our connection snapped. I didn't want him. I didn't even want to dance with him. His skill was not enough now, given everything he lacked. I had mistaken shallowness for sweetness. Substance for some semblance of style. And he was just another empty, pretty face, the pool reflecting up and him reflecting down.

The crowd thinned and relocated to some darkened residential lounge for after-hours dancing. I perched on a wooden table, watching like an anthropologist: Marty and his partner. The Mogul and the pretty girls of Providence and Princeton. The younger teachers who'd been kind enough to sway with me around the room that night. The divas and the tango witches with their long and feathered earrings, their Crayola-painted toes. In my clearance rack black dress and (now battered) Comme il Fauts, I felt as if the world were Technicolor and I was stuck in black and white.

I sat for hours, watching the line of dance go by, converting the Mogul into caricature. I was all alone and stuck in central Jersey — no train home, no home. I wanted that to make me stronger. But I did not feel strong; I felt small and frightened. Disconnected. Like an embarrassed schoolgirl in detention, dangling my feet beneath the hardwood desk and waiting out the clock.

The DJ played a really tricky Pugliese/Piazzolla *tanda*, to flummox anyone left dancing at that hour. It began deceptively with "Orlando Goñi" and "Adiós Nonino," as relentless as a leaden heartbeat, then spiraled down the late-night drain into the instrumental version of "Balada para un loco," which begins with thirteen seconds of the most poignant descending bass you've ever heard, before the strings encroach and come at you like ocean tides accelerated in a silent film. The *bandoneones* are hushed but lapping at the *síncopas* precisely, erupting just before the minute mark, where everything devolves into an instrumental fight, with solo fragments pleading: First piano, plaintive. Then the *bandoneones,* mimicking a single sinking leaf that falls in whole and halftone lilting. The strings come back up weeping, the mood goes bright for but a moment, then the dissonance begins, the strings fusing together at their highest pitch, sustaining softly and unbearably as all the other instruments ebb out and march away — until they fade into suppressed arpeggio, a major resolution immediately broken by a wall of horror strings ascending, for twelve seconds, through the end. It's like a manic lover's wail, blown backwards into hell. It kills the reverie the song creates with a violence that is almost comical.

The dancers brave enough to still be on their feet were caught mid-step in antic and unwieldy poses. Pugliese's signature *chan chan* resounded, hitting the first beat and muting the second into an echo of itself. The dancers groaned and cursed the DJ, a friend of mine who winked at me from across the room. This was later Pugliese, 1970, in his stint as Piazzolla's bandleader. He called "Balada" not a tango but a "super-tango." Tango nostalgic for itself. Tango more in *vals* tempo than tango tempo. Tango so tough it made me tired. I left and wandered up two sets of stairs to find a ladies' room, a private stall in case I had to cry. In case I'd made another irredeemable mistake in coming back. For this.

But I had not. I stared myself down in the mirror, strains of music coming through the floor. *Vení*, tango said to me. *Volá. Sentí.* Come. Fly. Feel. My step was steady; no tears came. When I reemerged downstairs, the Mogul offered me a ride. A few compatriots and I crammed into his car. I sat in the backseat with my eyes closed, pretending to be asleep until we'd cleared the empty Holland Tunnel. I wasn't happy, but I was relieved.

Chapter Twenty-Three

FOR TWO MONTHS, I LET MY LIFE GET VERY SMALL. I PARED IT down to almost nothing, going without the cardboard cartons full of clothes and books and furniture and memories in storage. I left them to must and rot, forgotten, as I built myself again from scratch. I went back to therapy for the first time since my adolescence. I no longer believed that I could outrun who I had been. I found a merciful psychologist with a background in early childhood trauma who cheered me through the rockier parts of my transition and charged me next to nothing.

To avoid employment in an office or a bar, I started cleaning house for Peter's mom. Her housekeeper had flown to Lisbon for a month or two to care for her sick mother, and I was helping her. Or she was helping me. I stayed holed up in the guest room until the family had finished their morning routine, then slinked down and, for the next four hours, cleaned and disinfected surfaces and toilets, did the grocery shopping, sent out dry cleaning, and kept the liquor cabinets full. I vacuumed, dusted, polished things, sent rugs away to be repaired, and put books back on the shelves. I did this with no small amount of love. It was meant to be temporary—just a few weeks or a month—but I would work there for a year.

Weekday mornings, listening to Baroque music on the kitchen stereo, I drifted through her huge and ornate space.

Sometimes I'd catch myself in mirrors, holding a toilet brush, and think I'd lost my mind. I'd gone from liberal arts school honors graduate with the world at her feet to this, a technically homeless substitute housekeeper with half an STD. But it was honest work, and I was grateful for it. It felt tangible, productive; frank. My afternoons were free for writing, teasing stories further from my childhood vaults. I had nothing left to lose, I thought, and watched the city pass the window of whatever coffee shop I happened to be stationed in. I put a fevered stream of honest words to paper, and hoped that they might be enough to buy a future.

I woke most days in panic, and ended several in tears, sure that I'd been wrong to think that I could live out of a suitcase, impose further on Peter's family, continue as their borrowed daughter, beat the system in this audacious way. The highs and lows began to wear on me. I could either make it or I couldn't. I belonged there or I did not belong. I was stronger than I thought I was, or weaker, so much weaker. I needed to find the fulcrum. Neutral. And I needed to do it on my own.

I took a second job, somewhat humiliatingly, working for the Mogul. Though we both seemed willing to ignore everything that had passed between us, he'd offered me part-time clerical projects in his meat plant — and I needed money, so I took it. Three days a week, I took a subway to a commuter rail to a taxi to a bleak landscape of industry — all loading docks and barbed-wire gates — and strode into his office as if immune to his indifference. I projected steely poise and spent some memorable afternoons on the phone with the Food and Drug Administration, trying to nail down the number of sodium nitrite parts per million to be added to kosher deli meat for a shelf life of ninety days.

I saved enough to move from my spare bed in midtown to a sublet room in Washington Heights. It was important that I pay my way again. I wanted to stop asking favors, stop accumulating debts. I took on yet another part-time job, collected transcripts, drafted admissions essays. I danced, but not as much as I'd assumed I would. Everything felt temporary, out of time, but tango was my rock. *Bailá. Vení. Volá.* Dance, come, fly.

One night I went out when I knew I shouldn't have. I was broken down, fighting a flu I'd caught for lack of outerwear, and doing it the cavalier way — with orange juice and vitamins in lieu of rest. I was sweating — and not because the room was packed and overwarm; it was a fever flush, clammy and brittle, and I danced through it as the whole place blinked and buzzed. The next morning, I was cured — as if tango had drained and purified my blood. I woke up to a wash of almost-winter rain outside my spartan room, and — for the first time, honestly and truly — it felt good to be alone.

I took a rare night off from tango to meet a friend and her boyfriend at a West Side Irish bar for scotch. Mostly to prove to her that I was not imploding up there in the nosebleed section of Manhattan by myself, when all my friends had moved to Brooklyn. We claimed our stools and ordered drinks.

"Well? What happened with Gatsby?" the boyfriend asked.

I cringed. This had been everyone's first question since I'd been back. And that, I realized, was my fault. I'd quit adulthood as I knew it, forfeited my possessions, the apartment, newspaper subscription, the big-girl nine-to-five, and left, flipping a sparked match over my shoulder as I did. But since I'd hopped the graveyard freighter into transience, and come back to New York the way I came the first time, with nothing but a suitcase and a prayer, all anyone could think to ask me was whether or not things had worked out with some man. This, too — the sores besides — was a pattern in dire need of breaking; I should add up to more than whether some or other man had touched me lately, and what he did or didn't want.

"I'm having a hard time remembering what I saw in him," I said, belting back a dram of liquid flame, and tried to change the subject. "How about those Yankees?"

He narrowed his eyes. I looked away, took one more sip. When I looked back, he was still squinting at me, in assessment. "You know what?" he said. "I release you."

"Excuse me?"

"I release you from the idea that you don't deserve better," he said. "You're a good-looking girl. You're smart. But you're attracting only douchebags."

I nodded. My mother could not have said it with more piquancy or pith.

My father's girlfriend said the same thing, only gentler. She'd taken to hosting me on her balcony once every other month for chilled Sancerre among her potted flowers. Her city was not my city. It lay before us, in manageable blocks, beneath a swath of sky, steadied by the secret tolling of a steeple bell across the street. From up there, everything was clean and made a kind of cordial sense. Whether it was the white woven tablecloth, the careful dish of salted nuts, or just the compassion she showed that lost young lady on her porch, I felt calmer when I left. More capable. More like the fish who didn't need a bicycle. More like I might make it after all.

I learned to relish being undecided. And when that uncertainty grew overwhelming, I withdrew to tango. Every *tanda* was an act of reinvention, and when the dance was over, I immersed myself within the rich, albeit rather superficial, social scene — the conversations carried from *milonga* to *milonga,* as if across a series of Victorian village balls. I sipped more cheap wine from plastic cups. This was my society, floating on the effervescent riffs of stately *valses,* carnival *milonga* tunes, sweet and brassy hummingbird renditions of "El esquinazo" and "El torito." These buoyed me even if I could barely dance to them, they were so fast.

It was time to chase the joy. I craned my ears for ebullient Biagi, for sweet-footed Caló, and beamed with every froth of violin. There were no rules in life, but there were rules in tango. There was an etiquette to follow, a code of dress, a social protocol, and that was comforting. I let that steady me.

When the time came, I closed the chapter on the Mogul in a single conversation. He'd asked me, after several weeks of silence, to join him at an Ethiopian restaurant on Tenth. He kept me waiting nearly thirty minutes and avoided eye contact as we sponged up pungent stews with handfuls of *injera*. He drove me to a Saturday *milonga*, circling a while before he pulled up to a meter several blocks away. Only when he put us into park did he explain: he was embarrassed; he was sorry; he was hung up on his ex. He never imagined anything like this could happen; he couldn't look at me or at himself. I steeled myself against the chest constriction that usually accompanies rejection, but it didn't come. He kept explaining. I was lovely, I was innocent, and he had been enchanted; he couldn't promise anything or offer anything, but maybe we could play it cool and unattached a while and wait and see? He just couldn't shoulder the responsibility of a relationship. I watched him struggle, make excuses, push his lacquered curls from his face. *If he is over forty and has not been married yet . . .*

"You know," I said. "I'm tired." If I was going to love someone, I wanted someone who was sure about me, without audition or condition. I wanted to be sure. I wanted to be sure. Solitude, with dignity, was preferable to this. I mumbled something about being better friends.

He fiddled with the gearshift, fiddled with his keys, flipped the toggle switch between "performance mode" and normal mode. And then I knew exactly what to say.

"Sometimes you just have to say no," I said. "I'm saying no."

Chapter Twenty-Four

I QUIT THE MEAT PROCESSING PLANT AND MOVED AGAIN, to Brooklyn, to a room no bigger than a double bed, with a door that latched just like an outhouse, in a five-bedroom Park Slope tango flophouse. Adam, the ginger-haired co-proprietor of Tango Café, ran the place. He lived there with his father and his father's girlfriend, a retired *tanguera,* plus a rotating host of tango dancers as they came and went from town. On any given night, there might be seven of us there, plus one or two or three itinerant *tangueros* on the couch. My room was the smallest, just outside the shared bathroom along the slender hallway from the living room to the galley kitchen. It cost four hundred dollars a month, and I was very happy there. I slept on a twin mattress on the floor with a view into the airshaft between our building and a pizzeria. The tiny window caught a hint of naked treetop from the back garden next door. I hung my clothes on wire hangers from a rod above the dresser and tucked my shoes beneath a metal folding chair, wedged into the only empty corner. When I closed the slide latch, locking myself in, I felt I had just room enough to breathe. I handwrote a line of Emily Dickinson and taped it on the wall. I was making my own prairie, out of nothing but my clover and my reverie. *The revery alone will do,* I wrote, *if bees are few.*

This was my second tango autumn, and how far off course I'd veered. It was grey; the days were getting darker. I wallowed a little in that gloom. Some nights, when everyone else went out to the *milongas,* I stayed home. I made myself dinner in the kitchen, if any of my groceries had survived the constant pilfering. I left Adam's father to his privacy, noodling on his guitar behind the curtain that delimited his alcove bedroom. I took my plate into my room and latched the door. Dim light shone through in a strip, but that was all that touched me there. An odd lick or two of folk music. Water running, or a toilet flush. The whoosh of city bus brakes at the corner. A teenage whoop outside the pizza place. I slept, and was awoken almost every time by troops returning before dawn. The lock, the footsteps, and the chatter. The open-shut of the refrigerator door. The smell of toast. Hushed giggles or full-throated conversation. Occasionally a *shhhhh.* But that was all beyond my door, and couldn't touch me. It was all part of the rhythm, the boarding-house feel of the place. Sometimes, after all, the late-night toilet flush and toast making was me. No one cared when I came or went, or what I ate, or where I worked. If I slunk in late or in the wee hours, I would often have to pick my way past bodies on the floor, a stockinged foot protruding from beneath a blanket on a couch. Piles of shoes, still-belted pants. Sometimes I chatted with the tango goddess in the adjoining room. We'd stand in each other's doorframes or the tiny kitchen, sipping from our mugs of tea.

Already, I suspected that my gamble had paid off. I'd started spending free hours at the Lincoln Center library, in the crypt quiet of the media room. Listening to Pugliese on headphones —*Ausencia* on repeat. Writing down the memories I'd never fully owned. The birth mother. The uncles. The cruel schoolyard taunts of youth. Some days I sat there, slumped into a swivel chair and staring at my laptop screen, stuck between imagined worlds. But I kept going back.

It got colder and colder. I shoved my hands deep in my pockets. I readied myself for winter, sealing off my doubts like window cracks. I called my parents every afternoon, walking to a train or a *milonga*. Mum had forgiven me for leaving her, and was so relieved that I had started writing, finally, about my past that she ignored her skepticism toward the rest. Dad was glad to have me back on neutral ground. We met for lunch and coffee at a midtown salad bar each Friday afternoon he was in town. He asked so little of me. Bought my lunch. Quizzed me about my applications. Said *attagirl* and tripped uptown to his girlfriend's place. I found the steady dates, the gentle monitoring a comfort. He bought a shin-length red down coat for me, as an early birthday present, to make sure I kept warm.

However uncertain these days were, they were—by far—my best in tango. Some barrier had broken. Sure, I wasn't nearly half as good at tango as the cool kids, and they were still a close-knit clique of friends with histories and jokes I'd never be a part of, but I went to their *milongas* and I slept in their fifth bedroom and I danced with them and they were kind. When I turned up, they greeted me with hugs, *saludos* to the cheek, a conversation. Edward made a new habit of treating me to sumptuous meals I could not afford, multiple-course tasting menus at places that took reservations until after ten. I wore one of my two clearance rack summer dresses over tights, and we laughed our way from *amuse-bouches* to *mignardises*. Marty and I talked through half our *tandas,* catching up on what we hadn't mentioned in our emails. The New York tango community, I realized, was generous, and I was part of it. At a *milonga* anyway, I never lacked for company. This was my corner bar, my social club. I was a god-honest regular.

· · ·

Without the trappings of accumulated stuff, ineligible men, and unfulfilling jobs, New York was kinder, too. I had hours to spend staring at the blinking cursor, and hours to dance. I danced my way to winter, into familiar sore-soled bliss. It seemed my only limitation was my body, imperfect and angular, but evolving, getting sturdier by the day. I wanted to quit my head, live only physically. Empty what I could to paper, keep the rest at peace. I stretched my arms above the yoga mat and stamped my feet into the floor. I tried to be fully present, not just on the dance floor — the owner of my axis and my every step — to walk slowly and with purpose, and to breathe. In each asana, I found new aspirations: I would be a warrior. A crow. A balanced tree. It was the same with dancing: I wanted to be great and sexless, self-sufficient. Holy and ascetic. An ecclesiastic bride of tango. I swore off men — particularly tango men (including a lanky Italian airline steward who had two dozen roses sent to me at a *milonga*). They were sirens trying to lure me off my boat; my mother could be right about the men and wrong about the dancing. And the dancing was the mast to which I'd lashed myself, resolving to get better, and maybe even — one day — strong.

Adam offered me a roommate discount for private lessons. I took him up on one or two, and met him at You Should Be Dancing, the daytime home of Tango Café, in the quiet of the dim and massive room. I brought us lunches from the bodega salad bar at the corner, and we sat on stools, ate half of them, then danced.

Adam was another leader in the school of less is more. He was small featured, pale and freckled, and born and raised in suburban Ohio. Like Dennis the Menace, he was all big eyes and crooked teeth and boyish mischief. He took my hand in his and led with slight and subtle movements, expecting force, expecting me to move with full intention in whatever manner he suggested. Close and open were no longer choices to be made but qualities through which the dance might pass. He reeled me in and out like fishing line — the trick being to maintain my axis — and led me to my single favorite moment in all of tango dancing: the return to pure closeness when a leader pulls you back. He invites and you accept. You reaccommodate each other and continue on in close embrace.

Adam sent me to his partner, Ciko, the former architect who'd awed me when I'd seen her dancing with Silvina Valz. Ciko was six inches shorter than I, but strong. She wore wedge sneakers with duct tape wrapped around the toe box when she taught. Watching the liquid way she moved while following, I had not expected so much steadiness or sheer might. She took me in her thin brown arms and led me, diagnosing weaknesses and teaching me to zip my core muscles like a corset. She was everything I aspired to be then: femininity and force in perfect balance.

We worked on generating power, and then we worked on smoothness. We turned and turned and turned until it felt least jarring to her, until my steps were level and my *molinetes* stopped careening from their circle track. *"Yes,"* she'd say, when I got the balance between taut and fluid right. It was our all-girl *academia,* and she my chosen *milonguera maestra*. She could tell me, with her body, how I ought to adjust mine — to make me feel how a follower should feel in a leader's arms. "Round, *round*," she'd say, breaking the stiff plane of my shoulders until my lat muscles were down and my wings curved in the embrace, as though she were a beach ball that I held. With her mismatched earrings brushing at my collarbones, she guided me. "Better . . . ," she'd say, in her soft Turkish inflection. "That was better." She stopped and started songs from portable speakers plugged into her phone on the floor. She gave me stretching exercises meant to loosen up the spine.

At the beginning of every lesson, we rolled together, laughing, as we twisted, slumping our limbs against the dusty floor. And at the end, we hugged.

I'd like to say I was thereafter looser and more generous, making inviting circles with my two long, bony arms. Not just pushing back, but opening, to create that magic vacuum column between me and a leader wherein we might merge and beam straight up into the tango heavens. Certainly I tried. But tango study is progressive; one never ceases drilling the most basic skills.

It didn't matter that I wasn't great and probably never would be. I was good enough. I had a place within the hierarchy of the tango circus — somewhere beneath the gods and monsters doing aerials between the rafters of the tent, somewhere above the plebes. I stopped apologizing for every mistake.

Chapter Twenty-Five

"SO WHAT DO YOU DO?"

I was at the Brooklyn equivalent of a cocktail party; thirty or so friends-of-friends stood awkwardly in the corners of a bar roughly the size of a meat locker, clutching Sazeracs and trying to make small talk above ear-walloping music in the dark. This had always been the dreaded question. "I'm trying to act," I'd say. And they would answer, "Well, what would I have seen you in?" And I'd say either, "Did you happen to catch the one about the circus act used car salesman? Written in verse?" Or, simply, "In an apron, in the upstairs bar at P. J. Clarke's." When I had a real job, it was almost worse: "I do marketing for a non-profit," which sounded perfectly legitimate. "Which one?" my interlocutors would ask, and I would answer, and they wouldn't recognize the name, and I would bite my tongue to keep from saying, "That's okay. It's badly run by a sexist bigot and I'm only marketing coordinator because they fired everybody else and I'm afraid of confrontation."

That evening, stumped, I stared into my drink. *Good question.* The short answer was: nothing at all. In the morning, I wore rubber gloves and cleaned my ex's parents' opulent apartment, all the while worrying I was making their lives awkward, abusing the complicated privilege of that gig—being their maid without them treating me as such. Midday, I did yoga and made breathing noises like the ocean. Afternoons, I sat deep in the library, either cramming review math for the GRE or writing and revising application essays. In the evening, I danced tango. That got an interlocutor's attention.

"Like, professionally?"

"No."

In my eagerness to set fire to my life, I had forgotten about cocktail parties.

Undeterred, I tunneled ever deeper into the tango tar pit— damn what anybody thought. I signed up for FeralTango, a six-month registration-only boot camp. This was hardcore technique taught by Sara and Ivan, a married couple from Zagreb and Mendoza, respectively, who focused mostly on body mechanics and the physical limitations of each student in an attempt to turn civilians without ballet training into proper dancers.

Ivan was short, slick, and pouty, but preternaturally talented —like an extremely agile mink. Sara was more professional, with an encyclopedic knowledge of anatomy. She would watch you walk around the room and scrutinize your foot bones. "You're leaning backwards," she would say. Or "You're collapsing into your forward steps." She was also perhaps the fiercest female follower I had ever seen for attitude and sheer physical power—dense and muscular, showing off the domination of her stretches, her intense control.

FeralTango was expensive—nearly two hundred dollars per month—but I'd been saving, and the instruction was invaluable. They spoke like physicians—about the psoas and the clavicle, the first and fifth metatarsal, the piriformis and the ever-elusive core. Every millimeter of the foot was called upon. By isolating every segment, every muscle, Sara and Ivan devised a system to identify every way a body could approach a tango step. Often, it seemed, they found the trickiest means to explain the most straightforward ends. It was a system of totalitarian simplicity requiring invisible arduous effort, coiling and recoiling around a center spring. Their methods took you so far into their anatomical vernacular that you almost lost your sense of what they meant to say. But what they taught was unavoidably correct — obvious once you understood it, albeit occasionally impossible to do.

The major concept of FeralTango was something called the membrane, the force field between the couple. Each step involved manipulating it. For Sara and Ivan, all movement went in multiple directions, like yoga: down into the floor, up through the body trunk, into the center of the couple, and out across the room. Every forward step was initiated by a backwards summons of intention to generate momentum, then a push through the arches of the foot, the legs following the torso, the front foot like a shock absorber, then a pulley system to bring the body back together. Backwards, it was the same, inverted. The leader would engage the lady with what they called "directional push," treating her center like a billiard ball. He targeted geometrical coordinates and moved toward her with specific force to move her a specific way. A Sara-and-Ivan leader could control each increment of movement. This was tango for math geeks and bankers, tango for investment strategists. Many of their students became a little supercilious — so turned around within the FeralTango framework that it was sometimes hard for them to dance with anybody else.

It was exactly what I wanted — a project, endless and profound. Some intangible repository for my monkish devotion, a gauntlet through which I'd goad myself, moving my boulder ever up the same unyielding slope. And so I spent two evenings a week in a low-rent studio with a buckling, bowing wooden floor, turning absurd circles with a partner, sweating and grunting, trying to approximate what I'd seen Sara do so gracefully — while she barked orders in my ear.

It took me quite some time to comprehend the difference between technique and style. When I first learned the eight-count box, I thought, *oh yes, that's tango*. I learned the box was wrong and thought, *well, this is tango*. I learned that there were only three steps — six, if you counted each in both directions — and *that* was tango. Then I met Sara and Ivan, whose instruction seemed to scream that everybody else was wrong.

But I was done assuming there was one right answer and that I needed someone else to tell me what that was. There was a difference between learning what was expected of me, and developing the skills to execute and choose. It seemed to me the best of tango dogmas were the same. There was only one technique, one toolbox, one way of moving that made movement tango. Enzo's "waiting for the train" and "waiting for the bus" analogy was just another way of saying "change your weight from foot to foot." And Mariela's "use the heel" refrain was just what Sara meant when she said we must engage the back foot to push through to the next step with the front. The fundamentals never changed: maintaining axis, moving the upper and lower body in opposition, staying in alignment, not relying on our partners' arms for stability — leading or following, stepping precisely, and keeping the movement ever circular in turns.

Beyond that, the smallest move was taught a thousand ways. As tango anthropologist Julie Taylor wrote: "It is up to the woman how she moves her body . . . . You could decide to make your legs cry, or laugh. A leg can weep." It matters where you put your foot; it matters more how you place it there. That was style; and there are as many styles as there are stylists. I could study technique with Sara and Ivan and still not dance as they did. Their style was their style; mine was mine. And that was good, because their dancing always seemed contentious. It looked like sparring. But it felt like hot knives through butter — or at least, it should.

I valued that physical rigor. I wanted my dance clear, corporeal, stripped of excess and emotion. To feel the fire of the music in my muscles, uncomplicated by the rest of me. Sara and Ivan's methods were invaluable for this. While Ivan tiptoed and scowled, Sara stood squarely in the center of the room and made me responsible for myself in tango in a way I hadn't ever had to be. Like Adam and Ciko, expecting me to power my own rocket in a shared orbit, Sara trained her followers to take almost nothing from a leader. There was no *ignorancia sagrada;* ignorance, sacred or otherwise, was not an option. If I wanted to dance in Sara's world, I had to *be* a dancer — not merely a follower who danced back.

Sara rejected the popular axiom that every follower's mistake was but the product of a leader's imprecision. "The woman's role," to her, demanded more. A leader should hew to his partner's level, but beyond that, he bore no further responsibility for how well she danced. "He does his work," she said. "I do mine."

That work was *moving.* The "directional push" exerted by the leader was more directional than push. He set the coordinates; she got there under her own steam. She did not rely on him for turns or pivots, pushing off against his hand to boost herself around. Sara could swivel into the floor like a heavy drill bit, entirely in control of her own force and speed. "Ladies, do your work," she'd say, like a proctor telling her examinees to keep their eyes on their own tests.

A lack of progress was due only to a lack of practicing. If a leader prevented us from moving properly, that was no excuse. We had to find a way. Balance, integrity, and execution — our tools were all we had.

Learning tango typically requires modern feminists to willingly suspend indignity. At first, we bristle. We take a leader's proffered arm in spite of a reluctance to be "led." Then, perhaps, we cotton to the merits of ceding control. Gender roles aside, it's nice to be exempted from decision making. Nice to trust someone to navigate us safely through the throng. Maybe then we get complacent, and forget ourselves. The world is tiring, so very tiring — how nice to sink into the role of *la sonámbula,* the sleepwalker, guided safely through the darkness in suspended animation. Lord knows I'd been seduced by that.

Sara took it on herself to wake the sleeping beauties of the tango world.

Tango, to her, wasn't *one plus one equals one.* It was *on our own and yet together.* There was no talk of submission. The dance was not a love affair, of any length, but rather a debate. A reasoned discourse. If one partner shouted, blathered on, or wouldn't let the other get a word in edgewise, then that particular exchange was futile and uneven. The mistake followers too often made was meekness, muteness, doing just as they were told.

Sara taught me to speak up in my dancing. Not to demur. Not to, say, muffle my voice or speak into my lap. My work was *moving.* Even if a leader gave me nothing. Dancing for myself and by myself, rather than in reply to being led. I should not alter my technique for anyone, no matter how a leader seemed to drown me out. If I did, my dancing suffered, and it would be my fault for relinquishing control. If I didn't like a leader's conversation, I simply didn't have to talk to him.

I started to apply this unforgiving framework elsewhere in my life. I was where (and who) I was by my own choices, my own steam. If I stepped ungracefully — if I erred, I was to blame. And oh how I had erred. So eager to close my eyes and trust someone to lead me better than I could myself, I'd yielded valuable ground. So eager to be loved, I'd lain there in the dark expecting someone to make love to me. I'd given myself over to the caprices of the tango currents and the tango cads, and let both carry me away.

Men lead and women follow. There are plenty of exceptions to this tango rule, but generally, the gendered lines are clear, reflecting — it must be said — the workings of a much less equitable world.

Back in the old Buenos Aires heyday, if a young man wanted to get a girl, he had to learn to tango. He went to the *academias* and danced with other men, established leaders keen to practice. He followed first — for months or years — feeling the echo of the lead before his own attempt. Only with the soundest skills would he be admitted to his first *milonga*. Women, who for many years were a minority, were forced to hone their craft with family members, in the privacy of the home. At the *milongas,* of course, they reigned supreme. This system was both worshipful of women and dismissive; it presupposed that leading was more difficult and thus the chore of men — even as it sought, above all else, to show the ladies a good time. Men fancied themselves patriarchal peacocks, and the girls a flock of plain brown pigeon hens just waiting to be wowed.

Call it chivalry or call it chauvinism; the custom has endured, often simply because of differences in height. In many ways, it *is* more difficult to lead. Not only is a leader liable for his dance, but he must also know the music well enough to plan it in advance, and equip his partner to react in time. He must skipper their shared boat across the counterclockwise sea of other couples. Could a woman shoulder this responsibility? Of course. I've never met the teacher or professional who couldn't—often better than the boys. Is there some deeper reason, then, why men are given tactical control, and women left to make the best of what is offered? No. Just the thicket of oppression at the heart of human culture. Just centuries of men calling the shots. But this is tango; this is the architecture of the dance.

It is deeply sexist. But potentially reclaimable as the vestige of another time. The worst of tango's trespasses against our sex are much more recent, the convention having long outlived its raison d'être. Nowadays, men lead because *that's how it's done*—by force of habit, rather than some deep and decorous respect, however condescending. This isn't true everywhere; there is a thriving queer tango community, where all gender lines are arbitrary and dancers are free to choose their roles—often swapping lead for follow in a single dance. Anyone, dressed up any way they like, can lead whomever else, be they gay, straight, bisexual, transgender, genderfluid, queer, or questioning, be they androgynous, butch, femme, or a little of all three. All avenues are open to expression. There are heroic professionals out there. Silvina Valz taking the lead in vest and flats or strappy heels. Leaders like Berlin's Astrid Weiske in her silken tailored shirts. Rebecca Shulman and Brigitta Winkler, who formed an all-lady tango company called Tango Mujer. Martin and Maurizio. And all the others who make tango a better, freer art, safe for everyone beyond the binary.

When I first signed up for tango class, I had no idea that new order existed. In my studio, there was no questioning. The men started leading on day one of Basic Section A. New followers like me had to abide their lack of skill, and improve in spite of it, until advanced enough to dance with better leaders. If followers outnumbered leaders in any given class, we sometimes had to skip a turn when changing partners, and stand between two couples, skiing in place on our own. It is the beginner's plight that's cruel, not following itself. Maybe everyone

— of any gender — should be made to learn to follow first. For weeks, or months, or years. Just like the old days. Maybe without following, a body cannot feel the implications of the lead.

The cool girls of the Robin Thomas crowd all learned to lead, and the men to follow, albeit later on. To internalize the structure at the heart of tango, you ought to learn both roles. I once asked Robin to teach me. "Okay," he said, and tucked himself into my arms. "Now move." He talked me, roughly, through two steps and the cross before dismissing me to practice that until perfection. I remember feeling flat and potent on my feet, almost burdened by the possibilities. *Should I move the queen's rook or the bishop?* I didn't want the cognitive burden of the strategy, the steering. I didn't want to think with anything but my body on the floor. I was in awe of those who did, and sought my share of lady *cabeceos,* reveling in their softness, their delicious skill.

While the idea of subverting the gendered orthodoxy at the heart of tango continually thrills me, I was also grateful for it. After four years of women's college theatre, building sets and hanging lights, and binding breasts — my own and others' — to play both male and female parts, I was no stranger to the idea that we might all benefit from blurring lines. That gender needs no roles or rules. But when I came to tango, I was twenty-five and terrified of men. If I could have learned to dance with women, I might not have bothered with the other half of the adult population. Not least because I can't imagine Astrid Weiske ever taking it upon herself to suck my toes without consent.

Though I didn't understand why at the time, I didn't want a choice of avenue. If I'd had one, I might still have chosen the outdated and unfair. I wanted gentleman-and-lady, he-leads-and-you-follow. I needed to choose contact with bristled cheeks and unforgiving chests, those cisgender aliens with furry forearms that felt like livestock to my untrained hands. I needed to know what a man's touch felt like, to decide whether I liked it, to imagine how my own might feel to him. On the dance floor, at least, we could, safely, relate.

If we ignore the veil of sex that surrounds tango, what we bring to the embrace is this idealized vision of who we'd like to be inside our own private vacuums of desire and expression: our sexuality without the sex. Tango can never quite be gender *neutral,* but it can be gender pliant. Gender fluid. It is a game of opposition.

Take the *parada.* That single moment holds the key to the dynamic at the heart of tango. There is nothing there but jazz. The needle catches in the groove. The pauser has become the paused. The dance is just a circle, changing course. For every time the leader lunges forward and the follower steps backward to receive, the leader opens up an empty space, inviting occupancy. The follower, in some cases *she,* accepts the invitation, but the leader, in some cases *he,* must follow the follower, wherever she or he has moved. At the very nexus of tango technique, leading is following.

Tango is a playground of paradox. Yin and yang. Geometry and sensuality. *Melodía y compás.* It is violent and tender. Humble. Swaggering. Insolent and deferent. The leader and follower both are free to experiment with all the conflicts they contain. Tango is Jung's union of opposites, and Heraclitus's *wholes and not wholes; brought together, pulled apart; sung in unison, sung in conflict; from all things one and from one all things.*

Still, in every dance, there is a leader and a follower. One proposes, one decides. One tracks, and one interprets. As Silvina Valz would put it, "As much as you will find both in both, the roles should be very clear." If not, there's simply too much noise. "As much as they are intertwined, they need to be defined." For better or for worse, these are the mechanics of the dance. One partner will propose "the trip," the other will "accompany" — with all the rights and responsibilities each role entails. "And if you don't like that aspect of this discipline?" she adds. "Don't do it."

Silvina takes enormous pleasure leading, but she prefers to follow. "When I lead," she says, "I feel the freedom of the musical interpretation, one hundred percent for me." She listens to her follower, but is wholly free to sculpt the song the way she hears it. "I am the musician," she says, "the first one." The follower is her instrument. Listening and moving are the same to her; both come from the music. Following is different; a leader hears the song his way, and she will hear it hers. As a follower, she listens to his listening. Sometimes a leader will have a lot to say, and on those occasions only — should he be worthy of the gesture — she may defer to his interpretation. Otherwise, she will impose her own.

Perhaps there's something deeply masculine and feminine at the center of the dance — perhaps there isn't. Both energies are and must be present. We all contain both, by degrees. Tango requires both. There is power and there is deference. Opposites align. Sometimes the follower goes around the leader. Sometimes the leader goes around the follower. Sometimes they go around each other.

Take Sara and Ivan. Ivan in his machismo could insist on Sara's absolute submissiveness, but she would never stand for it. His bravado, her defiance — both are just another part of their particular conversation. When his lead becomes unclear, she tells him just what he's done wrong. When he is snappish, she snaps back. And though Ivan is capable of all sorts of impressive footwork, Sara has the deeper understanding of the dance. She paints with movement, varying the color, quality, and quantity of light. Together with Ivan's lightning strokes and stabs of pigment, they make art.

This is what Silvina means. The follower is not a canvas

onto which her leader splashes paint. She wields a paintbrush too. The canvas is the space between them no one sees.

Because the roles had been presented to me as they were, I followed. I listened first when male beginners got to speak. Listening, however, taught me what it was I had to say. Eventually, technique taught me how to say it.

Other women come to tango more secure in what they want — some to somnambulate, some to seduce. Some to rehabilitate a broken heart. Some to use their sex and their stilettos to lord their power over men. Some to simply twirl in the dark. Still others, confident in femininity and feminism, have no need for tango; the embrace offers nothing to them and the music leaves them cold. No two women are the same.

I'd needed to fumble from one end of the spectrum to the next, then claw my way back to the middle, where I felt at home. I needed to be touched — within those safe and preestablished margins. The "woman's role" was not a prison to me; it set boundaries, koans for me to riddle out and, ultimately, transcend. Following gave me secret freedom. From Silvina, I took strident softness. And from Sara, sovereignty — of body and of aim. I was where I was. I was who I was. I could blame no one but myself for tossing me around. Not Peter Pan, not Enzo, not the Mogul. Not my landlord, my childhood, or my boss. Not even New York City. I bore the responsibility of living, dancing well, and putting in the work, but this was power: every step I took was mine.

The irony of following, for me, was that it forced me to take the tiller of my boat. No matter how difficult it had been to share an axis, to lean into a stranger's close embrace, in such proximity to unfamiliar flesh, and let him (or her) move me, it had been more difficult to dig my way out of that blind reliance, to find my axis and negotiate how I might move — both coupled and alone. Alone was hard. Coupled was harder, and confusing. Within that duality, though, I got to play. I got to be demure and deranged. I got to play the shrinking violet and the violent bloom, different in every dance until I finally realized the kind of dancer — and the kind of woman — I wanted to be.

Chapter Twenty-Six

I TURNED TWENTY-SEVEN ON A COLD AND CLOUDY FRIDAY, not quite winter. I went to an early yoga class, took myself to lunch, walked through the Village with a cappuccino. By some magic, the city smelled of woodsmoke, very faintly, and I remembered Buenos Aires, trying to conjure back a time before I learned this dance. I couldn't. I went to a shop instead, and bought myself a dancing dress, then walked east through the gloaming to meet friends for ravioli. On the way, I bought myself a massive chocolate cake. I'd take the leftovers with me to the Uke later, to share.

The more I learned, the simpler my dance became. A leader's touch no longer startled me. I was not afraid of men. I spoke to them and danced with them, and sought nothing in their *tandas* save the "supernatural joy" that all the maestros say tango inspires. I was ready for the single most important concept in my tango education.

Back when those first *porteños* put their arms around each other — when the lines of *candombe* came together into pairs, the double cylinders of waltz and foxtrot frame were welded into one pillar of touch — something special had transpired. Two bodies shared a single equilibrium. This is the contract at the heart of tango: *we will make one body for the duration of this song*. It is not so simple as *one plus one is one*. Sara was right. We do not sacrifice ourselves into the couple; we form the couple to make tango. Gloria and Rodolfo Dinzel, contributing founders of the tango renaissance, put it this way: "Between one and two, *three* is born." And that is tango. Because the dance is pure improvisation, it is altogether new, unique, alive for the three minutes of a song, then it ceases to exist. Whether any given *tanda* is a love affair, a conversation, or an outright war, it "consummates itself in its own creation." The canvas crumbles into nothing as the dancers part.

We know other dances by their form: a pattern of steps, the beats on which to step them—by *what* is being danced. But we know tango by its manner, by its *hows*. If you learn tango hewing to the form, you'll miss the dance entirely. *"Form,"* the Dinzels say, is "produced as the dance proceeds." The *manner* is the thing. And that takes two; that takes connection.

Like the fifteen Yup'ik lexemes for "snow," or the four words for "love" in ancient Greek, there ought to be a dozen definitions of "connection." It can refer to anything from the physical fact of fixing your chest to another's chest and listening for cues, to Sara and Ivan's membrane, to the idea of a particular rapport between two dancers, to being so deep in the music that the dance floor disappears, to opening your eyes after a *tanda* only to feel as though you've been asleep and dreaming in a timeless, private world. It's the catchall that describes the best of tango—from the corporeal to the divine. Without it, at its most rudimentary, there can be no transferring of weight—and thus no dance. And with it, at its most mystical, all things are possible between two people and their bodies and the music and the floor—total communion, total melting, total flow.

Connection was a term I'd heard so often it had almost lost its meaning. But after years of dancing, connection is the well that never parches. The last source of surprise. There are parts of tango I will never access as a white woman, an American, living in this sleek and terrifying age. The muscle memory of a nation. The recollection of the movement in the blood. I did not grow up listening to tango in the living rooms of my forebears; I will always hear the music differently for that. To the extent that poetry is national, these lyrics and Lunfardo aren't mine. They were not written for me or about me. When I dance, I borrow. Gavito once said that tango, as a dance of immigrants, has no nationality. "Its only passport is feeling, and everybody has feelings." This is true and false. My freedom to take from tango what I need is luxury, no matter how reverent my pillaging. Maybe we are all just playing dress-up, donning our imaginary cloche hats and fedoras to walk la Calle Florida to Corrientes. Perhaps we dance and see ourselves in sepia, faded by the old-time smog of soot and steam. Or maybe we imagine we can own our tango, independent, as a purely physical pursuit. We can't. We take one step and place ourselves in conversation with another culture — whether we are there to desecrate or pay tribute, to build something deeply personal that can never quite be ours. Connection, however, is for everyone. It cannot be exoticized, or bought or faked. It requires only honesty, humility, and willingness to let yourself be held.

I had come to tango so completely disconnected — from myself, my body, and the possibility of touch. (My mother would likely add "reality" to that list.) Now I nestled into other bodies nightly, offering my torso and my temple, my left arm, my right hand. Unflinching, as my breasts brushed against a male body, as my face fused to his. I could be held by anyone, hold anyone, and it was little more to me than shaking hands.

Which is not to say that tango had desensitized me. It deadened me, perhaps, to insecurity and inhibition, and asked me to suspend my sight and smell only to open wide my other senses and listen like a root thirsty for sun. The embrace becomes a normal act because what follows is exceptional. A kind of trance. A shared communion. The total dissolution of your differences.

Marty and I were like this, as familiar as lovers to the other's form. I knew that certain steps would cause our knees to bonk together, or our chests to pull apart. I knew that others would unite us perfectly, at full height, and I would drape my arm around his shoulder just the way he liked, and feel his jawline tighten to a smile. This is what our bodies taught us, once they'd spoken. It was intimate, but not romantic. Stirring, but not sexual. We shared a thumping passion for the dance, great mutual affection, and respect. But just as often, our dance was ordinary. Plain connection, the kind two people need to dock themselves together and start dancing, is a necessary prerequisite of tango. The deeper kind is something else — and very rare. Silvina considered it a luxury, a fragile "magic in between both people," wherein they read each other's very breath. We can't pretend that it is possible in every *tanda;* this magic is blind to skill, to preferred partners, to any strenuous attempt to tease it into bloom.

It is the sum of everything we seek in tango, the fifteenth lexeme, or the ideal word for love. It is what keeps us coming back. *All that anguish for three minutes' worth of joy.* But too much joy — the kind that turns your body into warm salt water and makes your organs quiver and your skin blur with the light. I could count the times I'd felt it on one hand: my first *volcada,* the magic All-Night dream of Enzo, my last *tanda* in Baltimore, and a moment or two with random strangers with whom I did not exchange a single word.

Marty felt it once, with me. It was a regular RoKo night, an end-of-the-evening Di Sarli set, sung by the immortal Alberto Podestá. Right away I knew that *tanda* to be special because we hardly moved. It wasn't amorous. Marty held me and we walked. Occasionally, we turned, tranquil and unflustered, like well-oiled hinges of the same enchanted door. We paused. Something was different. We did not speak between the songs. By the third, his eyes had glassed with tears. He will tell you that he shuddered, that he prayed I wouldn't notice. But our embrace held steady, heavy enough to sink through quicksand, diaphanous enough to float to sky. At the end, I took one look at him and felt the instant need to vise my heart to keep from bursting. He stumbled off, and I sat out "La cumparsita."

We speak of this occasionally. Marty says it was the first and only time his own dancing brought him to tears. It was also a gift, from him to me — that he could show me the transcendence I had wrought in him for those nine minutes, that I could cause that, I who had felt such paroxysms of grace myself, but only ever at the hands of swarthy leaders to whom I'd given so much power. I didn't need a man to breathe the dance, to create something so beautiful and then, by rights, destroy it. For a few months, I was *la bruja,* the good witch of Marty Nussbaum's tango, and I carried the dance like Di Sarli's "sentimental reason": *como una garra, hincada en la carne viva de mi emoción.* Like a talon, driven into the live meat of my soul. Though I felt a little bashful, and didn't quite know what I'd done to earn it, for those nine minutes Marty had abandoned all the acrobatics and athleticism to which he constantly aspired, and put everything he had into a single step. "No *sacada,* no *colgada, parada, volcada, soltada,* or *empanada,*" Marty joked. The simpler, the better. "You can take the simple," he said, "and *sanctify* it, elevate it, make it holy." We could put down our magnifying glasses, he seemed to say. We wouldn't need them anymore.

Marty's magic *tanda* didn't change the way I danced, but it changed me. I realized I didn't need a leader to transform me. I was yoga-strong and tango-strong and I was writing. I started to believe that, even if I could not see why or how, I might have something to give.

It's not always reciprocal. I felt this sometimes with a dancer I'll call L.K., a poet of a leader — though who knows what he felt with me. L.K. was a DJ with a lover's ear, tuned always to sweetness. He milked legato strings in a sinewed way that made me want to cease existing. For me, he always played the sweet stuff, the sad old songs with simple, candied melodies and sparkling pace. I couldn't name exactly what he did that made him different. But every so often, I would feel the magic saline tides lap at my chest. Dancing with him made me feel immortal, balanced, in firm possession of my axis and my faculties, and yet utterly lost in every song. I melted into him and he would melt right back. The room faded to white behind closed eyes.

L.K. was steady, understated, concerned only with my comfort. He had a musician's sensitivity to rhythmic texture underfoot, always leaving room to let me stretch, or to ad-lib with my heels against the floor. He listened for my interpretation of the song, for what I had to say, and gave me time. He helped me break my fear of dancing to *milonga* music, which often came up for our second *tanda*. "But I'm terrible at *milonga*," I cringed into his ear, remembering the jerky romp in Jupiter and how mortified I'd felt by my own lack of grace. He smiled and led me steadily through each bacchic labyrinth of beats. I stopped tripping, and came to love the intricacy of the syncopation, the precision of the footwork, and the fun. The "sass and the celerity." Nothing can change the energy of a room quite like *milonga*. A hundred tango grimaces soften as the frolicsome, pants-rustling engine of the *habanera* bass, the whisper of *candombe* drums, dare you not to smile. *Milonga*, pre-dater and precursor to tango, is Angolan for "argument" or "issue," Ki-Kongo for "circling lines of dancers," and the medium that syncretized the many cultures compromising at the time of tango's birth. How all the pieces fit together in conversant play. It was sparring, mischievous. *See, Mum?* I thought. *It's not all angst and emotionally stunted men.*

I had come full circle, from a beginner's first exhilaration with complicated sequences to the minimalism of maturity. The most thrilling moments of connection were the smallest. Henri Bergson once said that one *giro,* or *molinete,* told him more about the soul of a woman than ten volumes of Shakespeare. L.K.'s gift was listening for that.

Tango, I was beginning to understand, is something that you are, not something you do. At best, tango is the closest two people come to Plato's double being—joined at the navel, a four-armed, four-legged, round, revolving entity of soul satisfaction and sexual perfection. Form is irrelevant. Manner is what matters. The Dinzels claimed this came from two things: technique and *tangüedad.* Technique is necessary to control the body, to turn movement into dance, but *tangüedad* makes tango. José Gobello, a tango and Lunfardo scholar who passed away in 2013, called it "that which, if it were missing from tango, tango would not be tango." *Tangüedad* is the secret kernel at the center of the whole thing.

A simple walk across the floor is timeless, worth all the *ganchos* in the world. Even Chicho, glorious Chicho, tango's greatest improviser, took his dancing to the farthest boundaries of *nuevo* possibility, then retracted it, refined it, and went back to the stately bosom of the close embrace. He rebelled against the *milonguero* dogmatists, only to return to purity once he sensed that what he calls the *valor* of the dance had been endangered. He wanted to protect his art against the loss of the ineffable, the loss of the connection. To Chicho, the essence of tango was in *el abrazo y el otro,* the embrace and the other; between the two, we find ourselves.

I'd thought that tango was just another form of acting. It reminded me how it used to feel to lose myself onstage, and then to feel the audience's concentration — all their held breath in my hand. When the lines I spoke were both my own and some-one else's, when I moved with someone else's limbs. The deeper I fell into character, into that half possession, the deeper was the pleasure and the power. It was perfect, boundless, crystal-line. I'd always assumed that dancing was the same; the more control I gave up, the more control I'd feel. Together, very qui-etly, a leader and I would blur together, moving like one pup-pet without strings.

That feeling was connection. But it wasn't about being someone else. It was being perfectly myself in the moment when the lines of lead and follow melted, when technique was so well remembered as to be forgotten, when my eyes closed between two states of consciousness. And *that*, I decided fi-nally, was tango. The fusion of our intellect and physicality and creativity — our relationship to our bodies, other bodies, and ourselves. It was impossible, in that place, not to be honest. And that's what I was after now: finding the manner beyond form. Not in order to be held, or turn blind circles in the dark, or disappear, but to find a way, in all of it, to be sincere.

Chapter Twenty-Seven

I TAKE THE GRANITE BLOCKS IN FIVE-FOOT STRIDES. IT'S twenty-nine degrees at Lincoln Center, and I am charging through the plaza, past the library and the elevated lawn, past the winter-drained reflecting pool. My heels clack and my scarf flaps in the air behind me as I run. My date has been standing by the fountain for three-quarters of an hour, waiting to escort me to the opera. And I've been underground, stalled on an uptown C train, one car length into Canal Street — seventy blocks and over four miles south — at rush hour.

I was making an exception. His name was Barry Maguire and we had already danced and talked and gone for pints of Guinness in a Thirty-first Street Irish pub. He had already kissed me, twice. And I'd already told Mum about him, how he was kind and green-eyed, gentle, and how I dared to dream. He'd asked me formally to be his date to *Pelléas et Mélisande,* and I was forty-seven minutes late.

I sat there, helpless, on the hard, flat subway bench. Wearing my black cotton birthday dress, with heels and tights to match. The conductor garbled something unintelligible. We hadn't moved in half an hour. I crossed, recrossed my legs. I read and reread ads for hair loss remedies and bunion treatments and medical malpractice lawyers, staring at the useless cell phone in my lap. Even if I could have dialed out, my date was curiously old-fangled and didn't have a phone.

The woman next to me struck up a conversation. I told her I was late for my first proper date with a man I thought was really wonderful *and I was supposed to meet him at the Met at seven just like* Moonstruck *Cher and I couldn't call him and what if he thought I stood him up and he left and —* I took a breath.

Six or seven boorish men began to wrench apart the sliding doors, heaving and slapping until one side snapped back and we all belched forth into the station — one line, single file, polite — before the transit police could intervene.

It was after seven thirty by the time I sprinted up the stairs and onto Sixth, which was glutted with a four-lane mass of bumpers, taillights shining red and stretching all the way uptown. I scanned the intersection, the crowd, the stand of Christmas trees across the street.

"Split a cab?"

I nodded gratefully to the woman from the train. We found a vacant one by hand of providence and hurled ourselves into the back. I told the driver he should spare no speed in getting us to Lincoln Center. We had twenty minutes, tops, before the lights would blink and the lobby gong chime for the impending curtain rise.

"No way, lady," he said. "It's a parking lot."

I locked eyes with my taxi-mate. "What about the West Side Highway?"

"At this hour? Are you nuts?"

"Very possibly."

"Fine, but you ain't getting anywhere in twenty minutes."

"We don't appreciate your negativity," my new ally said.

The cabbie nosed his way toward the highway entrance, and my new friend fired up her BlackBerry, calling Lincoln Center bars.

"Hi, this is a strange request, but my friend here needs some help . . . . No we don't have a reservation." She tried half a dozen businesses. "His name is Barry and if you could just send someone to locate him at the fountain and tell him she'll be late . . . . It's their *first date!* We were stuck underground. There was *police activity.*"

When no one would help, and eight o'clock kept yawning closer, I called Peter. He was the only one I knew in walking distance.

"Sure, Biscuit," he said, and started north from Fifty-seventh Street.

Our battered yellow taxi found a window in the gridlock. The speedometer began to climb. Street signs bled behind us and, within minutes, we were pulling to the curb in front of Juilliard. I started ferreting in my purse for cash.

"It's on me," my new friend said, and handed me her business card. "Just tell me how it went." I started to articulate my thanks. She cut me off. "Go!" she cried. "Good luck!"

That's when I ran. It was important that I run. He was important. And he'd been waiting for an hour. I rounded the corner, skittering into the plaza. I raced toward the fountain, which was warm and iridescent in the winter dark. He was there, and pacing, both hands in the pockets of his overcoat. I saw him first and then he must have heard my heels because he stopped. He stood still and squinted at me through his lenses — a monument of tweed, a flash of red felt scarf.

I vaulted into his arms. "I'm so sorry!" I wailed into his hair. He held me back and murmured how it was no bother, how he thought it added certain glamour to the enterprise. Over his shoulder I spotted Peter, approaching the plaza fountain from the east. I smiled wide and gave the thumbs-up over my suitor's shoulder. Peter waved, I winked; he turned around and left.

We held hands and joined the line of dinner jackets wafting

up the stairs. We sat in the orchestra, and leaned our limbs together to the stark and somber strains of Debussy. First intermission, we stood out on the red plush carpet of the mezzanine
to survey the marble lobby underneath. We shared the half-
squashed cucumber and tomato sandwich he had smuggled
in his pocket wrapped in foil, gazing at women in elaborate
hats. Second intermission, we tapped the rims of two plastic
champagne flutes. We kissed again — just once, but in a manner
wholly inappropriate to our surroundings. I opened my eyes
and everything was red, velvet and twinkling beneath the crystal chandeliers.

We'd met in tango just a few months after I had sworn off men
— a month or two before the opera. The first time we danced,
we almost didn't. Which is to say, we chatted for half an hour,
and only halfway through "La cumparsita" did he ask me to
the floor. He trembled, a fact that he attributed to over-caffein-
ation, and I believed him, as he was three Styrofoam cups deep
into the RoKo coffee dregs. I cozied into his sandpaper stubble,
against his sprinting rabbit heart. We stood together, forming
a single lame and wingless bird, quivering between our steps.
And then the night was done.

I asked him to partner me for the next month's FeralTango
lab. It was an easy invitation, innocent. We were a match of
height and practice ethics and we made each other laugh. We
met to practice our "homework" at Mariela's *práctica* Saturday
mornings and stood chatting between bouts of drills. He kept
drinking coffee. I kept trying not to linger too long in his embrace.

I met my dad for brunch one of these Saturdays. As we sat
at the counter, tucked in to our omelets, he asked what I'd been
up to all that morning.

"Practicing."

"Tango?" he asked, salting his eggs. "With whom?"

Salting mine, as casually as I could muster, I told him it wasn't what he thought. I'd sworn myself to solitude, plus I was sure Barry had mentioned he was seeing someone. My father raised a knowing eyebrow.

"So what if he's a little dreamy," I admitted.

Barry Maguire was a shaggy and unshaven academic, roughly six feet tall. He wore third-hand baggy trousers, spectacles, and faded T-shirts often a size too small. He was manly and robust: wide-stanced, decisive in his movements, with kind eyes that held attention. He had a stomach condition that required him to take breaks from dancing to eat frequent sandwiches and bananas. Sometimes he got gussied up for tango in a rumpled collared shirt, half-unbuttoned to reveal a superfluity of auburn frizzle on his chest. He whistled, swaggered, and otherwise behaved as though he'd just dis-horsed and come out striding from the oeuvre of Austen.

He was finishing his doctorate in metaethics, working on his dissertation. He was also Scottish, so he explained this all to me in brogue. I remember chatting with him one evening at Nocturne, standing in the doorway to the DanceSport fishbowl. His hands behind his back, he scanned the floor for followers. I leaned against the door beside him — wide-eyed and slightly sweaty from a dance. We made sotto voce conversation about poetry. I said that every poem was a love poem. He disagreed. He had a Celtic sense of irony, every other word in jest, but was extremely literal where I was not. The philosopher and the artist. We bantered there, our backs against the dance floor door. I can't even remember if we danced. I do remember that his eyes looked seaglass green against his pinkish tattoo tee. Later, he would send a silly limerick and ask if it was not, definitively, an anti-love poem. *Rather not,* I wrote. *I rest my case.*

I knew he lived in Bushwick and commuted back and forth

to Princeton twice a week. He knew I lived in Adam's closet in Park Slope. I was writing, cleaning toilets. He was wrapping up his Ph.D. We talked about his work, my applications. We both liked rainy weather, tacos, Yeats. I wanted him more for his conversation than for tango. He was a lovely fellow — hale, well met. Occasionally we danced, and it was thrilling, easy, the ideal marriage of hilarity and heat. I danced back with him, active and expressive. We felt good together, giggling, dancing, pausing for a moment when the music asked us to, then, perhaps a little shyly, rejoining our hands. I ignored the way he made me feel, on the floor and off. I still didn't want to think of anyone that way.

Not surprisingly, our first kiss was a surprise. It was a Tuesday night, and blustery, with windchill in the single digits, and we were coming out of tango class. He slung an arm around my shoulders and tried to talk me into going to Sangria Practica, steering me downtown in roughly that direction. I had laryngitis and a plane to catch to Florida in seven hours; I should have been in bed, but I liked walking with him too much. It calmed me — our long-limbed gait, the light weight of his arm, wool at my neck. We paused together at a traffic light. He raised a wire-brush eyebrow, and drummed his fingers on my shoulder.

He nodded toward an Irish pub. "Fancy it?" he asked.

I assented and we lurched across the street into the bar. We unwound our scarves and ordered pints of Guinness. We took our stools and sat down, knees overlapping, and we talked, which is to say, he talked. I parried hoarsely. I was conscious of not trying to impress him. He was good, and charming, and I hoped we might be friends.

He took a great gulp of his Guinness, put the glass down on the bar, and slapped his knees. "So!" he volleyed, upbeat and looking right at me. "Tell me your deal."

"My deal?" I asked, taken aback.

"You know." He flapped his arms and shrugged. "Your life." I took a sip from my own frothy stout to hide the flush, the panic, and then stole a glance at his wide-open face. The human version of an animal with ears cocked and a wagging tail. I nearly fell back from the force of his good-natured curiosity. He had no interest in making small talk, about tango or otherwise. "You're a writer. What do you have to write about?"

"Well," I said, and started formulating a deflective yarn.

He didn't want deflection, didn't want a rehearsed tragicomedy routine. He was trying to figure what, if anything, I had to say about myself at twenty-seven. He thought all writers should aspire to novels, like the modernists, and was flummoxed by the whole mad enterprise of memoir.

"Erm, well," I stammered, feeble from the head cold, off my guard. "I had a fairly screwed-up childhood."

I tried then to change the subject, laugh it off. I fought the urge to crouch beneath my barstool. But he just squinted at me, asked me to say more. I saw my usual path through: the self-deprecating joke, the misdirection, a quick trip to the bathroom — timed just right — and, on return, a brand-new conversation. People didn't usually press. Then again, I had been writing it for weeks, typing steadily from my twin bed in the tango flop apartment. I'd woven details into sample essays for admission — still anonymous, addressed to strangers. If I could type it, if I could put it on the page and put my name there with it, then why not start saying it out loud?

I took a breath and told the truth. Not for him. Not even because of him, exactly. At that point, he was still a stranger — dreaminess notwithstanding. I did it for me. I didn't tell him everything, but I set the bones. He put his beer down, shone his full attention on me. Asked questions to which I gave unguarded answers. The truth tumbled out: a handful of plain sentences, alien and quick.

He was still there when I finished — this man who heard

me, saw me, took another sip of beer and then, with genuine compassion, had the good sense to make me laugh. "I turned out okay?" I offered.

"We'll see." He grinned. Never once did he say I was "well adjusted." Possibly I wasn't. Possibly he could tell. Possibly everybody could — with any insight. It didn't matter. But there was Barry, still perched on his barstool, eyes still smiling and his knees still leaned to mine. The way he looked at me — unflinching and unhesitating — hadn't changed. We cheersed to my resilience.

The conversation shifted naturally, but something in the air between us shifted too. I relaxed. I made dark jokes I don't usually get to make for years into a friendship, and he laughed at them, sincere. We talked about our work, our travels, art. I tried to explain my undergraduate thesis about the cult of Dionysos. He tried to explain a few finer points of his research. We laughed easily, swatting each other's legs and arms for emphasis. He continued being debonair and I continued croaking back retorts, almost as good as the old black-and-whites, and blushing every time I thought I caught a twinkle in his seaside eyes.

We debated whether my metaphor for leading versus following was right.

"*Is* it like chess?" he asked with a forehead scrunch, and I explained.

"You see what we close our eyes to," I said. "You stare, you steer, you peacock. We're free and off in flight." I added, "But it's impossible. Our objectives never match. You never feel what we feel. The moment can't be wholly shared."

He thought for a moment, frowned, then tapped his finger on my knee.

"Sexing chickens!" he exclaimed, the finger waggling in the air. "It's like sexing chickens." It was my turn to frown. He went on. "You have to look really really hard to see what sex a baby chicken is." Shared moments, he argued, were possible, as long as both parties were present. Leaders weren't always only navigating. There was a place in the dance, he said, where the lead bypassed technique and navigation, and he moved from somewhere else, inside the music. When he was no longer thinking to himself *boy, girl, boy, girl,* but seeing the conveyor belt of chicks and just *knowing* which was which—though not necessarily aware of why.

"That's the moment you feel," he said. "It is shared."

"You mean the moment of transcendence everyone in tango seeks is just the mutual sexing of chickens?"

"Exactly," he said.

"Sexing chickens," I said.

"Sexing chickens," he agreed, and clinked my glass.

The rest was effortless. I'd said already what I could have spent two years avoiding telling him. I wish that it were all I needed, that all my shame disintegrated in that one bright honest moment, lost in the December winds; it wasn't quite so simple. It was merely a beginning, our beginning—but for once, I'd started with the truth.

He was still there, my garrulous friend, with that arm over my shoulders, steering me toward a hotel bar somewhere on Tenth, a place that served us treacly off-season negronis. We were the only patrons, hunching together, elbows against the neon bar. We might as well have been the only two people awake and alive in Manhattan. When it closed, we trotted east, arms around each other's overcoats and shouting at the cold. It was the kind of cold that tears your eyes and floods your nostrils with the smell of sea. The stoplights blurred and it was Christmas, Thirty-fourth Street, Herald Square. When he bent his face to mine, honest to god, it still felt unexpected. I closed my eyes to sudden silence and the little watery blinks of red and green. Right there on Eighth Avenue. We missed I don't know how many traffic lights, how many little neon walking men. We kissed until it wasn't cold out anymore. And then we went inside Penn Station and kissed more, against a dirty pillar by a shuttered-up falafel shop.

I flew to Florida four hours later, for a visit, half-convinced that it had been a fever dream. I expected Barry to evaporate, as all other tango mirages had. He'd take a small piece of me with him, if he went, that gift of trust, and I was already scheming how to weather that loss gracefully. How to play it cool. I did an early gift exchange with my mother, my sore throat soaking up the warm, then headed home. But when I landed Sunday night, I took the subway straight to RoKo — just in case. He shot me a *cabeceo* laced with something between hunger and relief. We both trembled that time. The RoKorazzi caught us in the exact moment when we moved from close embrace to open, but had not opened our eyes.

I was dumbfounded. After the opera, we spent every night together until he flew home to Glasgow on the eve of Christmas Eve. Night one, we went for midnight wine and chatted, idly, as he twiddled with my Claddagh. At some point, I looked down to find it overthrown, likely accidentally, my heart now closed to village boys. I left it that way. He took me home, showed me his bookshelf, kissed me chastely, standing in his kitchen steeping cups of chamomile. At four that morning, his roommates burst across the threshold of his loft with cigarettes and bags of groceries and started popping cheap beer cans and chopping onions. They'd heard so much about me. Someone handed me a plate of *puttanesca,* and we all sat down to dine, just as the blackness beyond their massive window turned to blue. At dawn, we bundled up in woolen jumpers, and went upstairs to watch the sunrise turn the skyline salmon pink.

Night two, after a day of galleries, Neruda, napping: Nocturne. Night three, more dancing (RoKo), and then another late-night pasta dinner, a bottle of Korbel, a conversation about art. I set an alarm and fell asleep to Pushkin stories read aloud. Night four, a film, and mulled wine at a bluegrass bar. We traipsed from pub to pub with his roommates — gin and chips, a lunar eclipse. We sat around a Brooklyn bonfire, drinking hot spiked cider as the moon turned red, then back to white. We smelled of woodsmoke when we went to sleep. Night five was stolen, his flight home for Christmas canceled on account of weather. We spent it in his empty loft, sharing warm pie and prosecco, talking about his work, my work. We danced — slow — to Miles Davis while, outside, it snowed. He carried me upstairs.

I had to tell him then, before his hands removed the last lace barrier between us, how my body had been spoiled — and not just by the uncles. Part of me was sure that this confession, once uttered, would be the end of us, so I had steeled myself and put it off until I was there, beneath him, my nose in his neck. The thought of losing him burned in my chest. "Don't be daft," he said, and held me tighter, touched me more tenderly, wiped away my tears. He didn't want perfection. He wanted me, as messy as I was.

We made love. I wept, but those tears were warm and mild, and joyful. It wasn't dancing, but it was delicious — all the flesh and indecorum I had ever shied away from made suddenly luminous by mutual desire. My heart cleaved open with the ache of risk.

"I'll see you in a week, you wonderful creature, you," he said in the morning, kissing me goodbye. I stood on my toes, my naked legs goosefleshed and stretching up into his candy-red jumper. He flew downstairs *bah-rum-pum-pum-pumming* carols, and was gone.

Even then, I doubted him. I smoothed the quilt across his mattress, dressed, and left his jumper folded on his bed. I took the train back into midtown, where I cleaned someone else's house. I went back to my pantry, slept eleven hours. Danced. Spent Christmas Eve and Christmas Day with my father, who cautioned me to guard my heart; I was, after all, the daughter known for desperate, chancy choices, the daughter perhaps too eager to love.

A blizzard hit, and slowed the city to a stop. I couldn't dance. I took pictures of city buses stalled mid-street in drifts of snow. I studied math. The night before he came back, I was so nervous that I vomited up the bag of Skittles I had eaten at a movie, right into a snowbank. But the year drew to a close, and he returned, and there he was.

That afternoon I went to yoga class, lingering too long in *savasana*, breathing in the room sweat and the rubber mat, breathing out my doubt. I went home through the twilight of the new year, dressed, and went back out to his apartment, half-expecting to have made him up inside my head. But he was there, and he was still there with me later as we shot cheap champagne corks across the factory roofs of Bushwick, as we all linked arms and belted *auld lang syne*. He was with me when I shoved manila envelopes into a mailbox one Tuesday night outside an Office Depot in Times Square. With a little thump, there went my gamble: transcripts, letters, pages full of newborn prose. And then we danced. He was with me all that winter, while I waited for the news. He was with me so long past the point when I expected him to disappear.

Kerouac wrote, *"It's only later you learn to lean your head in the lap of God, and rest in love."* This took a while. Falling in love felt like a terminal disease. A beautiful flu I couldn't, wouldn't cure. Beside his nightstand built of books, we slept braided together as if the bed might plummet down the chute into the river Styx. It felt like lying in an empty field at the close of dusk, the world a quiet, windy blue, no sense of earth beneath us, no sense of world beyond.

It felt like a *volcada*.

We kept warm in the frozen grey of Brooklyn, hunkered in his loft, amid the squat industrial sprawl south of Flushing. We stayed in for cheap and cheerful suppers with his flatmates — more raucous dinner parties staged at dawn. We drank whisky out of jam jars. We read each other's work, drank tea, and sat together behind laptops at big wooden tables, shivering. We stood on his graffitied roof, with our hands stuffed inside each other's pockets, overlooking all the concrete buildings stacked like blocks of ice, and missed the moment of the sunrise, precisely when the pink eyelid of the island opened wide.

We weren't going to *milongas* much, but every day with him was dancing, one long *tanda* made for two. We played Canaro in the front room, with winter blowing in through cracks between the massive windows. We pivoted across the concrete floor in close embrace, dirtying our woolen socks. Unshowered, breakfast on our breath. We danced in the kitchen and the freight elevator, which swayed as we spun. We danced in the frigid corridor beside the dumpster. We danced in doubled sweaters, scarves, fingerless gloves. We hummed music to each other while we did *sacadas* on the subway platform, waiting for the L, the Q, the 1.

You might expect that we sang tangos to each other — or thought about our love in tango terms. We did not. Most tangos aren't for love; they're stories of poverty, injustice, long-lost lovers, broken hearts. Songs about betrayal — half hopeless and heart-shredding, the other half for dandies on the prowl, *conquistadores* congratulating one another on their well-oiled shoes and pompadours. One of my favorites, "Que te importa que te llore," begs, *"Déjame mentir que volverás, que volverás con el ayer,"* or, leave me with the lie that you'll return, that you'll return with yesterday. Love is an illusion. What does it matter to you, sweetheart, if I cry?

Then there's "Invierno," the most deceitful melody in all the world — knives out even as it spins its cotton candy web, sweet and reminiscent of a childhood carousel. *Volvió,* Maida sings, *el invierno con su blanco ajuar, y la escarcha comenzó a brillar en mi vida sin amor.* Winter has returned with its white veil, and frost now sparkles in his loveless life. The orchestra cascades into a weightless plunge, the painted horses sink from view, and the world continues turning as the lovers' laughter fades. It was a cruel parable for my winter — our winter, which I hoped might swallow the world in snow and stay forever.

The lovers in tango mourned and grieved, lamented, sneered. Varela's red-hot rendering of "Historia de un amor" was nothing more than passion spent, a heart relinquished to a woman gone. She gave him light then snuffed it when she left. There are songs like "Pasional" that speak of love-right-now, of love that breaks the chest, but that is tortured love; it isn't real. It is dying a thousand times of agitation. Lips whose kisses trammeled reason. Worship. Burning thirst. The famous line: *estás clavada en mí como una daga en la carne.* You are driven into me like a dagger in my flesh. "Pasional" asks you to die in someone's arms. It is a savage fantasy, and after three minutes it is done.

Barry and I were not a savage fantasy. We were something else, and I could find no song that summed it up. In stockinged feet, at home, we danced to "Farol," a song about a lonely lamppost in the *arrabal* whose light, with tango hidden in a pocket, was losing brilliance and had become a cross. Played by Pugliese, sung by viola-voiced Roberto Chanel, it's full of *síncopas* and soaring riffs above an almost plodding beat in the piano and the *bandoneón.* It's relatively simple, as tangos go — sweet in places, dramatic in the *variación* — and dancing it is no act of courtship. All the same, imagine being cheek to cheek and listening to the words of the elegiac Homer Expósito, his poem about the workers' dreams that mingle in the dim light thrown from a dark corner, conversing with the sky, while far away some clock chimes two. It is not about romantic love. And yet you reach your half-gloved hand up to your lover's neck. His arm tightens a little around your waist and you turn together, bundled in the dark fourth-floor hallway of a factory, in scarves and sweaters, unwashed hair. The romance is not in the music, but in how you feel the music — how you feel your own old world dying around you, how you feel yourselves agreeing how to move.

For the first few weeks, I will admit, we reveled in the amorousness of it. We kissed in practice rooms, kissed during dancing drills. There was that added edge of being lusty in a dance that lends itself so easily to lust. And maybe having held each other on the dance floor made it somehow easier for us to throw our arms around each other that first night in December, sprinting down the street. We already knew each other's bodies. What was left for us to learn was who we were beneath our clothes and bones.

I liked my body when it was with his body. It was cummings's *so quite a new thing.* And I liked his body, his *hows,* the thrill of him, our *eyes big love-crumbs* in the dark. Being with him made me want to shout and sob and laugh and recite verse — and all at once. I called Mum to explain my rapture, and she laughed at me. "Oh, Beanie," she chuckled. "You idiot. That's how it's supposed to feel."

She was right, I realized. She'd never wanted me to swing from chandeliers into the beds of men, or take to wearing racy leopard underpants, or to be "good" at sex. That province was hers. She'd only wanted me to find a way to feel loved enough to love somebody back. Enough to melt away the shame.

"But I'm too happy," I told her. "He's going to wreck my heart."

"So what if he does?" she asked. "At least now you know what you've been missing."

For a while, I feared sleep. The Barry in my dreams who came and went like tides. There was a lunar pull to him. I no longer feared being alone, but constantly anticipated how it ached when, finally, ultimately, he would leave.

There were times when — just to look at him — I could feel that saline warmth flood through me. We were connected even when there wasn't any music, even when we didn't dance. At some point, I realized, I had to make a choice. Whether to fear the unpredictable catastrophe, or close my eyes and trust. Not just him — myself. The choice that I had made, the choice of him. I stopped saying *when this ends* (because I was certain that it would) to my inquiring friends. Barry was my exception, my educated guess, a leap of faith — and would be, to whatever end. There was no armor to avail me. I had to stand right there in front of him, aloud and bare.

I worked mornings, all dishwater, dusting, and news radio. I went to yoga almost every day, using the mat, the wooden floor, the concrete angles of the walls to steady me, then ate the same three-dollar salad. Sometimes Dad joined me, and treated us to oatmeal raisin cookies and a latte. I enrolled in a night writing class at Hunter College, as a palate cleanser once a week, and spent my afternoons penning detective stories, in the library, in coffee shops, at my place, or at his. On Tuesday nights, before our tango class, we met to eat our brought-from-home dinners over paper cups of coffee at a deli on Seventh Avenue. Months later, long after we'd run out of money to finance FeralTango, I passed that deli, finally noticing its name. It was printed right there on the awning: The New Start.

There is a Fresedo song, "Buscándote," dated 1941. It may be the most beautiful tango ever written, the song that makes you stick with dancing despite the doldrums of your beginner Basic class. It's played often enough. It is steady and slow and good for practicing, for skiing across the room in socks. Maybe it was the first song that made your eyes well up in a *milonga*.

Three-quarters of the way through, Ricardo Ruiz comes in and in his satin morning voice sings, *"Vagar . . . ,"* which means to wander. He speaks of the *cansancio,* or weariness, of his endless "going," his *eterno andar,* and his *ansias enormes de llegar,* huge anxieties to finally arrive. *"Sabrás,"* he sings again. You'll know. *Que por la vida fui buscándote.* That all my life I've looked for you. Hastening his wandering, he strung long roads together, traveled leagues and leagues.

It is a song about finding love — searching for it without even knowing what it is or why — and resting there until you're sent away. It says, now that I've found you, love, if you prefer, I'll leave. It builds a yesterday into tomorrow, and hopes that neither ever comes. In two minutes and fifty-one seconds, it was the truest love song I had ever heard.

Chapter Twenty-Eight

WHEREVER THERE ARE BODIES, THERE WILL BE BODY HEAT. AT first I didn't understand this. I was afraid of sex and thought that it and tango could be separated, like two disagreeing children. This was, admittedly, naïve. They are inseparable.

In the *milongas* of Buenos Aires, and all over the world, men and women mine tango for romantic love, companionship, torrid dalliances, and one-night tussles. The dance floor is an easy place for lonely people to meet other lonely people. Despite what Robin Thomas said, rock climbing isn't worse; you may be bound to each other — physically, by rope — but the rules of basic math remain. One and one still make an even two. There is no heart-strung soundtrack, no instruments that wail with human anguish. And no pope ever tried to ban it on the grounds of prurience. The thrill does not come close.

A tango is not an act of sexual congress, but there are certain inalienable parallels. With few exceptions, you can learn a lot from how a person dances about how he or she makes love. And so the lines are sometimes blurred. A thousand girls before and after me fall for a thousand men like Enzo every night. The dance floor is rife with drama, coupling and uncoupling, betrayal and desire.

I think back to what Cesar Coelho said when I was still a

tango schoolgirl in my freshly ironed pleats, when I was too unripe to fathom what he meant by "secrets shared between the bodies." What is said and unsaid as we dance. *I don't know yours and you will not know mine.* Without words, and with a stranger, you dance everything you wished you'd written in every love letter you never sent. In every eulogy you never gave. You do this with your body — with the push and pull of your embrace, your breath, the pressure in your palms, your eyelids lightly, tightly closed, the tenor of embellishments, the manner of your step. Your *tangüedad.* We perform our pain, elation. Our sad thoughts dance. Perhaps you drag your heel in a wide arc around your leader's leg to slow a turn because the music moves you, or you caress his foot with yours. You're speaking the song, like Chicho, saying, *this is in here, and also this;* and often *this* is pain. Or reverie, or lust. Bitterness ebbing away. And when two dancers feel the same thing for the same pulse of piano, the same snarl of *bandoneón,* it doesn't matter whether they are talking *to* or *through* each other of some forgotten, private wound. The secret has been said.

If you're attracted to that partner, yes, of course, a tango — any tango — can be an overture. Just as any comment can be a come-on. Dancing does not manufacture feeling; it releases it. In the classic sense, a *tanda* is an act of romance: three minutes in the mysteries, remote from all things commonplace. A taste of courtly love. Imagine veils and corsets, a sword hilted at your leader's side. But consummation equals certain death. That's why tango flings cannot survive: a passion built on tango only is illusion — a game of love, not love itself.

It is easy to become confused. After all, you share an axis sometimes. You move in each other's arms, close enough to taste each other's breath. It is sensual and satisfying, and so easy to mistake the closeness of the close embrace for intimacy. I had done that twice. I'd asked *what if.* With Barry, now, there was no question.

. . .

When spring came, we took a discount bus to Washington, D.C., to ¿Por Qué No?, a new tango festival attended mostly by local dancers. As volunteers, we got in free. We turned up in the early afternoon and checked in to a room that we could only just afford. It was our first weekend away, our first shared suitcase — my half packed with tango clothes and newly purchased lingerie — and our first foray into the challenges of couples tango.

Our duties didn't interfere much with the festival. We helped set up the dance floor, lugging heavy wooden squares from loading docks up to the ballroom before drilling them in place. We rolled partitions in and out to form and unform classrooms, bolting them to brackets in the floor. We wore sweatpants and dance sneakers until the time came to shower and dress for evening *milongas,* where we validated passes at the door. We were otherwise free to do just as we pleased.

It wasn't lonely, as Baltimore had been, because we had each other. Though all the usual frustrations applied. Festivals are especially difficult for followers. For all the tango world celebrates women, shows them off, *deifies* them, even, the fact remains that, at least according to the *códigos,* the social dancing codes, the men do all the asking. A follower can't *cabeceo* if a leader utterly avoids her gaze. Once a man identifies his preferred followers, he has total freedom with his invitations. He asks whomever he wishes, when he wishes, to the music he finds most appealing. Women of his level, likely looking on from the perimeter, see him in action and accept. One run of bad luck sidelines a follower for hours. If you are not among the favored, it's easy to find this state of affairs unfair.

Barry was uncharacteristically shy, and so he sympathized. I'd slink along the *milonga*'s edge and he'd slink right behind me, like a child at his mother's pant leg. Even when you're attached, it is important to dance with other people — otherwise your tango stales. We goaded each other into dances. "Look," I'd say, "there's Midriff. Go ask her!" He'd say, "Red Trousers is free; stand over there where he can see you." He was genuinely sensitive to the plight of wallflowers. Months later, he would make an abortive attempt to start a movement urging the New York tango scene to try things Sadie Hawkins style. This degenerated into a contentious online gender war in which the chauvinists all bloviated about how the man *must* ask the woman *because that's just how it is done,* the feminists all railed against the patriarchy, but the consensus became clear: we all preferred the status quo. The convention isn't perfect, but it works.

When hunting for dances, Barry and I respectfully avoided eye contact across the crowd. He went his way; I went mine. For all his shyness and egalitarian ideals, he was the better strategist. Where I wandered aimlessly, half the time with eyes trained on the wainscoting, Barry had a system. When dancing somewhere new, he opted for a humble stratagem — decent followers who weren't getting many dances. He went for foreigners, or B-list ladies in the corners, culled from the flock at large. In his words, "the wee wounded gazelles."

I was much less organized, and still quite bashful with my *cabeceo,* but I managed. At first, when I saw him dancing with a string of beauties in bandeau tops and bangles, like bedazzled deities, it stung a little somewhere deep. Perhaps he felt the same to see me in the arms of tango dandies, asserting their tender grip around my hips. We adjusted. I cracked an eyelid from within the arms of someone else, to locate him across the room. He did the same. He had his peacock strut and so had I. Sometimes I performed a little if I caught him watching me. Sometimes we even shared a wink. We fell into the couple code, which is to say, we danced the first few *tandas* just to warm each other up, and then the last two, plus a special something in the middle — usually a *vals,* or something exquisite, like "Farol," which, by that time, had taken on the aching resonance of our romance. It was marvelous: checking in with him and flitting to and fro, receiving small and secret kisses on the sweaty brow. I had never been secure, but there, with him, I was. The *milonga* was our shared world where he was king, preening and lashing his tail against savannah flies, and I hunted like a queen. I stretched my yoga-sinewed haunches out behind me, flirted, danced. He was charming, strong, and threw pouncing leaps into his lead (like valiant house pets after vacuum cleaners) and bouncy wiggles that made the ladies laugh. At any point, however, we could unpuff, retract our claws, and fold away our plumage. We could dance together and the games of prey would fade to privacy. And when we tired of dancing, we went upstairs and sprawled out on our queen-sized bed, in various stages of undress, with take-out pizza, pale ale, and CNN. That felt like coming home.

By light of day, we took class with the unsinkable Silvina Valz. It was my first exposure to her in the classroom. She was as exacting as Mariela had been, but more brilliant, and much kinder — as if it actually mattered to her whether her students improved. Her ideology was radical, but her approach was not. She strolled about, coiling and re-coiling her thick lariat of hair, demonstrating, sometimes crouched beside us on the floor, how someone's leg should move. She sees herself as something of a missionary, a bannerwoman for Gustavo. When she speaks of him, she speaks in sentence fragments with emotion in her throat. Personally, Gustavo is "very touching," "very Argentine sentimental," "lovely." Professionally, he is a revolutionary.

"Gustavo and these kids," she calls them, meaning the *laboratorio* crowd, took "an intellectual approach." They are the theorists, the prophets and professors of the dance. They made teaching tango possible, but she will not call them teachers. If a student is not immediately capable of translating all that innovation into physical mechanics, he or she requires a peda-gogue. Someone like Silvina to take Gustavo's methodology, his "vocabulary for transmission," and help mere mortals access it. "In *this* specific body," she says. Her accent was pure *porteño castellano,* the *zhe* sound a straw broom swept across her "y's" and double "l's." Her approach was similar to Sara's, albeit more empathic. Her tango is a circle that begins and ends with who you are; she might as well add *in this specific soul.*

Silvina spoke more confidently than any woman I had ever met, even in English, which was her third language and dotted with Spanish syntax and random words in French. "Tango is *nostalgie,*" she said; a woman is sometimes *machiste.* She was contemporary tango's grand philosopher and muse, and, at the end of three days with her, Barry and I were ready to sell our worldly goods and follow her into the desert. We promised each other we would practice seven days a week until our bodies understood.

Technique seems such a tedious pursuit at first — rigorous and slow to learn, particularly when you signed up for amuse-ment. But without it, something will always be missing in your dance. Without it, there can be no *tangüedad.* Even if tango, to you, is just a hobby. "So what?" Silvina says. "You can get the best of pleasure that you can get, so let's go for it." Dedicate yourself to mastering even a fraction of its intricacy and you will begin to own it. That's how to get your body and your brain to disappear into your art. That's how to melt. Concentrating on tiresome fundamentals today internalizes them tomorrow, when you can truly sex your chickens. Move, unencumbered by your limitations. It is arduous, but worth it in the end.

I had idolized Silvina since the first time I had seen her lead. She was supernatural to me. She had so much power, a power she took such pleasure in relinquishing that her vulnerability made her even mightier. When asked about unfairness in the dance — men leading women, men doing all the asking — she dismisses it as play. "We cannot take that seriously," she says. Tradition is just another structure, the base from which we fly.

Then again, a woman never has to languish idly, waiting for a man to come and claim her. Every follower, regardless of her level, has the right to initiate the *cabeceo,* to choose a leader and stare pointedly in his direction until catching his eye. They both reserve the right to look away.

Your dance is very personal, a combination of how you're built and your imagination. And Silvina is traditional at heart. It is the paradox inherent in her tango. "I am *machiste,*" she says, "because I am absolutely so feminine."

More than anyone else, Silvina made me understand that there were some things one could only say in sex or tango. To do either well, you must present your body to another. There is little room for timidity or doubt. You have to know your body well enough to give and to receive — with restraint or with abandon. Lead and follow interlace and when it's good, a sweet equality occurs.

"That's all I ever wanted for you," my mother said, as if to explain her scandalizing candor about sex. "After everything you went through, I wanted you to stand a chance of feeling that way someday." She hadn't wanted me to hide in tango, to play dress-up with a fragile sense of sexuality, without learning the difference between physical act and intimacy, without working first to heal.

I had been afraid of touch, but there was nothing left to fear; the worst had already occurred. I'd craved touch, been overwhelmed by symphonies after years of silence. Enzo had unlocked a part of me that terrified me, so I'd shuttered it. But desires denied led only to disaster. I learned to want and need, and to assert, but not to wait for someone who would listen. And so I closed myself again.

The mistake I'd made was not in yielding to desire, to the

what if, but in failing to see beyond it to where physical intimacy turns into love and trust. That's what cannot happen on the dance floor — and will never happen off it unless you're ready with your body and yourself. Unless you're sure enough of each to share.

So much of the dance, according to Silvina, "*is* the relation of seduction." In the end, we can't avoid it. Sex is part of tango — and of life. "That doesn't mean it needs to end up there," she says. The dance is just a means of setting free the *pulsion,* as she calls it, the drive to show up, fully, in the presence of another human body, either naked or in dancing clothes.

I thought about my mother, about Robin Thomas, about wanting — needing — to be held. Dancing the so-called woman's role, I'd learned fragility, surrender. I'd learned how to be touched. But it felt like so much more. Learning to be half of one embrace had taught me to be whole. "It's not true what your mother says," Silvina told me — about the predatory men and desperate women, occasionally the other way around. That element exists in tango, but does not define it. "We all come back for this embrace," she said. "For this contentment." It is and isn't about joy. It is and isn't about sex. "You know when someone takes care of you?" she asked. I nodded; finally, I did. "Peaceful," she said, and I remembered Kerouac again. It wasn't all just man and woman, being held. For Silvina, tango was the path by which our lives were shaped. A way for "living honestly and deeply," in the embrace and out. In life and in art.

On the fourth and final evening of the festival, Barry and I danced until the clocks sprang back for daylight saving, then danced an hour more. Neither of us had landed any dances to write home about, but we'd dressed up every night and gone down to the ballroom anyway, hunting for partners and "sparkling in our muscles," as Silvina Valz had said to do. We danced until "La cumparsita," which, as the first we'd ever danced to, had become our song. It was just past three, by the new time of early spring. He caught my eye across the crowd. We found our way through all the milling dancers to an open patch of floor. He opened up his arms and took my right hand in his left. We stepped toward each other, torso to torso, heart to heart, and we stood still, listening, until the music told us where to go.

It was a quiet thing.

I closed my eyes, and thought about the *what if,* how it disappears only when your heart is tuned to someone. When there is no more need for make-believe. Our tango was bigger than three minutes. It unfolded, deepened, and became a space for everything we could not put to words.

The crowd applauded warmly to conclude the festival, and then receded. Barry and I took up a pair of power drills and set about stripping the floor. By the time we'd helped to ferry all the wooden flats down to the loading dock, it was nearly dawn. Too wired for sleep, we strolled the silent streets of Alexandria. It was cold still. We walked hand in hand, the whole world to ourselves. *Sabrás,* I hummed, wordless, as we crawled into bed, the music and the lateness pulsing in my ears, *que por la vida fui buscándote.* I had looked for him so long, but also for myself. The bad dreams were fading to belief, which was another very quiet thing.

Chapter Twenty-Nine

DAY ONE: A STABBING, UNWALKABLE PAIN IN MY LEFT HIP keeps me from RoKo on a Sunday night. I'm left behind with Barry's roommates at the dinner table, while he marches off into the night, armed with bananas and his tango shoes. He kisses me goodbye, the smell of ninety-nine-cent coffee on his breath. I dig my thumbs into the flesh around my joint, hoping to bore into the offending ligament and tear it out by fist.

Day two: I spend a humiliating afternoon in paper shorts, among the brittle elderly in an orthopedic x-ray waiting room. A surgeon consigns me to a chiropractor, both recommending ice and ibuprofen, a strict regimen of rest. It's just a muscle strain.

Week two: the chiropractor returns me to the orthopedist. The pain has started shooting up my vertebrae. An MRI shows one herniated lumbar disc, another slightly bulging—but neither serious enough to warrant surgery. "Good news!" he exclaims, before dismissing me. I am prescribed more bed rest, and more ice.

I cry. It seems a minor injury, but still I feel like my world is ending. I lie on bags of frozen peas. I read, and watch a lot of movies with my laptop propped up on my knees. No yoga, no fast walking, no bending from the waist, no lifting, carrying, sitting, stretching, strenuous behavior, sex — and, more damning: no tango. I panic, certain Barry will abandon me — and our new, ice-spun us — if I can't dance.

Week three: I still can't dance. The ibuprofen is making mincemeat of my stomach. I have chemical burns from overuse of heating patches. I have gained five pounds. I take a lot of taxis I cannot afford. I ride in elevators. I start having dreams of dancer's pose, *natarajasana,* only I'm in tango shoes. Then unkind morning comes. I lie in bed imagining myself in heels in downward dog. The surety of the yoga mat seems far away. I feel my muscles turn to pudding underneath my skin.

Week four: I stop counting weeks.

Barry cares for me, carries me downstairs, ferries me up in service lifts, and breakfasts me in bed. I write while he writes. I sleep while he dances. He has the patience of ten men, so I hate myself for hating him when he goes dancing, three, four times a week. I turn my face away from him, his metronomic heavy sleep, deep in the wee hours, to cry until the muscle drugs thud sufficient tiredness through my blood. Tomorrow he will dry my tears and make good-natured jokes at my expense. "You silly girl, it's just a bit of nature. You'll be back to normal in no time." We'll go see a violinist rassle Paganini one night in lieu of dancing. We'll spend some Sunday evenings eating garlic, drinking beer. I'll make elaborate dinners, start roasting meats in hopes that the smell will keep him home.

Eventually, I put two and two together. The D.C. festival. The dance floor and the power drill. The sixteen screws per every wooden square that we put down and then took up that weekend. The hours I spent, bent and drilling, still in heels. And Barry's voice repeating in my head. "Be careful, babe. Don't hurt your back."

· · ·

The weeks turn into months. I give up any hope of yoga, and shove my mat into the closet — without bending at the waist; I lower myself as one stiff trunk. I do everything at half speed, still cleaning house, but shoddily; the sweeping and the bending aren't good for me. I feel that I am taking up too much of people, of their sympathy. I spend hours and hours alone, not moving, with no way out of my own head. Three days a week, I see the chiropractor. Three days a week, I ask:

"Can I ride a bicycle?"

"No, you certainly cannot."

He kneels beside the exam table and gouges a thumb pad deep into my butt flesh. My gluteus medius and my psoas have pulled too tight, wrenching my spine, and my gluteus maximus has erupted into little fascial knots, hard blooms to be elbowed smooth.

"Ow," I say.

"Yeah," he says. "That's pretty bad."

When Dr. K has done all he can, he passes a giant vibrator over the soft tissue of my backside, pausing at my hamstrings, which are taut almost to snapping. He tells me about his wife and lawn up in Connecticut, both of which he tends evenings and weekends, and about his yoga practice. He is a yoga fiend. Well, I think. Bully for him.

"The elliptical machine?" I ask.

"Hmmm, no."

"How about running?"

"Definitely not."

I pay yet another co-pay.

"Have a nice weekend," we each say. He rummages through his supply closet and tosses me a blow-up lumbar pillow — royal blue — which I dutifully inflate whenever I am seated.

Weeks blur. I walk slowly, carry nothing. I lie on my back, my side. I cramp and twist, futilely rub whatever's sore. I am poked and plied.

"Can I do Pilates?" I ask, hopeful.

"No."

"Gyrotonics?"

"Maybe next month."

"Rowing?"

"Are you insane?"

Having a back injury means spending a lot of time flat out on hardwood floors, tears slipping from your cheekbones, as everyone who passes asks you why you're crying. It means not lifting anything, not even my new rolly backpack up the subway stairs. It means not buying juice or gallon milk without a chaperone to carry groceries. But, worse still, it means nights spent knees-up in your bed, lying with your laptop open, ice against your lumbars, while your boyfriend goes to the *milonga*. It isn't egotism; that world does quite literally turn without you.

Oh lead me to a quiet cell, Ms. Parker said. The silence fell with velvet heft. The lonely melancholy next. At first I was missed. *Where have you been? Why aren't you dancing?* And then nothing. No water cooler. No community. Just me inside my head.

I offered to work the door at RoKo, taking cash and names while perching on a swivel chair, just to be around the music, and to avoid staying at home. At some point, during one joyous romp of a *milonga tanda,* the little neurons started flaring up my back with greater force. I had to bite my lip to stop the sobs.

The worst part was the rush of insecurity. Barry both was and wasn't just another tango man. We both had and hadn't courted in the ballroom, on those polished floors. Tango both was and wasn't part of who we were. Before, we'd danced together, danced apart. It was fine then for him to dance with other women, when I was in that world with him. Now, suddenly, his nights seemed full of feral evening minxes in their up-slit skirts and strappy blouses — claws clinging to his shirt back, tongues lapping for his ears. A jealous Gorgon started weaving snakes into my hair. The corners of the room grew dark, acquiring the humidity of sex; I heard my mother's voice on loop again. I lashed out with the fury of a woman prematurely scorned.

Tango was the only thing we ever fought about. I picked fights and pouted. I was sour, angry, and impatient, but mostly I was afraid of losing him. *Not you too,* cried out my child's voice — but who could blame him if he left? In the act of making ugly faces, wincing walking up the stairs, I snapped at him. I was in pain. As if that justified my churlishness.

What was I afraid of? That he would really leave? Or that I had fooled myself into another dancing fantasy, turning daisy-plucking circles in the dark? He loved me not. He loved me. Surely he could not love me now.

"You'll chuck me to the curb with all the other useless junk and ugly lamps," I finally said, eyes dewing with embarrassment.

"Of course I won't," he told me. "Don't be daft." He objected to my lack of faith in him. "Honestly, Meghan. It's insulting."

He was right, of course. But doubt was my default. And without the daily yoga and the dancing, nothing could stop the rodents running through my head. Tango was the place where all the parts of me converged, and that place had been barred. Tango had sewn me back into my body, then taught me to live in it. Now I had been fettered there, strangled by its infuriating limits. Where before there was the *bandoneón,* now there was only silence. A refrigerator hum. There were no new *asanas* to reach for, nowhere I could move until my mind went blank. I missed the way I had once pretzeled into bliss. How I'd spiraled into meditation in a pair of practice shoes. Where before I'd found my stillness only in the movement, I now was faced with finding movement in my stillness.

· · ·

Because I couldn't dance, I started listening differently. I tagged along with Barry to *milongas* once a week or so and sat there watching. There, but not there. As though stuck inside some closed bud that refused to bloom, where tangos echoed wet and tinny, played from the outside in.

I listened to the lovers who lamented. About the woman who'd just left, the woman who was never theirs, the woman who threw away her girlish innocence to become a creature of the seedy streets and cabarets downtown. In "Milonguita," I was little Ester, girl-next-door, grown up to be a flower of the night, wasted on the men who took her home; if she cried they'd say it was because she drank too much champagne. In "Remembranza," I was shipwrecked, knowing I would lose myself in the horizon, but not yet willing to resign myself to being lost.

I listened to Pugliese's steady pulse of *bandoneón,* the nails-across-a-chalkboard strings, the singer wailing in the tenor-sphere about the *flor* of his illusion. The strings thump like a drumroll, and the singer curls his lips over his teeth, almost sneering the line: *Aaah! . . . olvida mi desden,* forget my scorn. He begs his lover to return so that their love can bloom again. He sings about his withered hydrangeas of pain. I'd danced that song a hundred times, in the last, show-stopping *tanda* of the night, with leaders I knew and some I didn't. I'd tightened my arm around their shoulders to the stretched-out keen of *"deeeeeeeeesden,"* playing the *milonguita* as I clutched their kidneys, raised my shoulders, pressed my face into their cheeks, and dragged my foot around theirs in one toe-curling arc of coquetry. I'd danced that song a hundred times, and now I heard it.

I listened to songs that mourned the plowed-over barrios of yesteryear, tangos of the old country, or the vanishing *arrabal.* "San José de Flores," about a man returning to the neighborhood where he grew up, only to find it changed. Like so many other tangos, it memorializes *la esquina,* the all-important corner where childhood games were played and innocence idealized. The barrio was witness to the singer's sum of loves, his dreams of triumph. Returning, he is poor and beaten, sorrow-laden, tired from so much wandering. *Más vale que nunca pensara el regreso, si al verte de nuevo me puse a llorar,* or, better to never imagine returning if seeing you again made me weep. If everything is lost, even the dream of home, no other wound will hurt.

"San José de Flores" begins with a quick little tag, four notes on piano, a flourish of strings dissolving into little trills, and then the singer does the first two lines mostly legato, like a dirge. He marches off from there, speeding and slowing at his whim, between the fluid and the guttural vibrato, between lament and recitative. It's a fairly schizophrenic song, not really danceable. It is a piece of theatre, a monologue set to music, urgent, grating, almost shouting toward the end. In both refrains the singer backs off to warble the final syllable, as if he were massaging it, holding it in a little globe of sound, an echo of vibrating vocal cords. As if he were saying *poor, poor me.*

And poor, poor me was how I felt.

I took refuge in all the poor, poor me that I could find in tango music. I'd spent two years learning the dance and all that came with it: history, tradition, music, *códigos,* the close embrace. I'd let it slink up my limbs and through my organs, until it had embedded green and leafy vines inside my chest. Now it was stuck inside me, threatening to wither. I didn't want to let it die.

The melancholy in tango is part of what had drawn me to it, carried me through countless hours of studios and drills, and forced the dance into my sluggish limbs. Dancing was communion, but also isolation. Every tango danced, while shared between the couple, had this private aspect: you, alone inside the music. The three-minute love affair is maybe less about your partner or your lover than about all you've lost and all you've never had. Loves, lives, places left, and former versions of yourself. Oscar Wilde would write — and Borges quote — that certain music made him feel that he'd been weeping over sins that he had not committed, mourning tragedies that were not his to mourn. "It creates for one a past of which one has been ignorant, and fills one with a sense of sorrows that have been hidden from one's tears."

It is *el poema de ayer*, the poem of yesterday. The *cuartito azul*, the blue little room inside your heart. Where the hero keeps his youthful love, his *primera pasión*. It is the door that no longer opens, the balcony he never sits on to reflect. There are a million songs as sad as this. Tangos mostly of goodbye. Most dancers ignore or never learn the lyrics, and songs are open to misinterpretation. I so often danced "Invierno" with a smile. But smiles are also grimaces in tango; there is always aching underneath.

I thought of how much of my own aching I'd uncovered. What I had not allowed myself to mourn: my splintered family, the poisoned stranger who gave birth to me, my buried shames. And then the silly stuff: banalities of growing up and learning to be lonely, the locusts, boils, and the relinquished dreams.

Tango has always been the underdog of social dances — subtle and serious where others are more frivolous and fun. Five hundred miles to the northeast of Buenos Aires is Porto Alegre in Rio Grande do Sul, a jolly port city in Brazil, the samba capital of the world. Ask a *porteño* why Brazil got the lime greens and shocking yellows of the samba and Argentina ended up with tango, and the answer will be melancholy. The deep current of drifters' sadness in the culture of that "grey" and "incoherent" nation and the means by which it claimed a national identity, how immigrants and Afro-Argentines, poor creoles and gauchos — the so-called "fraternity of the condemned" — all came together in a perfect circle of nostalgia. Mourning the paved-over places where pampa once met barrio and flowers grew. Missing the old world even as it disappeared. Out of oppression, poverty, and impotence in the face of the unjust: an art. Something beautiful from so much pain.

The world has changed since those days of boats and men and wooden instruments. The dance has ranged so very far and wide from where it started. Much has been lost, destroyed, forgotten. But we are linked to them and then. To the *minas* and the *milonguitas,* to the *compadres* and *compadritos,* to the gauchos and the *milongueros* of the Golden Age. We want to belong to something. They wanted to belong to something. The something we belong to is the same.

There is a word for it now, for the old men and *milongueros* who sit in worn wood-walled cafés in San Telmo, buried in a bottle of red wine, or staring at the sludgy dregs of strong espresso. The clouded mirror above the back banquette. The word is *mufa,* a black and bitter funk. A mood vital to the tango, to any man or woman dancing it, and to the soul of Argentina. An aesthetics of self-pity. A lineage of artful gloom. You won't find it in most Spanish dictionaries, though the closely related *mofa* translates as "mockery" or "derision." *Mufa* comes from the reflexive verb *mufarse,* which is a Lunfardo slang term encompassing a range of sentiments: moodiness, annoyance, crushed spirit, rotten luck, depression, boredom, neurasthenia, misfortune, listlessness, and pain. In short, "to mope." *Mufa* means depression with a healthy dose of cynicism, moping for the sake of moping, wallowing in melancholy because it feels so good to feel so bad.

I moped. I sat in street shoes at the edge of the *milonga* and boohooed about my lot. I drank plenty of Malbec — for effect.

There was no threshold-of-drunkenness to thwart my dancing, so I swirled the sediment at the bottom of my plastic cup and muttered *poor, poor me.* For a while I fancied myself some sort of mascot, the giant animated squirrel of New York tango, galumphing in and sliding to the center of the dance floor on my matted faux wool paws, then slumping on the bench, my head hung low. I'd smile big and wave whenever called upon, but everybody knew that I just wanted on the team.

The turning circles stopped and I was stuck in stasis, longing for what had passed, for what was irretrievable, for some simpler time and way of life. The old and very simplest sadness. In "San José de Flores," it was called *el ansia bendita,* the holy longing.

But mine were champagne problems; I raised a toast instead to all my blessings. To Barry, to my little room in Brooklyn. To Peter, and his family. To friends and parents who had suffered my indulgent tears. And to COBRA, however extortionate the monthly charge.

I tried another non-force chiropractor, Dr. B, who did not concern herself with rubbing knots and hardness out of tissue. Her patron deity was alignment. She would lay me face down on her leather table, send piano finger flourishes up my ribcage, and check my leg lengths with her thumb and finger at the heel. This was a very different kind of being touched. I'd lie faceup as she wedged leather blocks beneath my hips, settling my pelvis into place. As if two hands had reached up through machinery to levitate me and set straight my bones. Her adjustments lasted about a day before the muscles clenched and pulled the bones around.

Dr. B was brunette and petite, with birdish feet. Calmness was her criterion. She could tell in seconds that I wasn't calm. I'd come to her after months of lumbar pillows, butt-cheek kneading, ibuprofen, feeling breakable, and sitting up too straight to compensate for years of slouching. And after hours spent in awkward places stretching on whatever patch of floor I could find, doing my "exercises" three times daily because some doctor or other told me it might help.

I'd walk a lap around the table, sit, and then she'd scrutinize. I'd point my toes and flex my feet, open and close my mouth. I'd breathe: that seemed important. It felt as though I'd held my breath for months. Finally, she'd tap me two times on the ankle and, in her Upper West Side twang, dismiss me.

"Goodbye, bubble. Come back tomorrow."

Dr. B had joined the line of healers I had sought to grant my only wish: to fix my back so I could dance. The team included chiropractors (two), an overpriced masseur, one acupuncturist and then another (cheaper), an orthopedist, a D.O. with a sweating problem, a Korean ballerino/bodyworker, and a physiatrist who referred me to his number one — a man named Dariusz, who was a physical therapy bodhisattva. For twenty minutes he would move my bones in place, gently, using my limbs as giant joysticks, listening as a safecracker might for movement in my discs. When he was done, he'd cover me with electronic muscle stimulators and a weighted heating pad.

I had to let myself be touched in such a different way, medically, unmusically, as if all the doctors and the bodyworkers were leading me, but I could not respond. Whole afternoons evaporated in doctors' offices and waiting rooms. I had no money left for anything that wasn't spine-related. My body was a lemon; I fed it parts and oil. I poured money in like gasoline and watched it slowly power down.

It did get easier. One afternoon, when I was facedown on the leather torture table with Dr. K's elbow tenderizing my hamstring meat, I asked him, "Could I swim?"

He was silent for a second, then said, "Yes. I guess you could."

That very afternoon, I marched into a midtown T.J.Maxx and bought myself the only size 6 suit they had, plus a pair of goggles. I bought a combination lock, and queued up at the West Side YMCA to add myself to my father's membership for thirty bucks a month. I tiptoed down the steps from locker room to pool. I chose the slowest lane and lowered myself into the water, which was cold and tart with chlorine. I sank with a quiet plop and started treading water, sending little ripples out across the surface stillness of the all but empty pool.

I pushed off gently from the wall, not wanting to disturb the sleeping ogres of my lumbars. I pulled myself along by crawl stroke, barely kicking, gliding without swiveling my hips. To move was everything. It wasn't dancing; neither was it a naked cove in the South of France. But I felt the water on my body, the silken ripples as I swam. I found a quiet rhythm, an oh-so-gentle motion of the feet, just fluttering, not making waves. I felt like an old-time riverboat, bumbling along by paddle wheel. I tried to smile, serenely grateful, in the hypnotic push and swish. The little echoes made against the tile walls. I pushed my face into the water, as if it were a meditative cavern, or a yoga mat. It would have to be enough. I swam five hundred meters, then rejoined the hordes of nudists in the shower room.

There I confronted every nipple God had ever made, and every tufty patch of lady bramble — some mohawked with age, others diligently waxed. The ladies of the West Side Y were all about *au naturel,* so I acclimatized. Just like the *plage des naturistes* — only dark and windowless and moldering at the edges of the carpet. I went naked in the shower, naked to the lockers, and naked to the swimsuit-wringing-out machine. Women plodded up and down the aisles around me, their sagging once-pink flesh yellowed with age. Some stood naked even underneath the hair dryers. Others stood naked with towels on their heads. I could be naked there, without it being sexual or seen.

My body was just another body, whatever imperfections ailed it. Whatever hidden sores and hidden pain.

The Y became my refuge and the ladies' locker room my new community: a coterie of naked and imperfect women — droopy, wrinkled, or robust — all moving through alone, all favoring their limps and aches in the unanimity of the infirm. My body became loud to me, and almost ugly. As if I'd been a hologram in tango, a glittering ideal projected into leaders' arms. Here, I inhabited the real thing — the flesh without the fantasy. Without forgiving flowing skirts or harem pants that moved when I moved, the kinds of fabrics that once had made me feel like a string of prayer flags in wind. There was just nakedness — mine and everybody else's. I looked down in the shower at my skin and saw myself: pale flesh and vertebrae and discs and fingernails and hair and blemishes beneath fluorescent lights.

If this was all I had, then I would honor it. Tend it with gentle exercise, clean it, rinse the shame and chlorine down the drain. Slow. Crawl. Pause. In the pool, I didn't wait for impulses. I simply moved. The minutes passed in steady lengths. There wasn't any music. My thoughts washed with the tedium, and in that underwater stillness, I felt better. My skin would reek of pool water for hours afterward, which felt like victory. Even that small bit of moving, that fettered loop of exercise, was better than not moving at all.

Chapter Thirty

WHEN IT BECAME CLEAR, THREE MONTHS LATER, THAT NO amount of rest would make my back stop hurting, I decided to try dancing anyway. Barry took me to a quieter midtown *milonga* on a Friday night. I strapped on shoes, teetering a little in the ankles, like I had as a beginner, before my tendons learned stability. I took his hand. We danced—four *tandas* in twice as many weeks. We broke between them, rested at a table on the corner of the floor, and shared a drink. I'd brought a book, expecting him to start in on his *cabeceo*. "Dance?" he asked, and when I looked around the room to see which other followers he was passing up, he said, "I don't need to dance with anybody else tonight," and held me all the tighter. I woke up the next morning sore and knotted, but at peace.

The chiropractors both agreed. "As long as you're careful," they said, unlatching my cage, "a little dancing should be fine."

I hobbled my way back to tango. Sometimes I'd get an hour, maybe two, before the pain set in. Sometimes I didn't even try. I was rusty. I had fallen out of flow, and let my body lose its twist. I started favoring my spine, balking at *boleos*, cheating on my feet. I danced when I felt able, and then too carefully. One wrong leader, one bad *sacada*, and I worried I'd be benched again, for weeks.

It would be years more before I realized my injury was minor, before I saw a better doctor who explained the pain was much more likely caused by my deep canyons of anxiety than any bulging disc, and required only therapy. Ever more therapy. But that year, every *tanda* became precious to me as an hour of borrowed time.

Marty still grinned wide whenever we met eyes in *cabeceo.* If I stumbled and apologized, he only smiled. "There's nobody like the Kid," he said. He went to Buenos Aires and brought me back a pair of black-and-yellow four-inch Comme il Fauts that made me feel like a real *tanguera,* no matter how my skills had atrophied. I called them my Bumblebees and, when I couldn't wear them, displayed them on my shelf as a reminder of the hole that tango filled. I took things one day at a time.

I'd come to tango at the age of twenty-five, and couldn't fathom just how very young I was. I couldn't reckon with my past, or future, so I chose the dance that's strangled in the desultory present. The dance of *someday maybe* and of *I remember when* that erases past and future both in its oblivion. I wandered, ill-equipped, into the wilderness of man and woman. I grew bold. I learned how to say yes, and to embrace the things that terrified me: uncertainty, male flesh, surrender. I danced myself into a few precarious situations until I learned that "no" was also a word I could wield. I said "no" to all the things I had been holding on to out of fear: Peter, theatre, the steady job.

I let go of a life I thought I was supposed to like and went for one I thought that I could love. I turned my circles in the dark. I flew. And then I hit hard ground. I was at peace then, perhaps, with everything I couldn't comprehend, but no less lost. In my pursuit, there wasn't much I wouldn't throw away. I was Agave at the height of her *ekstasis.* I wasn't wandering because I'd lost the path, but because I'd come to love the losing and the being lost. Tango was old and it was new. It was movement and stagnation. I felt that anything could happen to me, and yet nothing ever would.

Tango is also empathy. You try on someone else's misery, strum someone else's melody, sing someone else's pain. It is not stealing; it's homage. Everyone who dances tango finds something there, and leaves something behind. New dancers fall in love with tango every day, and, despite my own obsession, I often wonder why. There are other dances, after all. Samba, salsa, bachata, lambada, swing. Tango is not considered cool. It is a little staid. An acquired taste. People enact, to fullest expression, antiquated gender norms. They do their hair and dress up nice. They are polite. Maybe that's what draws us to it, in this age of social media and false connection. It is a *social* dance. In Gustavo's words, we are drawn to tango *"porque aparta una solución para paliar la soledad"*: because it offers a solution to alleviate the loneliness. It exists beyond language and culture, beyond the march of time. It offers a release from all the pressures of our modern lives.

And so, at bottom, in the darkest chamber of my *cuartito azul,* I used the dance to fix the mess I'd made in it, that it had made in me. I figured out the kind of woman I wanted to be — in brain, body, and art — and then I fell in love. Dancing, for all of my mistakes, had taught me how.

Summer cracked its egg against the city. Heat and sunlight spilled into the valley built by skyscrapers, warming the pavement, bringing out the sewer smells. But the prospect of the season left me cold. Barry was leaving, for Berlin.

"Why is he going to Berlin?" my mother asked.

"For work," I explained. Nearly all his colleagues fled there in the summers. The rent and beer were cheap, the weather mild. It made for an idyllic place to finish dissertations over currywurst and *Küchen,* to go from drinking coffee on the sidewalk to drinking liter-bottled beer up and down the U-Bahn.

Plus, the tango there was good — almost as good as in Buenos Aires.

"Yes, but what is he going to do there?" she asked, and I tried to paint a picture for her of how philosophers spent their workdays — which was to say, hunched over books and laptops, batting arguments around, writing, pacing, thinking.

"So he's going to Berlin to think?"

"Basically."

"For two months?"

She had all of southern Florida guffawing over that one. When I visited later that summer, her friends were trained to say, when stumped, *Well, geez, I don't know, I guess I'd better go to Berlin and think about that.*

I didn't mind. My wild gamble had worked. The spring post had brought the fat acceptance envelope. I was starting school in the fall. I'd paid my deposit, signed my natural life away to loans, and sworn a private oath not to look back. I'd left my mother down there, basking on her plastic chaise longue by the pool, but it was right. I felt more at home in Barry's world of laptops than I ever could in hers. I'd leapt, finally, in the right direction.

I'd waited hours to tell Barry in person, at Tango Café. I'd turned up with the Bumblebees and found him dancing. I waited for his *cabeceo,* sauntered over, took his arm. "I got in," I whispered in his ear, nonchalant.

"You did *what*?" he said, and pulled us from the line of dance just as the song began. "You wee devil!" he exclaimed, and scooped me up and spun me round and round in circles, black-and-yellow heels flashing behind me. I smiled until my face hurt, then we danced. I pressed my forehead to his cheek and squeezed his hand. He gave my bottom a tender smack and we took off around the room. We danced so hard and happily that I forgot to wince through turns.

The night before he flew, I tried to make my peace with the impermanence of him. Of everything, of us. I tried to see myself as he saw me, he who'd taught me how to love, and who believed in my ability to rise. If the two months and the distance of the summer were to sink us, at least there had been this.

Despite my default state of doubt, I didn't lose him. I spent two months, solitary in the city swelter, shoring up. From the sidelines, I had a lot of time to think. Tango was, in many ways, a happy accident — in my life and in the world. Rodolfo Dinzel once called it an *"ansiosa búsqueda de la libertad"* — an anxious quest for freedom. A dance for the nomadic and the trapped. Immigrants seeking freedom. Gauchos, free by nature, pushed into the grid behind the wire fence. Descendants of slaves who were not free, but became so, and would shape the culture of a continent. Even women, breaking free of gendered confines of propriety. It was the product of a particular place and age, which happened to be Buenos Aires but could just as easily have been somewhere else, had circumstances changed. Another cruel port city, another cruel time. Even here, now — where not so much has changed.

Tango was born a partner dance of pure improvisation. There were clear roles and rigid structures, but within them, total freedom. A dancer claimed that freedom — in that movement, in that music — to move without orders and without constraints. A dancer was even free to *not* move. Stillness — *not* dancing — is, after all, the subtle undersoul of tango. The essence in the pause. And freedom in *la pausa* represents nothing less than "the faculty of free men [and women] to simply say no." These democratic structures seem so obvious to us now, but "in those days . . . such a dance was inconceivable." Tango was, as Rodolfo Dinzel wrote, "the last great breakthrough in dance in the history of humanity." Horacio Ferrer, poet and scholar, wrote that *"tango — previamente de ser arte*

— *es una actitud.*" Before it was an art, it was an attitude. No matter who or where you are, you're free to define yourself inside it, as it continues to define itself. For Argentines, it is a living history, written in them root and blood and earth. For everybody else, it is a many-layered labyrinth. From the cheesy tourist tours of Recoleta to the sainted memory of Osvaldo Pugliese with the red carnation placed on his piano every night he wasn't there. Without at least a tip of the fedora to tradition, tango ceases to be tango. Otherwise, the line of dance is wide and you are welcome. You could be eight feet tall, pink-haired, and pierced from stem to stern; you could dance in sneakers; you could be blind, or mute, or strange. Any gender, no gender. Anyone. Even the severest member of the *milonguero* orthodoxy will not disparage a new convert if shown adequate respect.

That said, there are those who'll find the wormhole into the *porteño* soul and *tangüedad,* and those who never will. There are those who'll never see beyond the stage — the hobbyists and the exoticizers — but they are welcome too. I would not take away their fishnets. May they find solace also, in red wine and Caló.

Tango was once the dance of former slaves and strangers coming to a foreign place. Now it is an oracle, an antidote for almost anything: For loneliness, connection. For nostalgia, future hope. For insecurity and wistfulness, the bawdy brag of ego. For surrender, self-possession. For braggadocio, submission. And for heartbreak, the warming memory of pleasure yet to come. It is a dance that moves in perfect circles. Mourning celebration, celebrating mourning. The music is often tragic, as if it means to say: "But beyond all that, I *hope.* And I dance. I hope, and I keep hoping."

Silvina told me once that tango is culture and culture is suffering. A mother feeds her crippled infant. A young man is abandoned by his lover, a gaucho driven from his land. Carlos Gardel dies young, too young, in an airplane crash. "Tango is talking about *unfairness,*" Silvina said, the cruelty of life. Tango deals in sadness. It salutes it. "And if I dance that," she asked me, "will we say tango is sad? No. Life is sad." Our combined experience is reflected in the way we move. In one side step, one simple *salida,* with two partners in perfect concert, "you will see if it is tango or not." Tango is a way of dancing, not limited to quantifiables. "A ritual," Silvina says. "A way of life."

The dizziest freedom to be found within the narrowest of frames. Maybe anything can be "tangoed." Maybe any song, from waltz to schottische to mazurka, can be played or danced with *tangüedad.* You could walk down the street with *tangüedad.* You could love that way.

My failures didn't lead to bigger failures but to better ones. Tango was my chosen implement for good and ill — the fusion of my worse and better natures. With it, I could face chaos unfettered. As a dancer, as a lover, as myself. And when I couldn't dance, I had to find a way to keep it with me. To stand sturdy even off the dance floor, balanced on both feet.

Peter may have said it best. We were having dinner at a bar a few weeks after Barry left, and I was hacking back the doubts. He was newly in love too, with the woman he would later marry. He was nervous he would lose her, almost nauseated. I laughed and told him what my mother had told me. Which is to say, I told him to relax, then said, "You idiot, that's how it's supposed to feel." We clinked our glasses to that fragile happiness. I was nervous too — about graduate school, money, yet another new beginning. I told him I felt I had been wasting time. That tango had taken up too much.

"But without tango, Biscuit . . . ," he said, trailing off. "Just look how far you've come."

·   ·   ·

The summer melted past. I made practice dates and was able to keep most of them. I swam. I cleaned. I wrote. I danced outside, and then met friends for picnics on the Christopher Street pier, as the diehards spun around the dock until the sun went down. I raised a paper cup to toast them from my blanket on the grass a hundred yards away. I went home to my closet bedroom, turned up the window air conditioner, and slept.

One Saturday I went to Nocturne and accepted a once familiar *cabeceo*. I was still a little rusty, and self-conscious, but I didn't care. I wanted to show him just how little his opinion weighed. *No hard feelings,* I thought, as I fit my chest against his chest. He still had that equine smell, though soured by the tang of half-skunked DanceSport red. I laid my arm across his sweat-damp shoulders. We danced one *tanda,* and it was just a dance. Music played; we moved. Enzo was just another body to me now, his touch devoid of memory, or heat. I danced with him as I would have danced with any other stranger. He didn't matter anymore. But somewhere near the end, he breathed into my ear. "I'm jealous," he said, "of whoever made you this good."

We thanked each other. I went back to my seat to stretch. More than any other benediction, here was proof that tango changed me. *It was me, Enzo,* I thought. *I made me that good.* My technique, my tango, it was mine alone. "Good" or not, I'd built it by and for myself, and no injury could take that work away.

I got home that night to a humble bunch of roses and white daisies waiting on my dresser, and a card that read: *"Until soon! Barry."* If I'd been asked just one year earlier to imagine life like this: living in a six-by-eight-foot room, and writing, living on tomato sandwiches, I could not. Where good days had once been judged by how much fun I'd had, or whether things had gone my way, now any day in which my spine felt strong enough to dance was good enough. Days without panic. Nights without catastrophic dreams. And Barry. In two weeks, I was getting on a plane to meet him in Berlin. We had grown our vines across the ocean from each other, knit together somehow midair in the wide Atlantic. We had made it. We were just about to bloom.

Chan Chan

EVERY NIGHT I DO NOT DANCE, I MISS IT MORE. FIRST THE missing is immediate, like hunger or the spread of sunburn, then it fades to something softer. This too is a quiet thing. A love I've given up. Or one that's cooled suddenly, unrequited.

I have never truly danced in Buenos Aires, or walked the streets of Boedo, Flores, or San Cristóbal. I've never taken taxis from *milonga* to *milonga*, or danced the checkered floors of Club Sin Rumbo, the basketball courts of Sunderland, or the pink lights of La Viruta, hours after dawn.

Then again, the Bumblebees and I have graced the floorboards of New York, Boston, Glasgow, Paris, Berlin, New Haven, Princeton, Los Angeles, Charlotte, and Washington, D.C. I sit and listen more than I used to; I dance five *tandas* now instead of fifty. But then I go outside, and see the world.

I continue grappling with my body, a body that, while dancing, allowed me to forget that we are made of fragile stuff indeed. Fat and veins and bones and organs. What thin shields we are given — and yet how astounding all that we are able to contain. Our flesh is home to shame and pleasure both, to pain and to the memory of pain. We are made of everything we've ever touched. It's like Silvina says: "When you touch a human being, you are in the presence of a miracle." And sometimes one touch has the power to erase a legacy of others.

As Cátullo Castillo wrote, and Roberto Goyeneche sang, *"La vida es una herida absurda."* Life is an absurd wound. Even if my muscles have lost most of their tango sureness, the good work of dancing sparkles in them still. I put on the Bumblebees and remember I was once a woman who danced tango — hard and long and late. Maybe someday I might be again.

The music stabs you in the heart. It is sad, but life is sad. Tango is life. The *bandoneón* expands; the *bandoneón* contracts. The old magic is never far away. Barry and I can still kill it to "La cumparsita," and our bodies own the bitter sweetness of each other, our secrets, all the songs we've ever danced. I move my embracing arm up past his shoulder, cupping fingers gently at his neck. This is a move reserved only for him.

I'd like to say that Barry and I were a tango love story. That we came together by the dance and for the dance. But I believe we would have come together otherwise. If you'd put us in a room together, any other room, we would have found each other, like two migratory birds. The *milonga* for us was just another room. Our blue little room. The place where we first moved together to the music. Maybe there's a yesterday built in to our tomorrow, but these are risks I no longer fear to take.

My mother told me once that tango could not be *all I had.* In the end, it wasn't. There was school, new aspirations, the act of putting words on paper. There was love. Real god-honest grown-up love. Love that asked for leading and for following. Those things should be good enough; they almost always are. Tango carried me — awake, asleep — to a place where I no longer needed it. Where I can glue all of the ripped-up pages of abandoned journals back together into one unapologetic self.

Where I can show up, listen to my partner, and dance back. One and one are one, but two make three — and that is tango.

We move to the Carolinas, where the community is small and the *milongas* are infrequent. A neuroma in my left foot consigns me to ugly practice sneakers, which make my feet feel like outsized hot dog buns. We practice our *colgadas* in the grocery aisles, which, being suburban, are plenty wide. We play Fresedo while doing the dishes, and Barry croons the occasional tango lyric in the shower, startling the dog. We've learned not to take ourselves so seriously now that a *tanda* is a semimonthly gift and not a nightly given.

There are still states of grace. Moments, rare and transient, wherein every breath is shared and I am bare and unafraid, and free.

Every time my father asks me what I want for Christmas, my first answer is still "tango lessons." Because tango taught me all these things and then it taught me to let go. Because it will always be there, beckoning. Because when I can, I hope. I dance.

All that agony for three minutes' worth of joy.

And then it feels like flight. It sounds like ocean dusk in one ear and Di Sarli in the other. A blind moment of bliss. Body, brain, and art all come together.

And all three disappear.

Acknowledgments

My working title for this book was always *For the Doubts,* and I've been lucky enough to find myself surrounded by those who've helped to assuage mine. For that, for all of you, I'm deeply thankful.

Tango friends and mentors, of New York and the Triangle and the world beyond, I hope you hear my gratitude in every word.

Particular thanks, in no particular order: To Jaime Green (my original one-hundred-thousand-dollar friend), Madeline Felix, Carena Liptak, Miranda Pennington, Caty Gordon, and Rebecca Worby—for reading me even when it wasn't homework anymore. To Richard Locke and Patty O'Toole, for coaching me through my first rough-hammered drafts with lavish patience (and for that matter, to Patty O'Toole, for . . . well, everything). To my teachers: Margo Jefferson, Phillip Lopate, Lis Harris, Ben Metcalf. To Ben Tarnoff, for championing my early drafts. To Bronwen Dickey, for the pep talks and the Jazzercise. To Nick Stang, for the avuncular pats (and Sharpie tattoos) on the head. To Naima Coster, for the karmic link of simply sitting there with me. And to Caroline Eisenmann, for her tireless faith and virtuosic fluency in corgi gifs.

Special thanks are due to Kris Dahl, warrior agent, for

the tough love and tenacious optimism. To my editor, Naomi Gibbs, for taking a chance on a new kid and the story she had to tell. And to the entire team at Houghton Mifflin Harcourt, for so gently guiding this tenderfoot through unfamiliar territory—especially the thoroughly wonderful Larry Cooper and my ace copyeditor, Amanda Heller.

This book could not have been written without the hand-holding of my dear friend Emily Holleman, who hates tango, but read more drafts than I'll admit to writing. Or without the "Christine Flaherty Writing Residency for Wayward Nieces," which is to say, the selfless gift of her bunker and a most critical few weeks of peace.

And finally, my family. I am nothing without my parents and their unshakable belief that I might (yet) amount to something. Dad and Mum, wherever you are, you gave me everything. And Barry James—father of my dog and child-to-be—you are my husband, partner, patient critic, steadfast inspiration, and the thorn tree to my birch. Here's a little extra love for you in print. You know, *por las dudas*.

A Note on My Research

I don't consider myself an expert on tango, either in theory or in practice. In writing this book, I have relied heavily on the generosity and kindness of the New York City tango community — its leaders, followers, and teachers, without whom I would still be skulking around the edges of the *prácticas* and dancing like a frightened deer. I have stolen so much understanding from my tango betters, and dearly hope my reverence shines through in the text. Where appropriate, I have mentioned tango professionals by their real names, so that you may seek them out and learn.

Dialogue and insights from Silvina Valz and Robin Thomas come directly from personal interviews conducted in 2012. Quotes from tango greats like Chicho, Fabián, Sebastián, and Gustavo were pulled from published interviews, in Spanish and in English. All other dialogue is reproduced to the best of my most fallible recollection.

This is a work of nonfiction, featuring real people with real feelings in real places. It is also a work of memoir, and hamstrung by the imperfections of my memory. I have tried to recount events as fairly and as truthfully as retrospect admits. To protect the innocent, I have changed the names of friends and intimates. If you are reading this, men of my past, thank you, *vos absolvo,* and I hope you learned as much from me as I have learned from you. Everyone is a lesson, as my mother liked to say.

There is a wealth of tango scholarship and theory, mostly in Spanish, some in doctoral dissertations or master's theses in sociology or anthropology. I've tried to honor as much of this erudition as possible, though much of great interest, regrettably, would not fit within these pages: the work of Marta Savigliano, Maria Carozzi, Simon Collier, Carolyn Merritt, José Gobello, Christophe Apprill (in French), Maria Susana Azzi, Donald Castro, and Christine Denniston, among hundreds. As well as everything I could not quote from Robert Farris Thompson's superlative *Tango: The Art History of Love,* Gloria and Rodolfo Dinzel's *Tango: An Anxious Quest for Freedom,* and Julie Taylor's *Paper Tangos.* Nevertheless, this material has shaped me as a dancer and a thinker, and I emerge from this process more and more convinced that tango takes a lifetime — at very least — to learn.

Generally speaking, translations of tango lyrics are mine. I erred often on the side of resonance, rather than precision.

Had I but world enough and time, I would have spent months upon months in Buenos Aires, dancing. I can speak only from my experience dancing where I've danced, and for that I humbly apologize. Tango is a big wide world awaiting you. This was just my little slice.

Notes

PROLOGUE

page

viii *Tango is a sad thought danced:* Though it should be translated more faithfully, this phrase has become standard in the English-speaking tango community.

CHAPTER ONE

2 *"Bahía Blanca":* Music by Carlos di Sarli, recorded by Orquesta Carlos di Sarli in 1957 (RCA Victor).

7 *watching two* porteños: Denizens of Buenos Aires, port city on the Rio de la Plata delta (in adjective form, singular: related to that city or its people).

CHAPTER THREE

27 *conventillo:* A large shared tenement house of lower-class families, often immigrants, arranged around a center common space. In 1880, at the peak of *conventillo* housing, there were 1,770 such buildings in Buenos Aires, housing nearly 52,000 people in half as many rooms.

28 *the great whitewashing:* The slave trade in Argentina was robust. By the early 1800s, an estimated one-third of the Buenos Aires population was of African descent. This number began to drop soon after slavery ceased in 1853—but this precipitous decline in population was no accident. It was covert genocide. There was indeed a deadly yellow fever outbreak in 1871, but blacks were also forcibly conscripted into a series of regional wars, and lashed to poverty by domestic policy. Eighteen eighty-seven was the final year Afro-Argentines were recognized in the census—forming roughly 2

percent of the Buenos Aires population. By 1895, the black population was too low to be registered.

"more civilized": Domingo Faustino Sarmiento, *Facundo: Civilization and Barbarism,* trans. Kathleen Ross, 1st complete English ed. (Berkeley: University of California Press, 2003), 51. Even the 1853 constitution — drafted eight years before slavery in Buenos Aires was fully abolished with the unification of the country in 1861 — declared that the *gobierno federal* would vigorously promote European immigration. Article 25 goes on to add, "and it will not restrict, limit, or burden with any tax the entrance of foreigners who come to work the land, improve our industries, and introduce and teach the sciences and arts."

30 *Afro-Cuban* habanera: "Nurtured by musicians of color in Cuba and brought to the River Plate by sailors, sheet music, and Spanish light opera . . . the pulse of the earliest tangos." Robert Farris Thompson: *Tango: The Art History of Love* (New York: Vintage, 2005), 217.

from the Ki-Kongo: Ibid., 97.

cortes *and* quebradas: "Cuts" and "breaks," core elements of the Afro-Argentine and Euro-Argentine fusion that made tango. Both are still visibly present in the dance. Ibid., 10.

31 *"Tango starts rhythmically"*: Interview with Sebastián Arce and Mariana Montes, "Entrevista con S.A. y M.M., dos reconocidos bailarines de tango," https://actualidad.rt.com/programas/entrevista/view/59200-Entrevista -con-Sebastian-Arce-y-Mariana-Montes%2C-dos-reconocidos-baila rines-de-tango (accessed April 2013).

ocho: Legend also credits Afro-Argentines with this move, for the figure-eight patterns left in the road dust from their winding and turning during Carnival *comparsas,* or parades. It is also said the figure took its name from ladies' skirts doing the same swish pattern in the late nineteenth century — this time on the dirt floors of cantinas. Thompson, *Tango,* 285.

CHAPTER FOUR

37 *"intolerable for a decent society"*: Billy Sunday, quoted in Virginia Gift, *Tango: A History of Obsession* (North Charleston, S.C.: Booksurge, 2009), 245.

"'old gipsy dance": Vernon and Irene Castle, *Modern Dancing* (New York: Harper & Brothers, 1914), 83.

"correctly . . . especially repose": Ibid., 83–84.

just plain suggested sex: Joanna Dee, "Transatlantic Encounters: The Triangulated Travels of the Tango, 1880–1914" (master's thesis, New York University, 2008), 41.

38 *"that reptile from the brothels"*: "Ese reptil de lupanar como lo definiría Lu-

gones con laconismo desdeñoso." Jorge Luis Borges, "Historia del tango," in *Evaristo Carriego* (Buenos Aires: Gleizer, 1930), 117, referring to Leopoldo Lugones, *El payador* (1916).

tanga . . . tangana: Robert Farris Thompson, *Tango: The Art History of Love* (New York: Vintage, 2005), 82.

or claims to be: A 2005 study concluded that an estimated 10 percent of the Buenos Aires population had some identifiable black ancestry, according to DNA analysis of a sample group. Laura Fejerman et al., "African Ancestry of the Population of Buenos Aires," *American Journal of Physical Anthropology* 128, no. 1 (September 2005): 164–70.

39   *cara fea:* Thompson, *Tango,* 222.

Continental intimacy and Bakongo control: Buenos Aires elites got this backwards, assuming the salacious closeness came from the dance culture of the blacks, rather than from the waltz and polka: "Continuous body contact in dance had been a Western phenomenon; Bakongo couples danced far 'apart' (*tatuka*)." Ibid., 157.

CHAPTER FIVE

50   *"Tu íntimo secreto":* Music by Graciano Gómez, lyrics by Héctor Marcó. Recorded by Orquesta Carlos Di Sarli in 1945, sung by Jorge Durán (RCA Victor).

55   *"La bordona":* Music by Emilio Balcarce, recorded by Orquesta Osvaldo Pugliese in 1958 (Odeon).

56   *Pugliese finish: Chan chan (tshia tshia* in Ki-Kongo), the verbal expression of the last two beats of any tango. Usually a dominant cadence, *sol* to *do* — in close succession, the second heavier and more pronounced. Pugliese messed with this most famously; in his signature ending, the *do* is muted, barely audible, and follows a long, arrhythmic pause.

CHAPTER SIX

61   *men . . . outnumbered women:* Virginia Gift, *Tango: A History of Obsession* (North Charleston, S.C.: Booksurge, 2009), 198.

CHAPTER EIGHT

73   *"Poema":* Music and lyrics by Eduardo Bianco and Mario Melfi, recorded by Orquesta Francisco Canaro in 1935 (Odeon), sung by Roberto Maida.

76   *canyengue, orillero:* For further discussion of these terms, see Christine Denniston, "Canyengue, Orillero and Tango de Salon," 2003, http://www .history-of-tango.com/canyengue.html.

"Mi noche triste": Music by Samuel Castriota, lyrics by Pascual Contursi, recorded in 1917 (label unknown) and again in 1930 (Odeon). Established the "tango song" and the tango singer. Robert Farris Thompson calls Gardel's rendering "a decisive moment in *porteño* art history." Robert Farris Thompson, *Tango: The Art History of Love* (New York: Vintage, 2005), 31.

social protest . . . "racial mixing": Social protest and the general bemoaning of injustice was present in tango lyrics from the first *payadores*. Though the rise of the tango *canción* and singer made tango trend toward romantic tragedy, there was often an element of social critique just beneath the surface. Tango was considered, on occasion, a tool for political radicalization, inciting worker strikes and encouraging other aberrant "democratic" behaviors. Carolyn Merritt, *Tango Nuevo* (Gainesville: University Press of Florida, 2012), 34.

77　Guerra Sucia: The Asociación Madres de Plaza de Mayo, a group of mothers of the disappeared, have marched in their white kerchiefs outside the Casa Rosada, the executive mansion in the capital, every Thursday since 1977 demanding justice for their missing children. http://madres.org/.

Astor Piazzolla . . . Nuevo Tango: Piazzolla returned to his roots but broke ranks with the *orquesta típica*, tango singers, dancers, and public opinion. For thirty years, he developed his controversial tango, cross-bred with jazz and electronica and infected with the same atonality and chaos that shaped much of twentieth-century classical music.

78　*all but impossible:* "There was 'nowhere to study,'" recalled Rodolfo Dinzel, according to Carolyn Merritt. "[Dinzel] also claimed to be an anomaly as a young man in the *milongas* in the late 1960s . . . . [T]he youngest dancers were in their sixties" (*Tango Nuevo,* 40).

80　milonga *to a* milonga . . . *tango to a tango:* Tango, milonga, and *vals tandas* are arranged in predetermined order (tango, tango, *vals,* tango, tango *milonga* . . . ad infinitum). *Tandas* can be of three or four songs, depending on the DJ and community preferences, which are occasionally controversial.

81　*"the man stood still":* Maria Nieves, quoted in Thompson, *Tango,* 265.

fifty-fifty: The rebellion of the tango women in 1940 led to the "sharing of action" trend; see ibid., 257.

partnering her broom: Ibid., 260, quoting Dena Kleiman, "It Takes Two Who Tango," *New York Times,* October 15, 1985.

CHAPTER NINE

85　boleo *is tangospeak:* Sometimes spelled *voleo,* occasionally *latigazo,* from *látigo,* "whip"; possibly related to *boleadoras* (or *bolas*), the whip-like throwing weapons used by gauchos with their herds.

CHAPTER TEN

96   *TriANGulO had a mural:* Painted by Russell Buckingham, 2007.

CHAPTER ELEVEN

105   *"La cumparsita":* Music by Gerardo Matos Rodríguez, lyrics by Pascual Contursi and Enrique Maroni, 1924. There are dozens of recorded versions.

CHAPTER FOURTEEN

133   *the word* canyengue: Also, in Angolan, "step it down" or "start to party." Robert Farris Thompson, *Tango: The Art History of Love* (New York: Vintage, 2005), 151.

137   Please, God: Dorothy Parker, "A Telephone Call," in *The Portable Dorothy Parker* (New York: Penguin Classics, 2006), 119.

139   They don't like you to: Ibid., 122.

141   *"worn-out" or "tired":* Thompson, *Tango,* 158.

143   wings fanned . . . it was praying: From Charles Bukowski's "the mockingbird," in *Mockingbird Wish Me Luck* (New York: Ecco, 2002).

CHAPTER FIFTEEN

144   *I was humbled . . . hardly knew of what:* Paraphrased from Jane Austen, *Pride and Prejudice* (New York: Penguin Classics, 2009), 271.

145   Yet I have slept with beauty: From Lawrence Ferlinghetti's "I have not lain with beauty all my life" (no. 10), in *A Coney Island of the Mind* (New York: New Directions, 1958).

153   *godfather of* "nuevo": His methods became known as *Nuevo Tango,* a misnomer. That name, by rights, belongs to Piazzolla's music. Gustavo himself is sometimes called *"el Piazzolla del baile,"* the Piazzolla of the dance, a title he disavows: "That would be very pretentious. Piazzolla did something devastating . . . a wonderful development, worthy of a true genius." Gustavo Naveira, quoted in an interview with Carlos Bevilacqua for the magazine *El Tangauta* 9, no. 119 (September 2004), www.rincondeltango .com.
   Programa Cultural headquarters: The Centro Cultural San Martín in the theatre district of Buenos Aires.

154   *tomes of surgical directions:* In 2008, Christine Dennison published *The Meaning of Tango* (London: Anova Books, 2008), a volume traversing twenty years of research and including a seventy-two-page "how-to" section.

155   *"opened all the doors":* Fabián Salas, in a 2001 interview with Keith Elshaw, http://oabrazo.blogspot.com/2005/01/interview-with-fabinsalas.html.

materials already piled: That said, Gustavo found more than ninety-eight possible *boleos,* discovered the "fourth" *sacada,* and even threw in the occasional foreign element. "Out of the three choices you normally have," Salas once said, use "the one that nobody used before in such a way" (ibid.). Gustavo, *el renovador,* is frequently credited with being the first to try each step *al otro lado,* to the other side. Also important to note: the degree to which the number and participation of highly trained followers made this possible.

"The 'basic step' . . . all you can do": Ibid.

156   *the dancehall music hasn't changed:* The *dancing* music hasn't changed. Listening music and art music continue to develop: for example, late Pugliese, Piazzolla, Pablo Aslán, Pablo Ziegler, El Arranque — and electronic tango — among others.

"athletic but not sensuous": Gustavo Naveira, quoted by Terence Clarke in "The Greatest Maestro of Tango in the World" (2007), http://blogcritics. org/the-greatest-maestro-of-tango-in/.

158   *A banker and a bricklayer:* Petróleo (Carlos Alberto Estévez) and El Negro Lavandina (Félix Luján), respectively. Robert Farris Thompson, *Tango: The Art History of Love* (New York: Vintage, 2005), 247.

CHAPTER SIXTEEN

162   "What was once orgiastic devilry": Popular translation of Jorge Luis Borges, "Historia de tango," in Emecé Editores, *Evaristo Carriego* (Buenos Aires: 1955), 146.

165   Oh the comfort: Dinah Maria Mulock Craik, *A Life for a Life* (London: Hurst and Blackett, 1859), chap. 16.

CHAPTER EIGHTEEN

172   *march for carnival:* Penned in 1916 by Montevidean Gerardo Matos Rodríguez, who gave the song its martial beat, then premiered in Buenos Aires under Roberto Firpo, who spliced in tags from two of his tango "misses" plus a bit of Verdi's Miserere. A contentious vocal version, named "Si supieras" (If You Knew) and recorded by Carlos Gardel, came along in 1924, with lyrics by Pascual Contursi and Enrique Maroni, and another in 1926, with lyrics by the composer.

"lo más espantosamente pobre": "'La cumparsita' cumple 100 años: Un clásico más allá del tiempo," *Clarín,* April 18, 2004, https://www.clarin.com/ extra-show/musica/cumparsita-cumple-100-anos-clasico-alla-tiempo _0_rJz_g7ECe.html.

dozens of recordings: I mention Firpo (1917), De Caro (1930), Troilo (1943), Di Sarli (1955), and D'Arienzo (1951 and 1963). Also mentioned: Varela (1956) and Díaz (1974).

CHAPTER NINETEEN

183 *"break his legs"*: Gustavo Naveira, in an interview for the website Dance of the Heart, http://www.danceoftheheart.com/naveirainterview.htm.

188 *"La milonga de Buenos Aires"*: Recorded and composed by Francisco Canaro in 1939, lyrics by Ivo Pelay, sung by Ernesto Famá (Odeon).

CHAPTER TWENTY

193 *"Historia de un amor"*: Recorded by Hector Varela in 1956, sung by Rodolfo Lesica (Discos CBS), music and lyrics by Carlos Almarán.

stayed in Mississippi: Bob Dylan's "Mississippi," originally recorded in fall 1996 and January 1997, not appearing on an album until *Love and Theft* (2001) and the bootleg album *Tell Tale Signs: Rare and Unreleased, 1989–2006* (vol. 8, 2008).

199 *Rodríguez whose little parade:* "La cumparsita," music by Gerardo Matos Rodríguez, lyrics by Pascual Contursi and Enrique Maroni. Recorded in 1943 (Odeon).

CHAPTER TWENTY-ONE

207 *DUM bah dum bum:* Robert Farris Thompson gives it as *bang-ki-ging-ging* in a 2005 interview with Ned Sublette, http://www.afropop.org/8392/rob ert-farris-thompson-interview-2005/.

CHAPTER TWENTY-TWO

214 *"Orlando Goñi"*: Music by Alfredo Gobbi, recorded by Osvaldo Pugliese in 1965 (Philips).

"Adiós Nonino": Music by Astor Piazzolla, lyrics by Eladia Blázquez. There are multiple recordings, including several with Pugliese on guitar.

"Balada para un loco": Pugliese's 1970 instrumental version of the Piazzolla tune (Philips).

215 Vení . . . Volá. Sentí: From Horacio Ferrer's lyrics to Piazzolla's "Balada para un loco," most famously sung by Roberto Goyeneche (RCA Victor, 1969).

CHAPTER TWENTY-THREE

218 Bailá. Vení. Volá: Also from "Balada para un loco" (see note to p. 216).

219 *"El esquinazo" and "El torito"*: Two of my favorite *milonga* tunes, recordings by D'Arienzo and Canaro, respectively.

CHAPTER TWENTY-FOUR

222 The revery alone will do: From Emily Dickinson's "To Make a Prairie" (no. 1755).

CHAPTER TWENTY-FIVE

230 *"A leg can weep"*: Julie Taylor, *Paper Tangos* (Durham: Duke University Press, 1998), 111.

236 wholes and not wholes: Heraclitus, *Fragments*, translated and quoted in Daniel W. Graham, "Heraclitus," *The Stanford Encyclopedia of Philosophy*, ed. Edward N. Zalta (Fall 2015), https://plato.stanford.edu/archives/fall 2015/entries/heraclitus/.

CHAPTER TWENTY-SIX

241 *"Between one and two"* . . . *"its own creation"*: Gloria and Rodolfo Dinzel, *Tango: An Anxious Quest for Freedom*, trans. Martin Harvey (Stuttgart: Abrazos Editorial, 2000), 82–83.

"Form": Ibid.

242 *Lunfardo*: A dialect and slang developed in turn-of-the-twentieth-century Buenos Aires, Montevideo, and surrounds. Originally prison jargon, popular among criminals and the lower-middle classes, but spread widely through its dominance in tango poetry. Notable for its Spanish derivations and cheeky wordplay (*vesre*, from *"al revés,"* making "tango" *gotán* and *"café con leche" "feca con chele,"* etc.).

"Its only passport": Carlos Gavito, quoted in an interview with Carlos Quiroga, "Tango Is a Shared Moment" *ReporTango*, no. 2 (January 2001), http://web.ics.purdue.edu/~tango/Articles/Gavito.pdf.

244 *Di Sarli's "sentimental reason"*: From "Motivo sentimental," lyrics by Carlos Bahr, music by Emilio Brameri; on *Di Sarli con Podestá* (RCA Victor, 1944).

245 *"sass and the celerity"*: Robert Farris Thompson: *Tango: The Art History of Love* (New York: Vintage, 2005), 131.

Milonga: Ibid., 134–35, could also be translated as a plural of the Bantu *mulonga*, for "words" or "wordiness." Ana Cara, "Entangled Tangos: Passionate Displays, Intimate Dialogues," *Journal of American Folklore* 122, no. 486 (Fall 2009): 438–65.

246 *the soul of a woman*: Quoted in Virginia Gift, *Tango: A History of Obsession* (North Charleston, S.C.: Booksurge, 2009), 248.

"that which": José Gobello, quoted in Cara, "Entangled Tangos," 438: *"eso que hace que algo sea tango y no otra cosa; eso que si le faltara al tango, el tango ya no sería tango; la esencia del tango, en fin."*

valor *of the dance . . . we find ourselves:* Interview with Milena Plebs, "Mariano 'Chicho' Frumboli: Mano a mano con Milena Plebs" *El Tangauta*, no. 182 (2009), http://www.eltangauta.com/nota.asp?id=1412.

CHAPTER TWENTY-SEVEN

259 "It's only later": Jack Kerouac, *Maggie Cassidy* (New York: McGraw-Hill, 1978), 37.

260 *"Que te importa que te llore"*: Music and lyrics by Miguel Caló and Osmar Maderna, sung by Raúl Berón, recorded in 1942 by Orquesta Miguel Caló (Odeon).

"Invierno": Music and lyrics by Horacio Pettorossi and Enrique Cadícamo; recorded in 1937 by Orquesta Francisco Canaro, sung by Roberto Maida (Odeon).

261 *"Pasional"*: Music by Jorge Caldara, lyrics by Mario Soto (1951).

"Farol": Music by Virgilio Expósito, lyrics by Homero Expósito. Recorded in 1943 by Orquesta Osvaldo Pugliese, sung by Roberto Chanel (Odeon).

262 so quite a new thing: e. e. cummings, "i like my body when it is with your," in *Complete Poems: 1904–1962* (New York: Liveright, 1994), 218.

263 *"Buscándote"*: Music and lyrics by Eduardo Scalise; recorded in 1941 by Orquesta Osvaldo Fresedo, sung by Ricardo Ruiz (RCA Victor).

CHAPTER TWENTY-NINE

277 Oh lead me: Dorothy Parker "Portrait of the Artist," in *The Portable Dorothy Parker* (New York: Penguin Classics, 2006), 95.

279 *"Milonguita"*: Music by Enrique Delfino, lyrics by Samuel Linnig (1920); recorded in 1953 by Orquesta Alfredo De Angelis, sung by Carlos Dante (Odeon).

"Remembranza": Music by Mario Melfi, lyrics by Mario Battistella (1934).

"flor . . . olvida mi desden": From the 1956 Pugliese recording of "Remembranza," sung by Jorge Maciel (Odeon).

280 San José de Flores: Music by Armando Acquarone, lyrics by Enrique Gaudino (1936). I'm partial to the Pugliese recording, sung by Alberto Morán (Odeon, 1953).

281 *"It creates for one"*: Oscar Wilde, "The Critic as Artist: With Some Remarks upon the Importance of Doing Nothing" (1881), http://rebels-library.org/files/the_critic_as_artist.pdf.

cuartito azul: From "Cuartito azul" (1939), music by Mariano Mores, lyrics by Mario Battistella. My favorite version is the Fresedo, sung by Ricardo Ruiz (RCA Victor, 1939).

282 *"fraternity of the condemned"*: Virginia Gift, summarizing José Hernández, "El gaucho Martin Fierro" (1872), in *Tango: A History of Obsession* (North Charleston, S.C.: Booksurge, 2009), 182.

CHAPTER THIRTY

289 "porque aparta una solución": Gustavo Naveira quoted in an interview with Cecilia Hopkins, "Bailar el tango es una forma de comunicarse," *Página 12*, June 22, 2004, http://www.pagina12.com.ar/diario/espectaculos/6-370 48-2004-06-22.html.

291 "ansiosa búsqueda": Rodolfo Dinzel, *Tango: Una danza. Esa ansiosa búsqueda de la libertad* (Buenos Aires: Corregidor, 2008).

gendered confines of propriety: Opposition to tango was also "rooted in a fear of women's independence and how that would affect traditional gender boundaries." Joanna Dee, "Transatlantic Encounters: The Triangulated Travels of the Tango, 1880–1914" (master's thesis, New York University, 2008), 41.

"faculty of free men" . . . "history of humanity": Rodolfo Dinzel, *Tango: An Anxious Quest for Freedom*, trans. Martin Harvey (Stuttgart: Abrazos Editorial, 2000), 104 and 97.

"tango — previamente": Horacio Ferrer quoted in Ana Cara: "Entangled Tangos: Passionate Displays, Intimate Dialogues," *Journal of American Folklore* 122, no. 486 (Fall 2009): 455.

292 *every night he wasn't there:* Because he had been locked away or banned. See, for example, his obituary in *The Independent* by Andrew Graham-Yooll, July 30, 1995, http://www.independent.co.uk/news/people/osvaldo -pugliese-1594093.html. Visit his grave in La Chacarita cemetery, Buenos Aires, and lay a flower yourself.

CHAN CHAN

297 "una herida absurda": From "La última curda" (1956), lyrics by Cátullo Castillo, music by Aníbal Troilo.